Residential Lighting
A Practical Guide

Randall Whitehead, IALD

WILEY

John Wiley and Sons, Inc.

This book is printed on acid-free paper.

Copyright © 2004 by John Wiley & Sons, Inc. All rights reserved

Published by John Wiley & Sons, Inc., Hoboken, New Jersey

Published simultaneously in Canada

No part of this publication may be reproduced, stored in a retrieval system, or transmitted in any form or by any means, electronic, mechanical, photocopying, recording, scanning, or otherwise, except as permitted under Section 107 or 108 of the 1976 United States Copyright Act, without either the prior written permission of the Publisher, or authorization through payment of the appropriate per-copy fee to the Copyright Clearance Center, Inc., 222 Rosewood Drive, Danvers, MA 01923, (978) 750-8400, fax (978) 750-4470, or on the web at www.copyright.com. Requests to the Publisher for permission should be addressed to the Permissions Department, John Wiley & Sons, Inc., 111 River Street, Hoboken, NJ 07030, (201) 748-6011, fax (201) 748-6008, e-mail: permcoordinator@wiley.com.

Limit of Liability/Disclaimer of Warranty: While the publisher and author have used their best efforts in preparing this book, they make no representations or warranties with respect to the accuracy or completeness of the contents of this book and specifically disclaim any implied warranties of merchantability or fitness for a particular purpose. No warranty may be created or extended by sales representatives or written sales materials. The advice and strategies contained herein may not be suitable for your situation. You should consult with a professional where appropriate. Neither the publisher nor author shall be liable for any loss of profit or any other commercial damages, including but not limited to special, incidental, consequential, or other damages.

For general information on our other products and services or for technical support, please contact our Customer Care Department within the United States at (800)-762-2974, outside the United States at (317) 572-3993 or fax (317) 572-4002.

Wiley also publishes its books in a variety of electronic formats. Some content that appears in print may not be available in electronic books.

Library of Congress Cataloging-in-Publication Data:

Residential Lighting : A Practical Guide / by Randall Whitehead.
p. cm.
Includes bibliographical references and index.
 ISBN 0-471-45055-3 (Cloth)
 1. Dwellings--Lighting. I. Title.
 TH7975.D8W49 2003
 747'.92--dc22
                                2003019195

Printed in the United States of America

10 9 8 7 6 5 4 3 2 1

Residential Lighting

FOREWORD

In the 1990s "home sweet home" had become the place to be, according to a Roper Reports survey about the preferences of mainstream Americans. People are now spending more time at home, using it to fulfill a greater number of individual and family needs.

Home is a place to socialize, with larger kitchens to accommodate resident and guest cooks, and great rooms for informal parties. More than ever, home is now also a place for work. It is estimated that between 20 million and 40 million people currently do some type of work at home, whether in a separate room furnished as an office or at a desk in the corner of the living room. People also want "home" to mean a safe place, as well as one where they can enjoy the great outdoors in the evening after a hard day's work by extending entertaining into the patio and garden areas.

Throughout all these varied spaces, lighting is essential to making them both enjoyable and functional. Well-designed lighting can transform a glare-filled, shadowy, annoying place into one that is comfortable and flexible, enhancing the occupants' feelings of well-being. Advancements in technology have resulted in the development of specialized tools that simplify installation and help lighting reveal the best aspects of the environments in which we dwell. The designer will learn how to use this technology to visually shape a home to meet flesh-and-blood human needs.

Presented here is a valuable, detailed approach to lighting the home that is unique because it not only explains the how of lighting design but also provides insights into the why behind design choices. The details of the technology of light must go hand-in-hand with aesthetics and the overriding philosophy that lighting is for people. The author, Randall Whitehead, has the advantage of being not only an experienced lighting designer but a master communicator and teacher as well. Read on, and revel in bringing lighting to its full potential in the most important place in all of our lives-the home.

Wanda Jankowski
Author of *Designing with Light*, *The Best of Lighting Design*, and *Lighting Exteriors and Landscapes*; former managing editor-in-chief of *Architectural Lighting* magazine; editor of *Commercial Kitchen and Bath* magazine.

Dedication

I would like to dedicate this book to my family, who learned how to put the "fun" back in dysfunctional.

Acknowledgments

My deepest gratitude to Anita Synovec who held down the fort as I pulled what was left of my hair out putting this book together. And especially to Steve Rao for absorbing my misplaced frustrations and talking me away from the edge of the abyss.

My appreciation also goes to Judy Anderson, Naomi Miller, Alfredo Zaparolli, and Fran Kellogg Smith. They were my wonderful technical experts, who know how to get an idea across without loading us down with technical jargon. Marian Haworth, a teacher of lighting design, was invaluable as the eyes of a student, making sure I got the information across without confusion.

I would like to thank Dennis Anderson, the extraordinary photographer, who captured all the amazing images in this book. He is the artist behind the lens.

I would especially like to thank our team at John Wiley and Sons; Amanda Miller, for championing the project; Paul Drougas, for being such a great editor; Jennifer Ackerman for all her helpful suggestions and editorial expertise; and everyone else we worked with to make the project a success.

I would also like to thank Clifton Lemon for working so closely with me on this text over the course of many years, and for turning a plain manuscript into readable art.

Residential Lighting

Contents

Introduction

ENJOYING LIGHT

There are three elements within each space that need lighting: art, architecture, and people. Think about lighting the people first—you must humanize the light.

This book is intentionally different from the many books written on lighting design. The emphasis here is on the art of lighting, not just the technical aspects.

Think of this manual as a guide to Applied Aesthetics. Light is an *artistic* medium. What you will learn is how to paint with illumination, using various techniques to add Depth, Dimension, and Drama (the three D's), while at the same time humanizing your environments. Remember, you're not only lighting art and architecture, but the people within the space as well. This book will show you how to create rooms that feel instantly comfortable and are flattering to your clients, with the ability to dazzle at the touch of the button.

Today, all architects, interior designers and other related design professionals need to know at least the basics about good lighting design. Nothing you learn will have more impact on your designs than lighting, because illumination is the "straw that stirs the drink." You give every single object or space in a home its appearance, tone, and impression through how you light it. Yet people still add lighting as an afterthought, "Oh, yes, let's also do some lighting," after the architecture has been laid out and construction has begun.

This is a huge mistake. Lighting design needs to be brought in as an integral design element, along with all the other design components at the beginning. The lighting budget, too, should be comparable to the other main design elements of the project. Lighting is not just an option; it can make or break your project.

Homeowners need to learn something about lighting design as well, so they will not be lost when making important decisions about their living spaces. There are many architects, interior designers and contractors who will say they know all about lighting design, but have had little training; the homeowners are often left with poor lighting that works against the overall feeling they desired.

All the new technologies of the past decade have increased lighting's importance. Who needed lighting expertise when the only thing available was a ceiling socket and a light bulb? That's all changed, but people's thinking has not. Fluorescent lighting alone has gone through a revolutionary change, and, with energy considerations and construction codes, is now a must for a home.

People have also changed the way they live and entertain, often congregating in the kitchen or a *great room*. Sometimes the house is designed as an *open plan*, where the kitchen, dining room, living room, and family room all flow together. People tend to move more from space to space, instead of staying in one room. The new entertainment centers and control systems have also changed the way people use their homes. People are cocooning more. Good lighting design has to take all these needs into account, and you can use the new technical advances to make lighting versatile enough to accommodate everything.

Overview—What to Expect
The first half of this book deals with design tools you will need to put together a well-designed lighting plan.

The second half of this book explains what to do on a room-by-room basis for single-family homes.

Remember, it's the aesthetic approach to lighting design that will be stressed. This book is a springboard to your imagination. The possibilities are limited only by your own creative abilities...and, of course, the client's budget.

A Guide to reading this textbook: The first time a lighting term is used within the content of this book it will be shown in bold print. This is an indication that a further explanation of this specific term is included in the glossary section.

Section One

UNDERSTANDING LIGHT

"Arthur, I think I liked our little nest better before we put in track lighting."

Reprinted by permission of
The New Yorker Magazine.

Chapter One

THE FUNCTIONS OF ILLUMINATION

Light performs these basic functions: decorative, accent, task and ambient—the well-integrated layering of the four within each space will create a unified design. "The mark of professionalism in lighting is the absence of glare." -General Electric.

The new developments in lighting over the last decade have created opportunities for approaches to ways of creating illumination that have only been dreamed of in the past. Lighting technology has greatly evolved from the times of table lamps and track lights, yet many homeowners have not updated their thinking much beyond that stage. We can now achieve lighting effects that are as flexible as our lifestyles, energy-efficient, and less intrusive in remodel situations. Plus we can do it within a reasonable budget, without dramatically changing the way we live. At the same time we can increase the comfort and convenience level in our living spaces.

Lighting can be a tremendous force in architectural, interior, and landscape design. It is the one factor that helps blend all the elements together. Yet, it has for too long been the second-class citizen of the design world. The results have left many homes drab, uncomfortable, and dark. Often the blame goes elsewhere when improper lighting is the culprit causing the discomfort. Helping people become aware of what lighting can do is the first step. Most of us simply accept what light there is within a given space instead of realizing that we can change and improve the situation. The main objective of this book is to crate a "language of light" that is easily understood by design professionals, homeowners, and contractors.

Light has four specific duties: to provide decorative, accent, task, and ambient illumination. No single light source can perform all the functions of lighting required for a given space. Understanding these differences will help you create cohesive designs that better integrate illumination into your overall plan.

The following sections explain the four functions.

The Museum Effect: when art becomes visually more important than people within the space. Even museums now add additional illumination beyond accent light to help reduce eye fatigue by cutting contrast in the overall environment.

Decorative Light

Luminaires such as chandeliers, candlestick-type wall **sconces**, and table lamps work best when they are used to create the sparkle for a room. They alone cannot adequately provide usable illumination for other functions without overpowering the other design aspects of the space. Think of them as the "supermodels" of illumination. Their one and only job is to look fantastic. Another way to visualize them is as architectural jewelry.

For example, a dining room illuminated only by the chandelier over the table can create a **glare-bomb** situation. As you turn up the **dimmer** to provide enough illumination to see, the intensity of the light from the decorative fixture causes every other object to fall into secondary importance (see Figure 1.1). The wall color, the art, the carpeting, and especially the people are eclipsed by the supernova of uncomfortably bright light. No one will be able to see any of the other elements in the room, no matter how beautiful or expertly designed.

By its very nature, any bright light source in a room or space immediately draws people's attention. In the best designs, the decorative light sources only create the illusion of providing a room's illumination. In reality, it is the other three functions of light that are actually doing the real work of lighting up the space.

Another common example of poorly done lighting is the overuse of table lamps and wall sconces with **translucent** shades. Filling a room with translucent shades makes the room look like a lamp shade showroom. It is partly because translucent shades such as those made of linen draw too much attention to themselves (see Figure 1.2). When incorporating this type of decorative fixture into a lighting design, consider using an **opaque** shade with a perforated metal diffuser fitted on top. This will direct the illumination downward over the base, the tabletop, and across your lap when you're reading.

Filling a room with only table lamps to provide the main source of illumination is bad lighting design, as it uses only one available light source. The other three functions of illumination must come into play. This is called "light layering," where a number of light sources are blended together to create a comfortable, inviting environment.

Accent Light

Accent light is directed illumination that highlights objects within an environment. Luminaires such as track and recessed adjustable fixtures are used to bring attention to art, sculpture, tabletops, and plants. Just like any of the other three functions, accent light should not be the only source of illumination in a room.

If you use only **accent light**, you get the **museum effect**, where the art visually takes over the room while guests fall into darkness. Subconsciously, people will feel that the art is more important than they are. Of course, some of your clients may indeed feel that the art is more important than their guests. Their desires must be taken into account, even if they seem to be incorrect. You may compromise on a more layered design that provides some ambient light. If not, their guests will just have to try to be witty or profound enough to compete with the art.

Figure 1.1
The hanging fixture over this eating area with its translucent shade visually overpowers the space, forcing the other elements in the room into darkness. This is an example of why decorative lighting alone creates an uninviting environment.

Figure 1.2
Here we see the same style of
wall sconce, manufactured by
Boyd Lighting, with three
types of shades. The fixture
in the center has an opaque
black shade, the fixture on
the right has an opaque
metal shade, and the fixture
on the left has a translucent
linen shade. Of the three,
your eye is automatically
drawn to the translucent
shade.

Figure 1.3
This is an example of an
opaque wall sconce, by Boyd
Lighting, that offers ambient
light from a shape that
appears to be an architectur-
al detail.

How many times have you had to sit down or run for a latte after going through three rooms in a museum? People can get really exhausted when looking at illuminated art next to non-illuminated walls. Even museums are now adding additional illumination beyond accent light to help reduce eye fatigue, thus cutting the contrast in the overall environment. They too are learning the advantages of light layering.

Remember that accent lighting thrives on subtlety. A focused beam of light—directed at an orchid or highlighting an abstract painting above an ornate chest of drawers—can create a wondrous effect. People won't notice the light itself. They will see only the object being illuminated. The most successful lighting effect achieves its magic through its very invisibility. If you see the light source, then there is no magic.

In the movies, if we can tell how a special effect has been achieved, we feel cheated. We don't want to know how it's done, because we want to think it's supernatural. In lighting design, it should be no less the case. We want to see the effects of light, but the method needs to remain unseen. This subtlety is what will create a cohesive wholeness, allowing the design, the architecture, the furnishings, and the landscaping to become the focus of a space, not the luminaires or the lamps glaring out from within them.

Task Light

Task light is illumination for performing work-related activities, such as reading, cutting vegetables, and sorting laundry. The optimal task light is located between your head and the work surface. That's why lighting from above isn't a good source of task light, because your head casts a shadow onto your book, computer keyboard, or ransom note.

Overhead lighting or incorrectly placed **task lighting** often contributes to what is called **veiling reflection**. It occurs when your eyes try to accommodate the contrast between black print on white paper. This happens when light comes down from the ceiling, hitting the paper at such an angle that the glare is reflected directly into your eyes, causing eye fatigue.

Veiling Reflection refers to the glare and eye fatigue resulting from overhead light hitting directly on white paper with black print, as if you were trying to read through a veil.

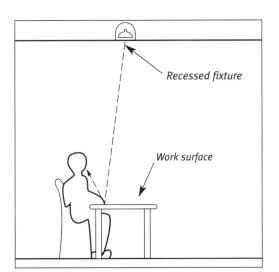

Recessed fixture

Work surface

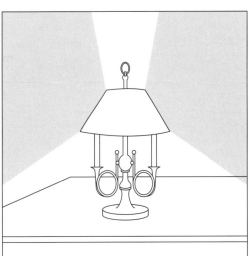

Figure 1.4 (left)
Veiling Reflection (glare) occurs when task lighting is improperly placed directly overhead.

Figure 1.5 (right)
A Bouillotte lamp is a traditional lamp that performs a good job of providing task light.

Ambient light is the soft, general illumination that fills the volume of a room with a glow of light, and softens the shadows on people's faces. It is the most important of the four functions of light, but is often the one element that is left out of the design of a room or space.

Think of it as the mirror-like reflection of a light source on a shiny surface. The plane may be a glossy magazine page or any matte surface that has markings of shiny ink, pencil lead, or other glossy substance. Veiling reflection is a way of describing the resulting brightness that washes out the contrast of the print or picture. The term comes from an uncomfortable situation where you are trying to read something while wearing a veil (see Figure 1.4).

Another related term is **photo-pigment bleaching**. When you try to read a book or a magazine outside, sometimes the brightness of the sunlight on the page makes it difficult to read. You end up moving to a shaded spot or tilting the magazine until the sun isn't hitting it directly.

A reflective surface is always a reflective surface, which means you can't eliminate glare if you are focusing light onto a mirror-like finish. What you can do is redirect the glare away from the normal viewing angle. That's why a light coming in from one side or both sides, instead of directly overhead, is more effective. It directs the glare away from your eyes. The best task light comes from a light source that is located between your head and your work surface.

Portable tabletop luminaires (this is what everybody but lighting designers calls table lamps) with solid shades often do the best job for casual reading, because they better direct the light and don't visually overpower the room when turned up to the correct intensity for the job at hand. You may be thinking, "That's fine and dandy for some Euro-chic interior, but what about my Louis XVI library?" Well, a **Bouillotte lamp** (see Figure 1.5) does a great job of task lighting, as does a banker's lamp (see Figure 1.6). Fluorescent or incandescent linear lights are also a good source of task illumination when mounted over a work surface with a shelf above or in the kitchen with the fixture mounted under the overhead cabinets.

As we go from room to room in Section Two, you will get examples of properly placed task lighting.

Figure 1.6 (left)
Banker's Lamp
Another traditional type of luminaire that provides good task light.

Figure 1.7 (right)
An RLM fixture coupled with a ceramic bowl reflector lamp provides a wide splay of ambient light without relying on the reflective qualities of the ceiling itself.

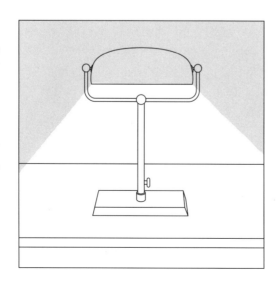

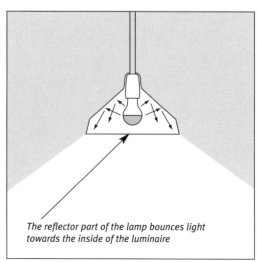

The reflector part of the lamp bounces light towards the inside of the luminaire

Ambient Light

Ambient light is the soft, general illumination that fills the volume of a room with a glow of light and softens the shadows on people's faces. It is the most important of the four functions of light, but it is often the one element that is left out of the design of a room or space.

The best ambient light comes from sources that bounce illumination off the ceiling and walls. Such luminaires as opaque indirect wall sconces (see Figure 1.3), **torchères** (floor lamps), indirect **pendants** (see Figure 1.9), and cove lighting can provide a subtle general illumination without drawing attention to them. You could call it the **open hearth effect**, where the room seems to be filled with the light of a roaring fire.

Keep in mind that filling a room with table lamps does not provide adequate ambient illumination. These are decorative fixtures that can double as task lights when needed, but they cannot provide ambient light. They can provide ambience, though. This is what helps people create an impression of a space. Using them alone in a space creates the feel of a lamp shade showroom. Let these portable luminaires be a decorative source, creating little islands of light. Using opaque shades and perforated metal lids can turn these luminaires into more effective reading lights. Utilizing other sources to provide the necessary ambient light lets the decorative luminaires create the illusion of illuminating the room without dominating the design.

The inclusion of an ambient light source works only if the ceiling is light in color. For example, a richly hued aubergine ceiling in a Victorian dining room or a dark wooden ceiling in a cabin retreat would make indirect light sources ineffective, because the dark surfaces absorb most of the light instead of reflecting it back into the space.

One solution to this situation is to lighten the color of the ceiling. Sometimes the answer is to alter the environment rather than change the luminaire. Instead of the whole ceiling being eggplant-colored, how about a wide border in that color with the rest of the ceiling done in a cream color or similar light hue? Using a traditional chandelier with a hidden **halogen** source could complement the design while adding a 90s sensibility.

A wooden ceiling could be washed with a light-colored opaque stain, giving it a more weathered look without taking away from the wood feel itself, as simple painting would.

If your clients are dead set against changing the color, a luminaire such as the ones shown in Figures 1.7 and 1.8 will provide its own reflective surface. If you were faced

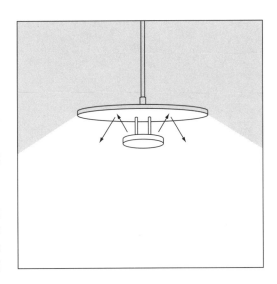

Figure 1.8
A more modern version of an RLM fixture uses frosted glass or a white metal to bounce the indirect light down into the room.

Figure 1.9
Pendant fixtures with translucent shades can often serve the dual purpose of providing both the decorative lighting and ambient illumination. Here an example of a very modern Italian fixture, by Artemide, would be a good choice for an interior with very clean lines.

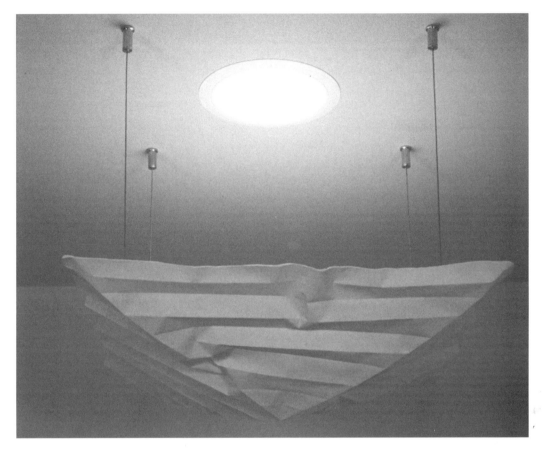

Figure 1.10
An existing recessed down-light becomes a source of ambient illumination with the installation of a paper thin cast cement decorative reflector by Parker Paper.

with a situation like this, a possibility would be to use a luminaire that essentially provides its own ceiling.

One such luminaire has been out on the market for many years. It is a metal shaded pendant generally known as a **RLM** fixture (Figure 1.7). It has a white-painted interior fitted with a silver bowl reflector lamp (lamp is the lighting industry's term for a lightbulb). A silver bowl reflector lamp is a bulb that is coated on the top to project light toward the base of the bulb. The illumination from the reflector lamp is bounced off the inside of the shade itself, instead of the ceiling, to provide an adequate level of ambient light.

There are more modern versions of the RLM, such as the one shown in Figure 1.8. The halogen source fitted within an integral reflector bounces light off the dish-shaped reflector and down into the room below. Sometimes a recessed fixture can be turned into an indirect light source, by installing a decorative reflector below it (see Figure 1.10).

There are many ways of getting ambient light into a room. Ambient light, just like the other three functions, should not be used by itself, because you end up with what is known as the **cloudy day effect**, where everything in a given space appears to have the same value, without any depth or dimension. Here again, ambient illumination is only one component of well-designed lighting.

Light Layering

As was mentioned earlier, lighting design is successful when all four functions of light are layered together within a room to create a fully usable, adaptive space. Good lighting draws attention not to itself, but to the other design aspects of the environment (see Color Plates 1.2, 1.3, 1.4, 1.5, 1.6 and 1.7).

Once you have a good understanding of these functions of light, you can decide which are needed for a specific area. An entryway, for example, desperately needs ambient and accent light but may not need any task light because no work is going to be done in the entry. However, there may be a coat closet, which would need some task-oriented illumination (see Plate 2.33).

What we often see is a house lighted for entertaining only. It has a very dramatic, glitzy look. Many of the design magazines show this type of lighting design. Every vase, painting, sculpture, and ashtray glistens in its own pool of illumination (see Plate 1.20). Yet the seating area remains in darkness. What are these people going to do for light when they want to go through the mail, do their taxes, or put a puzzle together with their family?

Also, you should know that the photographers for design magazines often use supplemental lighting specifically for photographing the rooms. Those lights won't be there when someone is living in the house, and the effect won't be nearly as wonderful as it seems on the printed page. What it does do is give clients a false sense of what type of illumination recessed **downlights** alone can provide, which is often all that exists in the space.

People entertain only part of the time. The rest of the time these rooms in a house are used to do homework, go through drawers, and interact with other family members. Highly dramatic lighting is not effective for normal day-to-day functions.

This doesn't mean that you should eliminate accent lighting. Just don't make it the only option. Simply putting ambient light on one dimmer and accent lighting on another provides a whole range of illumination level settings. The addition of decorative lighting and task lighting completes the design (see Plates 1.23, 1.24 and 1.25).

As your clients become more sophisticated about what lighting can do, you should have the knowledge to give them what they want and what they need. If once the project is finished someone walks in and says, "Oh, you put in **track lighting**," it means that the lighting system is dominant. If they walk in and say, "You look great!" or "Is that a new painting?" then you know the lighting has been successfully integrated into the overall room design.

The Bottom Line

Light layering is the key to effective lighting design. It is the true art of lighting.

Chapter Two

THE COLOR OF LIGHT—PAINTING WITH ILLUMINATION

Color temperature is a way of describing the degree of whiteness of a light source. Those sources that produce a bluish-white light have a higher degree color temperature and those that produce a yellowish-white light have a lower degree color temperature.

Color Temperature

Color temperature and color rendering are two of the most critical aspects in understanding how light and interior design are intertwined. The technical definition of color temperature is as follows: "as a piece of metal (black body) is heated, it changes color from red to yellow to white to blue-white. The color at any point can be described in terms of the absolute temperature of the metal measured in degrees of **Kelvin**. This progression in color can be laid out on a color diagram and now can be specified." Say what? It would seem that those engineering geeks have been cooped up in the lab too long and have forgotten how to speak plain English.

What does it really mean? The bottom line is this: All **lamps** (remember, this is the correct term for lightbulbs) emit a color. That color affects the colors you choose in your design. Understanding this interrelationship could dramatically alter how you select your color palette for any project (see Plates 1.15, 1.16, and 1.17).

Color temperature is a way of describing the degree of whiteness of a light source. Color temperature is measured in the Kelvin temperature scale (often abbreviated as K). Sources that produce a bluish white light have a high color temperature, and those that produce a yellowish white light have a low color temperature.

Understanding color temperature means unlearning your concept of temperature in terms of heat. An oven that is heated up to 5,000° Farenheit would be very, very hot. In terms of color temperature 5,000° Kelvin is very, very cold. The higher the number in Kelvins, the cooler the color of light. The lower the number in Kelvin, the warmer the color of light. Try to think of **daylight** as "freezing" and incandescent light as "hot." A little confused? Don't worry—once you've finished this chapter, you'll have a clearer understanding.

CRI — Color Rendering Index — A scale that shows how well a light source brings out a true color as compared to daylight.

Daylight

Let's start with the sun. If you were handed a box of crayons and asked to draw the sun, what color would you choose? Most people would choose a deep yellow. In reality, sunlight is a yellow-white light. It looks yellow compared to the blue sky around it. Daylight is blue-white, because it is a combination of sunlight and bluish light from the sky. Yes, it is true that in the early and waning hours of the day, there is a golden glow that occurs as the sun nears the horizon and is filtered by the atmosphere. But this is not what we are talking about when we refer to color temperature. So just get that out of your head.

Blue-white light is best for reading true color. That's why when we want to determine the true color of a carpet sample, a sweater, or a bad dye job we run over to the window. You will hear the term "daylight fluorescent," meaning that this lamp comes close to the color temperature of daylight. However, the proportions of colors that make up this blue-white light may be significantly different from the proportions in true daylight, so the color rendering may surprise you. If you expect a warm, sunlight-yellow color of light from these lamps, you will be very disappointed. The color will be much closer to that of cool white fluorescents, as in the greenish glow of a subway terminal, than a lazy summer's day as dusk approaches. It's great for color matching, but not so good for skin tones.

Daylight Versus Artificial Light

Have you ever gotten dressed before the sun was out or in a closet with no natural light and then looked down later in the day and realized that what you thought was navy blue was really black, or that two reds you chose didn't really go together? You mentally blame yourself for not being careful enough or being too sleepy at the time. The truth is that under incandescent light, the colors shift so dramatically that you couldn't tell the difference between navy blue and black, white and yellow, or blue-red and orange-red. Trading your incandescent light source for a good color-rendering daylight fluorescent source will allow you to choose your colors more carefully. Please note, though, that the color of this light is not particularly flattering—so it's best not to entertain guests in your closet.

Why do we all rush to the window when selecting a color? Because we want to see the real color. This is the correct thing to do—daylight does the best job of color rendering. The quality of light is intense and includes the complete color spectrum, so in daylight your material will be able to reflect its own special hue of the spectrum.

Color Rendering Index

All other light sources get rated on their ability to show color hue as compared to daylight itself. This is called their CRI rating (**Color Rendering Index**). Daylight is the best, so it gets a 100 (a 100 percent score). The closer the other sources come to daylight, the higher their score on the CRI. An 85-90 rating is considered pretty high.

How does this affect your design practices? Looking at your samples in daylight is fine for daylight situations, but it can be totally inappropriate when choosing colors for nighttime or interior settings without any natural light.

A Sampling of Often Used Lamps and Their Color-Temperature Ratings Measured in Degrees of Kelvin (K°)

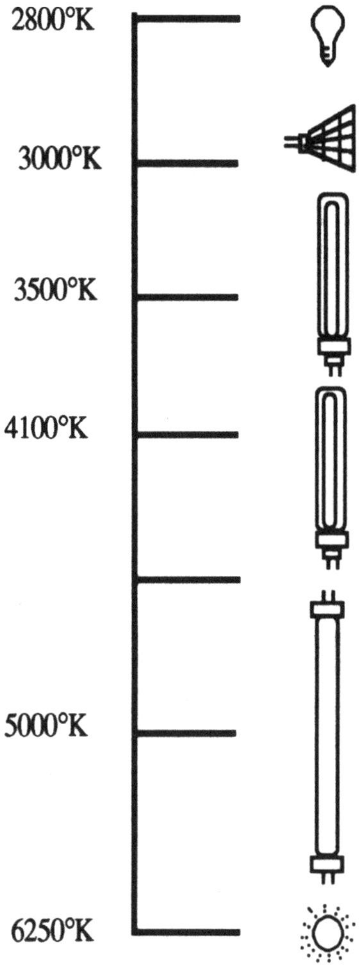

2800°K — Standard Incandescent
(Sample catalogue #: 60A19IF)
Yellow light; what most people are used to and feel safest with.

3000°K — Halogen
(Sample catalogue #: 50-watt MR 16 EXN)
Slightly whiter than standard incandescent, but turns yellow when dimmed.

3500°K — Color-corrected fluorescent
(Sample catalogue #: F39 BX SPX 35/RS)
A good color temperature for skin tones and color-matching, but not best for either—a compromise that is widely used

4100°K — Color-corrected fluorescent
(Sample catalogue #: F39 BX SPX 41/RS)
A good color temperature with enough red tone to keep skin color from turning greenish. Popular for offices, where color matching is slightly more important than correct skin tones

5000°K — Full-spectrum fluorescent
(Sample catalogue #: F 34T8/D
Comes close to daylight. Excellent color-matching, not great for skin tones, slightly greenish

6250°K — Daylight
(Sunlight mixed with the color of the sky)
Best color-matching capabilities

Rule of Thumb:
The lower the number, the warmer the color of light.
The higher the number, the cooler the color of the light.
Reds and peaches look better under a warmer color temperature, while blues and greens look better under a cooler color temperature.

Figure 2.1
Color Temperature Chart
The lower number in degrees of Kelvin indicates a warmer color, the higher number in degrees indicates a cooler color.

Rule of Thumb: The higher the Kelvin rating, the whiter (cooler) the light; the lower the rating, the more yellow (warmer) the light.

Much of the time designers use incandescent sources (including halogen), which can be thousands of Kelvins warmer than daylight. Under incandescent light, color selections will shift tremendously. White can go to yellow, red can turn to orange, blue shifts toward green, and grays can turn to tan. Then all your hard work and hours of color selection are down the drain. The bottom line is to make sure to select colors and show your colors to clients under both natural light and incandescent light so that they will see how these colors shift in the various light sources. Most people think that daylight and incandescent light are the same color. This couldn't be further from the truth. They are almost at opposite ends of the color spectrum. This difference will greatly affect how these colors are interpreted (see Plates 1.9, 1.10, 1.11).

Take a look at Figure 2.1. It shows how some sample lamps compare in terms of color temperature. At the top of the chart, you will see incandescent and **fluorescent** lamps, which give off a warm (yellower) color. At the bottom of the chart are the more blue-white sources of light, such as daylight and full-spectrum fluorescent, which are very cool colors. Incandescent, fluorescent, and high-intensity discharge lamps come in many colors. Chapter 3, you'll get more information on the various lamps that are available.

Rule of Thumb: The higher the Kelvin rating, the whiter (cooler) the color of the light will be; the lower the rating, the more yellow (warmer) the color of the light will be.

There are colored lamps, such as red or yellow **LEDs** (light emitting diodes), and some colors of HID (high-intensity discharge) sources, such as **low-pressure sodium**, that are off this scale. HID and LED sources are not normally used in residential design except sometimes in landscape lighting. They are most commonly selected to light large public areas or industrial facilities.

A large variety of lamps are available with color temperatures that fall in between the two extreme ends of the color spectrum. These colors can be good for skin tones and color rendering at the same time, but not perfect for either. A little compromise is needed to make the right choice. The purpose of this chapter is to help refine your ability to make a good choice in terms of color temperature for a particular situation.

Halogen Exposed

One lamp you hear a lot about is halogen (also known as quartz or tungsten halogen). It is promoted as the "white" light source. This is true when compared to standard household bulbs, but only slightly. Standard incandescent is 2,800° K, halogen is 200 degrees cooler (3,000° K). Also note that halogen is an incandescent source and, like all **incandescent lamps**, becomes more amber as you dim it. So it is only whiter than regular old incandescent when operating at full blast. Yet compared to daylight it is 2,000 degrees more yellow. That's a huge difference. So **white light** is a relative term. Daylight is the definitive white light.

Lamp	CRI (approx.)	Color (approx.)	Whiteness	Colors Enhanced	Colors Greyed	Notes
Warm White	52	3000	Yellowish	Orange, Yellow	Red, Blue, Green	—
White	60	3450	Pale Yellow	Orange, Yellow	Red, Blue, Green	—
Cool White	62	4150	White White	Yellow, Orange, Blue	Red	—
Daylight	75	6250	Bluish	Green, Blue	Red, Orange	—
SP30	70	3000	Yellowish	Red, Orange	Deep red, Blue	Rare-earth Phosphors
SPX27	81	2700	Warm Yellow	Red, Orange	Blue	Rare-earth Phosphors simulates Incandescent
SPX30	82	3000	White (Pinkish)	Red, Orange, Yellow	Deep Red	Rare-earth Phosphors
SPX35	82	3500	Red, Orange, White	Yellow, Green	Deep Red	Rare-earth Phosphors
SPX41	82	4100	White	All	Deep Red	Rare-earth Phosphors
SPX50	80	5000	White (Bluish)	All	None	Rare-earth Phosphors simulates outdoor daylight
Warm White Delux	77	3025	Yellowish	Yellow, Green	Blue	Simulates Incandescent
Cool White	89	4175	White (Pinkish)	All	None	Simulates outdoor daylight (cloudy day)
Chroma 50	90	5000	White (Bluish)	All	None	Simulates sunlight, sun-sky-clouds
N	90	3700	Pinkish	Red, Orange	Blue	Flatters complexions, meat displays, semi-"cosmetic"
PL	-2	6750	Purplish	Blue, Deep Red	Green, Yellow	Plant/Flower enhancement & growth

Figure 2.2
A sampling of Lamp Color Specifications.
Courtesy of G.E. Lighting, Nela Park.

A lightbox is a cube, painted white inside and equipped with different lamp sources that are switched independently. Holding your material swatches or paint chips inside the box under the various lamp sources will help you in the correct lamp decision.

Selecting Colors Intelligently

So how do you choose colors for a project that will be used in both daylight and evening situations? The answer is actually very straightforward. Before you show your color choices to your clients, look at the samples under an incandescent source as well as a daylight source. Choose hues that are acceptable in both situations. That way, you end up with a design that looks right both at night and in the daytime hours (see Figure 2.2). If the space you are designing uses fluorescent, then the color samples should be viewed under the selected color temperature.

Remember to show your clients your color board under both sources as well. If you have only daytime meetings, they may be unpleasantly surprised by the way the colors shift at night.

The terms "color-corrected" and "daylight" do not mean the same thing. "Color-corrected" means that the color rendering of the lamp is good to excellent, intended to complement the skin tones of the people and the colors of the surfaces within the space. "Daylight" means the source is close to the color temperature of daylight, but it does not render skin tones pleasantly.

Many lighting showrooms now have light boxes or color boxes which are display cubicles that show a variety of color temperatures and color rendering abilities from a number of different light sources. This is a great way of seeing how the numerous lamps compare to each other. Think of them as a series of cubes, painted white inside and equipped with different lamp sources that are switched independently. Holding your material swatches or paint chips inside the cubes, under the various lamp sources, will help you choose the correct lamp.

Color Temperature and Plants

Plants love white light. They look lush and healthy under whiter light sources. Unfortunately, most lamps that are used to light plants are incandescent, which, as you now know, has an amber hue. This yellowish light turns the green color muddy, and plants end up looking sickly (see Plates 1.12, 1.13 and 1.14).

What can you do? The answer is to change the color temperature of the light source to a cooler version. Here are some techniques:

1. Have you seen the grow-light bulbs that they sell in hardware stores? These are incandescent sources that have been coated to filter out the yellow wavelengths emitted by incandescent. Replace the existing lamp with a grow-light version.

2. Use a color-correcting filter to alter the color temperature of the lamp. They are known as daylight-blue **filters** or ice-blue filters, among other names, and come in sizes to fit everything from MR11's to MR16's to HID luminaires. You'll learn what each of these lamp terminologies means in Chapter 3, so don't wig out yet.

3. Use luminaires that accommodate fluorescent or HID sources that come in cooler color temperatures.

Remember that daylight is white light and that moonlight is the same, because it is just a reflection of sunlight. So if you want to create a moonlight effect with your landscape lighting, here again you need to consider color temperature of the lamps. This technique will be explained in detail in Chapter 15.

Color Temperature and Skin Tone

Even though we grew up with incandescent light and are used to it, it is not the best color for skin, because it adds a slightly sallow, waxy cast. A hint of peach or pink in the light is a more flattering light that complements a wide range of skin tones.

For example, do you or someone you know have a drawer full of makeup that looked great when it was applied in the department store, but when you got home it was just slightly off? Why do you think this happens? Do you just assume you made a bad choice? No, it's not really your fault. When those in-store cosmeticians put you in front of that illuminated mirror, do you know what light source they were using? It's halogen! How often are you seen in a totally halogen environment? Almost never! You are more likely interacting with others in a daylight situation or an evening situation with standard incandescent lights. That's why the colors seem wrong. You need to select makeup under a light source that matches the environment in which you will be seen.

A knowledgeable store employee will explain the difference in color temperature between daylight situations and evening situations. Then he or she may recommend two sets of makeup—one for day wear (the office, the park, boating, etc. when you are seen in a color temperature around 5,000° K), and one for evening wear (theaters, restaurants, singles bars, etc., when you are most likely seen in a color temperature around 2,800° K). You, as an informed customer, will look at yourself in daylight and incandescent light to see how that particular shade of lipstick really looks. Don't trust the mirror lights!

The Bottom Line

1. Be sure to look at all surface colors (carpets, walls, furniture, etc.) under the lamp color specified, as well as daylight.

2. Warm color schemes should use a lower Kelvin source, while cool color schemes need a higher Kelvin source.

3. Let your clients see your selections under both lighting conditions, so that there will be no surprises or disappointments when the project is installed. Yes, this is being repeated for the third time. So take the hint—this is important!

Chapter Three

CHOOSING THE CORRECT LAMPS

When specifying lamps for a project, be sure to stay with the same manufacturer for each type of lamp. That way, the color quality will be consistent from lamp to lamp.

Lamps, a.k.a. Lightbulbs

Welcome to the fascinating world of lamps. This is the lighting industry's term for light-bulbs. That's why we call table lamps "portable luminaries," just so we don't confuse ourselves. So from this point on when you see the word "lamp," think "bulb."

In just the last ten years, a broad spectrum of lamps has been developed that we can incorporate into our designs. Still, you must understand that there is no one perfect lamp. Even though there are thousands of lamps to choose from, you will find that there will be favorites that you use again and again because they work well for your particular style of lighting design. As in interior design, there are few absolute rules—only guidelines for selecting colors, creating furniture layouts, and developing other aspects of the design process. The same goes for lamps and luminaire selections. We can offer guidelines but what you ultimately do will come down to your skills as a designer.

Getting to know the various properties of the lamps that are available will help you in choosing luminaires, since the choice of lamp will determine your choice of luminaire. After all, it's the lamp that provides that all-important illumination. Often luminaires are designed around new lamps that are introduced by the lamp manufacturers.

All lamps fit into four categories: incandescent, fluorescent, high-intensity discharge (HID), and light-emitting diode (LED). LED technology will be discussed in Chapter 7.

Incandescent Lamps

Incandescent lamps are what we are most familiar with. This group includes the standard household bulbs you have been screwing into light fixtures your whole life. They come in many sizes and shapes, as well as wattages and voltages beyond the standard household bulb.

Figure 3.1
Sample excerpt from the
GE Lamp Catalogue.

Watts	**75**	—
Order Code	**38207**	*It is important to use this five-digit code when ordering to ensure that you receive the exact product you require*
Description	**75R30FL**	*This information includes the lamp's burning position. It also includes the abbreviations BDTH (Burn lamp in Base Down To Horizontal position) and BU (Burn lamp in Base Up position only). Also shown in this column is packaging information (48PK, Carded, tray, etc.)*
Volts	**120**	*Each lamp's voltage is listed.*
Case Quantity	**24**	*Number of product units packed in a case.*
Filament Design	**CC-6**	*Filaments are designated by a letter combination in which C is a coiled wire filament, CC is a coiled wire that is itself wound into a larger coil, and SR is a straight ribbon filament. Numbers represent the type of filament-support arrangement.*
Maximum Overall Length	**5-3/8 (136.5)**	*Maximum Overall Length in inches and millimeters.*
Light Center Length	**—**	*Distance between the center of the filament and the Light Center Length reference plane, in inches and millimeters*
Rated Average Life Hours	**2000**	*Average Life Hours figure represents the lamp's median value of life expectancy.*
Initial Lumens	**900**	*Initial Lumens figure (in lumens) is based on photometry of lamps operated for a brief period, at rated volts. mean lumens: Also listed in Fluorescent and HID sections.*
Additional Information	**Reflector Flood Inside Frost**	*Typical application and/or other important information.*

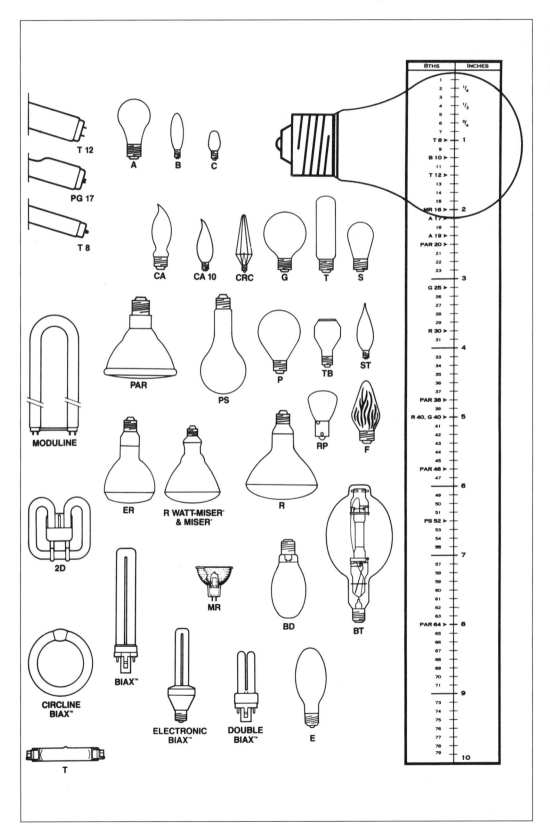

Figure 3.2
Lamp Diameters and Shapes
All lamp diameters are
expressed in eighths of an
inch. Note these lamps are not
drawn to scale.

Courtesy of GE Lighting, Nela
Park.

All lamps fit into three categories: Incandescent, Fluorescent and High Intensity Discharge (H.I.D.).

Cracking the Code

You can tell a lot about an incandescent lamp from its name. Let's start with a plain-vanilla household bulb. A 100-watt version is called a 100A19 IF 120V. The 100 refers to the wattage. If you wanted a 75-watt version, the first number would be 75. The A refers to the shape of the lamp (in this case the A stands for "arbitrary"). The chart below gives some of the most used abbreviations. The 19 refers to the diameter of the lamp. All lamps are measured in increments of 1/8 inch. So our standard household bulb is 19 eighths of an inch, or 2 3/8 inches in diameter. The IF stands for "inside frost," and the 120V means that it is a 120-volt lamp. This is standard house current (the voltage of the electricity that runs through your house).

Here's another example: *75R30 SP 120V*. The first number, 75, specifies wattage. The *R* stands for "reflector" and *30* tells you that the glass envelope is 30 eighths of an inch in diameter. The *SP* stands for "spot," and the *120V* refers to the voltage.

So just to review: The first number indicates wattage, the letter(s) indicates shape of the lamp, and the second number is the diameter, measured in eighths of an inch. The next letter or set of letters indicates the coating and the last number indicates the voltage (see Figure 3.1). A sampling of shapes of the most commonly used incandescent, fluorescent, and HID lamps is shown in Figure 3.2.

Here are some abbreviations you should get to know:

A = Arbitrary

IF = Inside frost

SB = Silver bowl—the crown of the lamp is coated to reflect light up

G = Globe— a lamp with a round envelope, like a ball

T = Tubular— a lamp with a tubular envelope, like a hotdog

R = Reflector— a built-in reflective surface that helps control the spread of light

ER = Ellipsoidal reflector—focuses light more precisely than an R-type lamp

PAR = Parabolic aluminized reflector—a lamp with a glass envelope of very heavy glass that controls its light **beam spread** using an integral reflector and lens

MR = Mirror reflector—a halogen lamp using faceted mirrors to control the light pattern

S = Sign—a lamp for use in signs, normally longer lasting than standard lamps

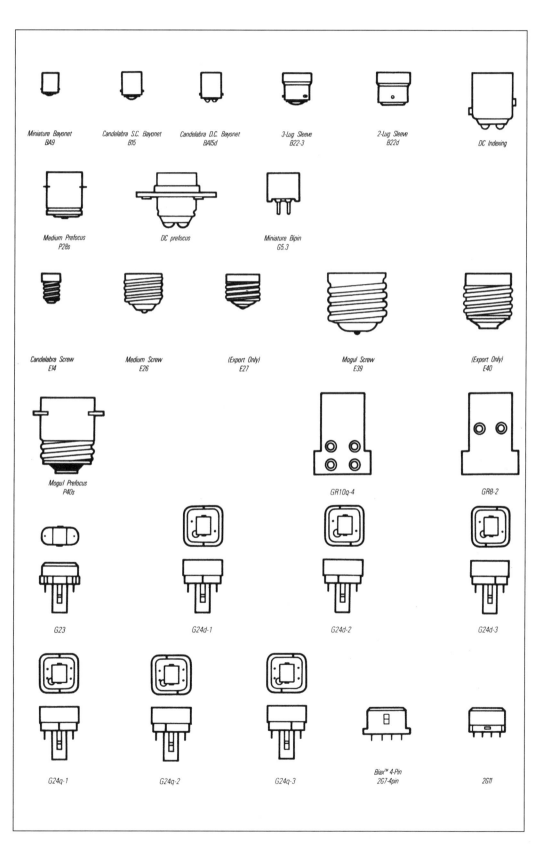

Figure 3.3
A Sampling of Lamp Bases
Lamp bases come in a wide
variety of shapes and sizes.

Courtesy of G.E. Lighting, Nela
Park.

*Figure 3.4
Here are even more
bases to study.*

*Courtesy of GE Lighting Nela
Park.*

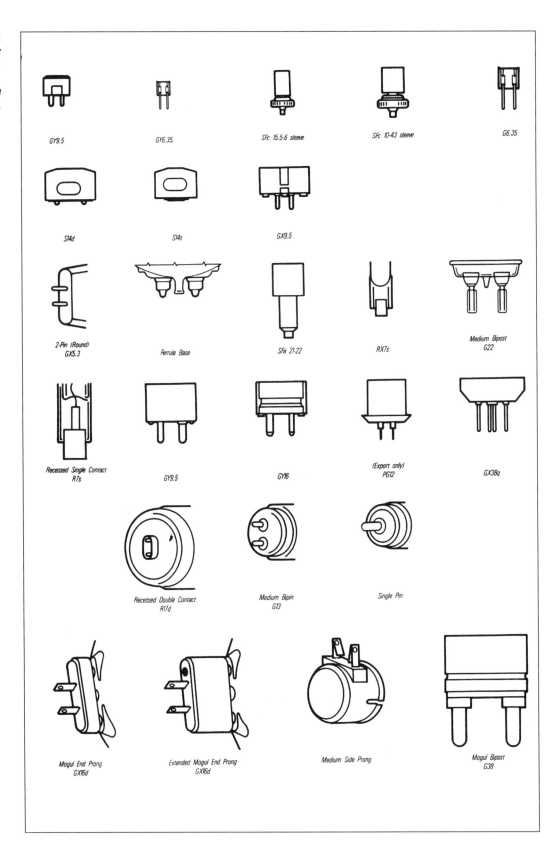

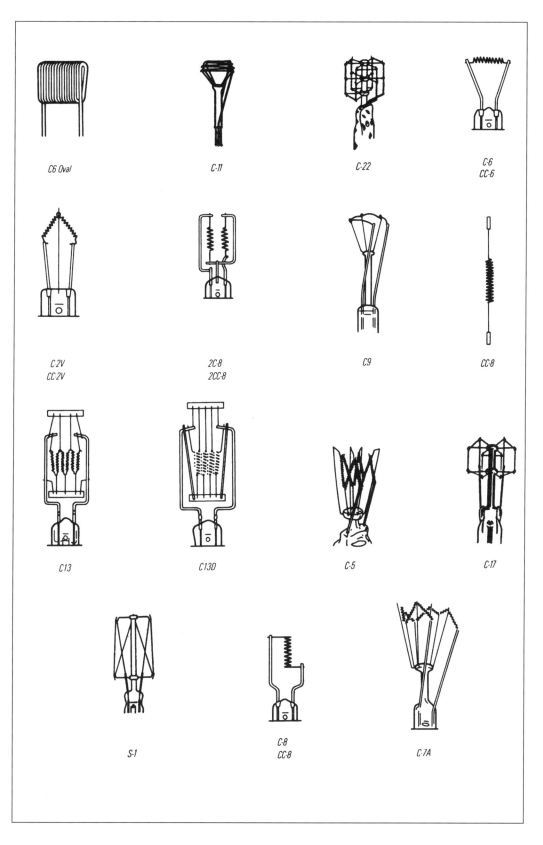

C6 Oval

C-11

C-22

C-6
CC-6

C-2V
CC-2V

2C-8
2CC-8

C9

CC-8

C13

C13D

C-5

C-17

S-1

C-8
CC-8

C-7A

Figure 3.5
There are a wide variety of filaments being used today. This is a good sampling for reference purposes.

Courtesy of G.E. Lighting, Nela Park

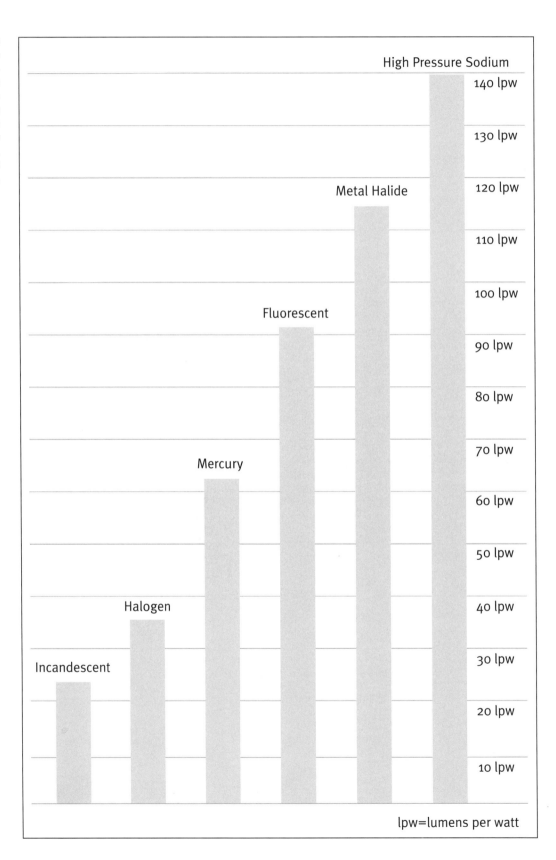

Figure 3.6
Lamp Efficacy
This chart compares the various lamp categories and their respective efficacies. Mercury, metal halide and high Pressure sodium are H.I.D. (High Intensity Discharge) sources. Incandescent gives us the least bang for the buck.

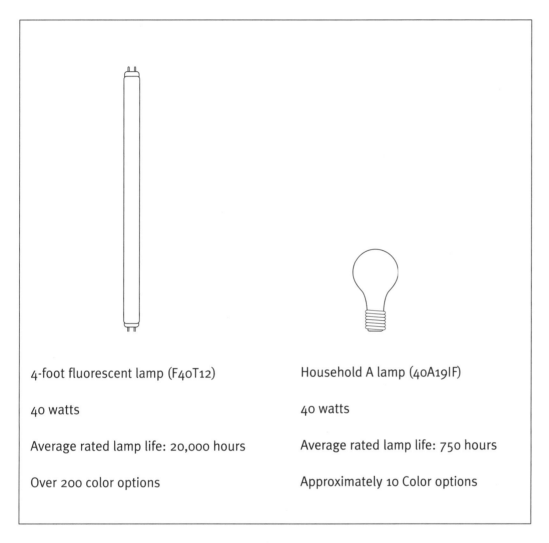

4-foot fluorescent lamp (F40T12)

40 watts

Average rated lamp life: 20,000 hours

Over 200 color options

Household A lamp (40A19IF)

40 watts

Average rated lamp life: 750 hours

Approximately 10 Color options

Figure 3.7
Efficiencies
Here is a comparison between a 40 watt household lamp and a 40 watt fluorescent lamp. The new lower wattage T-8 fluorescents are even more energy efficient.

Lamp Bases

Along with wattage, shape, and size, base designations are also important. The base is the part of a lamp that makes the connection with a socket. A household bulb has a screw-in base, also known as a standard base. An MR16 lamp, a very popular low-voltage lamp, has a bi-pin or bayonet base.

A candle-shaped or flame-tip lamp can have a medium base or a candelabra base. Just to make things more difficult, European countries use different sized bases than the United States. When selecting a luminaire, knowing what type of lamp fits into it is important (see Figures 3.3 and 3.4). The fixture manufacturers will tell you in their catalogs which lamp(s) fit into a particular luminaire.

Which Lamp to Use?

Often you have a variety of lamps that will fit the same luminaire, so it will be up to you to decide which lamp will work best for your purposes. This will come from experimentation more than from anything you will read. Go to lighting showrooms where they have recessed luminaires installed to see what the various lamps do. Check how bright they are, how tight or diffuse the beam spread is, and what color quality of light they produce. When you are working for a design professional or out on your own, manufacturers' representatives will come to your office to show you the latest models in their line. There are often trade shows that will show luminaires and lamps, such as Lightfair International (www.lightfair.com). This tradeshow happens every year, alternating between New York City and Las Vegas. It is a fantastic way to see lighting components from a lot of manufacturers in one location.

Lamp Filaments and Hum

A chart of filaments (see Figure 3.5) is shown here just as a point of information. In the lamp specification guides the type of filament is usually noted. The main thing to think about in regard to filaments is potential hum. Some lamps hum when they are dimmed. Some manufacturers offer lamps where the filament is attached to a central stem to keep it from vibrating. It is this vibration that causes the lamp to emit a sound. These lamps are often referred to as "rough service" lamps and are readily available.

Another approach is to select a lamp with a thick glass envelope. Usually the hum can't be heard through the heavier glass enclosure. It is often the lamp's interaction with a dimmer that increases the tendency to hum. This aspect will be addressed more fully in Chapter 6.

Voltage Choices

Voltage is also important when specifying a lamp. Many lamps come in multiple voltages: 6V and 12V for small lamps, 110V for residential, 130V for "rough service" (these bulbs tend to last longer than 110V lamps because they are operating at less than full brightness), and 220V to 240V for industrial or commercial use. If the luminaire is 120V, the lamp also needs to be 120V. If you try to screw a 12V lamp into a 110V fixture the bulb will probably explode when the fixture is switched on.

All lamps in the four categories have their advantages and disadvantages. Understanding what those differences are and communicating that information to your clients is a key element to making intelligent design selections.

Incandescent Revealed

This is the type of lamp with which we are all very familiar. It's what we grew up with, and it is the visual image that pops up above our head when we get a great idea. Incandescents are the least efficient of the four categories (see Figure 3.6 to compare how well they do the job of illuminating).

The standard household lamp, which you now know is referred to in the industry as an A lamp, has been around since the late 1800s.

Incandescent lamps come in hundreds of shapes and sizes and many different voltages. Halogen sources are in reality incandescent. They were touched on briefly in Chapter 2, but will be discussed in more detail separately later in this chapter.

In an incandescent lamp, heating the filament to a visible glow generates light. The hotter the filament becomes, the brighter the light. However, lamp life is shortened by heat. Their glass envelopes are usually clear or frosted but can also be colored to provide a wide variety of hues. A basic incandescent lamp emits a light that is yellowish in color. When you dim an incandescent lamp, the color turns more amber, meaning its color temperature becomes lower. This color shift will dramatically affect the look of objects being illuminated. You must take this into consideration when designing a space. This cannot be stressed enough.

Standard incandescent lamps are:

1. A good point source with good optical control

2. Easily dimmed at a relatively low cost

3. Very versatile in regard to shapes and wattages

There are drawbacks too:

1. Short lamp life: 750 – 2,000 hours

2. The least efficient of the three lamp categories (see Figures 3.6 and 3.7)

Yet we love it for that golden glow that takes us back to the time of candles, and maybe even further back, to the days spent in our caves around a roaring fire.

Due to concerns over energy conservation and advances in technology, certain lamps have been replaced by newer, more efficient light sources. Yes, this means fluorescent lamps, but don't be so quick to brush them off. Today's fluorescents are not like the ones we grew up with.

It is important to know that fixtures you specify can use many of the new lamps now on the market. This is true for fixtures already existing on a project. For example, 150R40 spots are now replaced by 75PAR30 spots. These more efficient lamps offer comparable light levels at half the power consumption. The old F40T12 cool white and warm white fluorescents are being replaced by lower-wattage lamps in T8, T5, and even T2 versions with wonderful color temperatures.

In 1995, certain lamps were outlawed by the Energy Policy Act of 1992 (EPACT), including R40's and R52's as well as cool white and warm white fluorescents. These lamps have been replaced with more efficient light sources. These new sources have found their way into the general market.

Note: All low voltage systems have some inherent hum. That hum comes from the transformer, the lamp, the dimmer, or any combination of the three. MR16 and MR11 lamps hum less than PAR36 lamps. If the transformers are installed in a remote location, then their hum is contained in the attic, basement, or garage space.

Figure 3.8
MR-11's and MR-16's.

Multi-Mirror Reflector Lamps

MR11's	Wattage	Type	Beam
FTB	20-watt	MR11	10° narrow spot
FTC	20-watt	MR11	15° spot
FTD	20-watt	MR11	30° narrow flood
FTE	35-watt	MR11	8° narrow spot
FTF	35-watt	MR11	20° spot
FTH	35-watt	MR11	30° narrow flood

MR16's	Wattage	Type	Beam
EZX	20-watt	MR16	7° very narrow spot
ESX	20-watt	MR16	15° narrow spot
BAB	20-watt	MR16	40° flood
FRB	35-watt	MR16	12° narrow spot
FRA	35-watt	MR16	20° spot
FMW	35-watt	MR16	40° flood
EZY	42-watt	MR16	9° very narrow spot
EYS	42-watt	MR16	25° narrow flood
EXT	50-watt	MR16	15° narrow spot
EXZ	50-watt	MR16	25° narrow spot
EXK	50-watt	MR16	30° narrow flood
EXN	50-watt	MR16	40° flood
FNV	50-watt	MR16	55° wide flood
EYF	75-watt	MR16	15° narrow spot
EYJ	75-watt	MR16	25° narrow flood
EYC	75-watt	MR16	40° flood

PAR 36 shape lamps

LAMP	Wattage	Type	Beam
25PAR36/NSP	25-watt	PAR36	narrow spot
25PAR36/WFL	25-watt	PAR36	wide flood
25PAR36/VWFL	25-watt	PAR36	very wide flood
35PAR36/H/NSP8°	35-watt	halogen PAR36	narrow spot
35PAR36/H/VNSP5°	35-watt	halogen PAR36	very narrow spot
35PAR36/H/WFL8°	35-watt	halogen PAR36	wide flood
50PAR36/H/VNSP5°	50-watt	halogen PAR36	very narrow spot
50PAR36/H/NSP8°	50-watt	halogen PAR36	narrow spot
50PAR36/WFL8°	50-watt	halogen PAR36	wide flood
50PAR36/VNSP	50-watt	PAR36	very narrow spot
50PAR36/NSP	50-watt	PAR36	narrow spot
50PAR36/WFL	50-watt	PAR36	wide flood
50PAR36/WFL/4	50-watt	PAR36	wide flood
50PAR36/VWFL	50-watt	halogen PAR36	very wide flood

Numbered	Wattage	Type	Beam
4405	25-watt	PAR36	very narrow spot
4406	29.5-watt	PAR36	very narrow spot
4411	29.5-watt	PAR36	spot
4414	14.9-watt	PAR36	oblong spot
4415	29.9-watt	PAR36	oblong spot
4416	25-watt	PAR36	ovoid spot
7600	42-watt	halogen PAR36	ovoid flood
7606	50-watt	halogen PAR36	oblong flood
7610	50-watt	halogen PAR36	wide flood
7616	37.5-watt	halogen PAR36	ovoid spot

*NOTE: All PAR36 lamps listed above are 12 volts

Figure 3.9
Par 36 Lamps.

It is important that you do not touch the glass envelope of a halogen lamp with your bare hands. The oil in your hands, transferred to the lamp when touched, could create a weak spot on the glass. This point of weakness in the envelope could cause the lamp to explode.

Halogen

Halogen (also known as tungsten halogen or quartz) is also an incandescent lamp and might be considered an advanced or improved incandescent lamp. According to General Electric Lighting, "They are just like standard incandescents but contain a halogen gas which recycles tungsten back onto the filament surface. The halogen gas allows the lamps to burn more intensely without sacrificing life."

There is a lot of misinformation about halogen that needs to be cleared up. It is often labeled a "white" source of light. That's a relative term. As was mentioned in Chapter 2, it is whiter than standard incandescent lamps by 200°K, but it's 2,000°K yellower than daylight. That's quite a large difference. Also, it is only whiter than standard incandescent when it is operating at full capacity. When dimmed, it becomes as yellow as any regular incandescent source. You need to treat halogen as basically a warm source of illumination in your design scheme.

Halogens have a number of advantages:

1. Halogen sources tend to be smaller in size than standard incandescent sources of comparable wattage.

2. They produce more light than standard incandescent sources of comparable wattage.

3. They have better optical control than most standard incandescent, fluorescent, or HID sources.

4. Halogens come in a variety of shapes and sizes.

Halogens also have disadvantages:

1. The light yellows when dimmed, as with all incandescent sources.

2. Dimming may shorten lamp life; lights should be turned up full at regular intervals to maximize lamp life.

3. The glass envelope should not be touched without wearing gloves.

4. They have to be shielded or enclosed in a glass envelope to protect the area around it from its intense heat.

It is important that you do not touch the glass envelope with your bare hands. The oil in your hands, transferred to the lamp when touched, could create a weak spot on the glass. This point of weakness in the envelope could cause the lamp to explode.

If you do touch the lamp, the surface can be cleaned with alcohol. Wearing gloves or using a clean cloth will prevent this problem. There are now what are called "double-envelope" halogen lamps available that eliminate this handling precaution, because they have a second layer of glass around them. These are also great to use when humming from a standard incandescent lamp is a problem.

Some other things you should know about halogens:

Beam spreads. With the right reflectors, halogen can produce a wide variety of beam spreads and a good punch of light.

Mirror reflector lamps (MR16's and MR11's). Halogens are being made in almost all the shapes and sizes of incandescent lamps, along with a few that are unique, such as MR16's and MR11's. The MR stands for mirror reflector. These particular lamps have been the hot tickets in the lighting world for the last 14 years. Their technology improves with each passing year. Their small size and beam control enables luminaire manufacturers to create a variety of compact fixture styles.

MR16 lamps were originally made for slide projectors, so their catalog numbers often refer to the machinery for which they were designed. They have American National Standards Institute (ANSI) letters such as EXN, EXT, and FJX. These are not as familiar as other lamp designations, which, as you now know, correlate to wattage, shape, and size. See Figure 3.8 for a list of MR16 and MR11 numbers and what wattage and beam spreads they represent.

PAR36 lamps. Another group of lamps, made originally for other uses, are PAR36's. They are available in standard incandescent and halogen varieties. They look like small automobile headlights. Not surprisingly, they were used as airplane landing lights and fog lights on tractors. They too have ANSI designations that don't readily give us information about the lamp, while other PAR36 lamps, produced later specifically for the lighting industry, do have the designations that are readily recognizable.

For example, a 25PAR36 12V WFL means a 25-watt lamp with a parabolic, aluminized reflector that is 36 eighths of an inch in diameter. It operates at 12 volts with a beam spread that produces a wide flood of illumination. See Figure 3.9 for some of the more commonly used PAR36 lamps. These lamps are used less frequently than the MR lamps because they don't last very long and they have a tendency to hum.

Here are some straight answers to commonly asked questions on halogen lamps:

What kind of wall dimmer can be used with low-voltage halogen lights?

It's best to use a dimmer that is specifically made to control low-voltage lighting. It will say on the dimmer box whether it is specifically designed for low-voltage lighting. Be aware that there are two types of low-voltage transformers used with halogen lamps: electronic and magnetic. A transformer is a device that changes 120 volts down to a lower voltage. Make

Average Rated Lamp Life means that halfway through a test of a certain group of lamps, 50 percent of them are still working and 50 percent are burned out.

sure you choose a dimmer that is compatible with the system you select. Otherwise, the system may emit an audible hum.

Occasionally, darkening of a halogen lamp may occur. If this happens, simply turn on the lamp at 100 percent illumination for ten minutes. The black residue (the result of tungsten evaporation) will disappear. Darkening of the lamp does not affect lamp life.

All low-voltage systems have some inherent hum. That hum comes from the transformer, the lamp, the dimmer, or any combination of the three. MR16 and MR11 lamps hum less than PAR36 lamps. If the transformers are installed in a remote location, then their hum is contained in the attic, basement, or garage space.

What is the light output of a 50-watt halogen desk light with a high-low switch when on low?
The high-low switch cuts the light output approximately in half.

Do halogen bulbs last longer?
The average rated life for a halogen lamp is 2,000 hours. A standard A lamp (remember, this is a regular old household bulb) is rated at a life of 750 hours. Remember that "average rated life" means that on average a particular lamp lasts for the number of hours listed in the lamp manufacturer's catalog. For example, in a hypothetical group of halogen lamps rated at 2,000 hours, after 2000 hours half of the lamps might be burned out and half will still be working. That's why some lamps seem to burn out right away, while others of the same kind tend to go on forever.

Do halogen bulbs use less energy?
Not really. The amount of money you'd spend to power a 50R20 lamp and a 50-watt MR16 is the same. The difference is that the MR16 lamp can produce a more concentrated beam of light, creating a better visual punch.

Do halogen bulbs use more electricity? Will you notice a difference in the electric bill?
You can cut your energy bill by using smaller-wattage halogen lamps to give a similar amount of light in luminaires that use higher-wattage standard A lamps and R lamps.

Is halogen safe to use in a bathroom? Does moisture affect the bulb?
Yes, it is as safe as any other lamp used in bathroom applications. The National Electrical Code requires that the luminaires be waterproof when located over wet locations. In the lighting industry these are known as fixtures that are "rated for wet locations."

Are halogen bulbs readily available? If so, where?
Lighting showrooms and electrical distributors will carry a ready stock of halogen lamps. Hardware stores and grocery stores are beginning to carry a limited variety.

How can I determine the width of the beam from various sources?

Lamp and fixture manufacturers have graphs and charts to show beam patterns of different lamps in their fixtures. The narrowest beam spreads come from the PAR36 VNSP (very narrow spot) or the 4405 (pin spot). The next smallest beam spreads come from MR11 spots. Almost all lamp sources can provide a wide beam. It depends on how wide you want it, what type of lamp the luminaire you're using can accommodate, and how far away you are from the object that you want to light. There is no set answer to this question (see Figures 3.8 and 3.9).

How far out from the wall should I locate the recessed cans?

The height of the ceiling and the type of lamp and luminaire being used determine distance from the wall. Each luminaire manufacturer has charts to show distancing and spacing requirements for their luminaires.

Look at recessed adjustable luminaires as a good source of illumination for a variety of functions. These can provide accent lighting, wash walls with a soft spread of illumination, or create pools of light to help direct visitors. These fixtures have a lot of flexibility compared to a fixed recessed downlight fixture. People today move their furniture and art around much than their parents did. The lighting needs to be more flexible to match today's lifestyle.

Are there disadvantages to MR16 and MR11 lamps?

The "dichroic" reflectors project heat back inside the luminaire itself. This is a special coating. The luminaire must be designed to withstand that heat.

Also, the dichroic reflector can project a colored light out the back. Open or vented luminaires will allow that color to be projected onto ceilings and walls. Fixtures that are sealed won't have this problem.

These dichroic reflectors ("dichroic" refers to a special coating) often vary the color of the light they project forward. Using one specific company's lamps instead of mixing manufacturers will lessen this problem but may not eliminate it. MR16's and MR11's are available with aluminized reflectors (solid backs) to help combat the color fluctuations and backwash problem.

The circle of illumination from some of the tighter beam spreads may not be consistent. Often, coronas of color and refractions can be seen along the perimeter of the beam of light. The addition of one of the many **spread lenses** or **diffusion filters** that are available can help soften or eliminate this problem. Some luminaire manufacturers include a diffusion filter as a standard part of the fixture.

In the future, we will probably be seeing incandescent light being used primarily for accent and decorative functions. Task and ambient lighting will fall on the shoulders of fluorescent and LED sources.

Halfway through its life, a fluorescent lamp may produce 20 percent less light than when it was new.

Figure 3.10
Here are some of the
fluorescent lamp shapes that
are available.

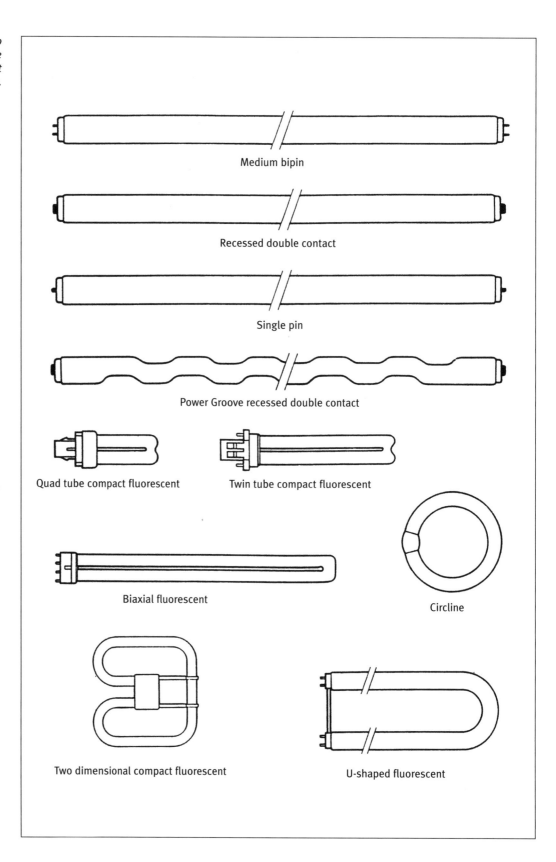

Medium bipin

Recessed double contact

Single pin

Power Groove recessed double contact

Quad tube compact fluorescent   Twin tube compact fluorescent

Biaxial fluorescent

Circline

Two dimensional compact fluorescent   U-shaped fluorescent

Fluorescent

Using electricity to energize a phosphor coating on the inside of a glass envelope creates fluorescent light. Inside the envelope are droplets of mercury and inert gases such as argon or krypton. At each end of the fluorescent tube are electrodes. When electricity flows between the electrodes, it creates an ultraviolet light. The ultraviolet light causes the phosphor coating to glow or "fluoresce," releasing the characteristic fluorescent light from the whole tube. The color temperature of the light will vary depending on the phosphors used.

Ballasts for Fluorescents

Fluorescent lamps require a **ballast** to provide extra power to start the lamp and to control the flow of electricity while it is operating. Early magnetic ballasts were partially responsible for giving fluorescents a bad name because they hummed and caused the lamps to flicker. The ballast is usually installed in the fixture **housing**, but in situations where space is very limited they can be located remotely. Also, some ballasts can operate more than one lamp.

There are two ways ballasts can be manufactured: pre-heat and rapid-start. Pre-heat ballasts warm the electrodes to a glow stage activated by a starter switch (located on the fixture itself). These are used primarily in small fixtures such as under-cabinet lights. Rapid-start ballasts have a circuit that continuously heats the electrodes, resulting in faster illumination of the lamp. Almost all modern fixtures using 26-watt or higher lamps have rapid-start ballasts.

There are two variations of the rapid-start ballast: magnetic (the first generation of ballasts), which unfortunately, tend to hum and cause lamps to flicker; and electronic (also known as solid-state) which have no hum and make flickering a thing of the past.

Dimming Fluorescents

Before, a magnetic **dimming ballast** was very expensive and might flutter if dimmed beyond a certain point. Now, with the advent of new electronic dimming ballasts, many of the old problems have been resolved.

For dimming purposes, solid-state ballasts are the best available (and, of course, the most expensive). The dimmable version allows for 90 percent to full-range dimming (depending on the manufacturer), with no hum or buzzing, and you can dim different lamp lengths together. Before, you could only dim all 4-footers or all 3-footers together. The solid-state ballast allows you to dim most lengths together. Chapter 6 will deal further with fluorescent dimming.

The latest technology coming from the lamp manufacturers is the advent of self-ballasted compact fluorescent lamps with screw-in bases that can be dimmed with an incandescent dimmer. A high-priced fluorescent dimmer is not required. One such lamp is the Earthlight by Phillips Lighting. This cutting-edge technology will be explained in more detail on the following pages.

There are cold-weather ballasts and well-sealed luminaires available that should be used if the project is located in a region with below-freezing temperatures.

Caution: HID
sources shift in
color over their
rated life.

Improvements in Color Selection

It is true that early fluorescent lamps were awful, but times have changed. There were just two colors available in fluorescent for the longest time: cool white or warm white. Cool white gave you a greenish cast, while warm white gave an orange facsimile of incandescent. Their colors were obtained using different phosphor powders. These two choices were (and still are) just poor interpretations of the two ends of the Kelvin color temperature scale. As noted before, both these lamps are no longer manufactured in the 40-watt T12 version for the U.S. market. There are new, improved fluorescents out there just waiting for you to embrace them and make them your own. Now there are many alluring colors available in fluorescent. Some are wonderfully creamy peach-toned hues, which are great for skin tone (but not the best for color rendering).

You have so many colors to choose from that you can "paint" with light, using a very broad palette. These colors are obtained from a mix of phosphors. Tri-phosphor fluorescent lamps (using a mix of three phosphors) have some of most usable color temperatures for residential use.

Compact Fluorescents

Compact fluorescent lamps (known in the industry as CFLs) have opened up a whole range of uses that were not possible with larger-sized fluorescents. We are seeing them now being incorporated into small-diameter recessed luminaires, wall sconces, pendants, wall-wash luminaires, and many more. This type of lamp is being improved more quickly than any other source on the market (with HID and LED sources running a close second). See Figure 3.10 for the common fluorescent lamp shapes available.

The first compact units on the market had a noticeable hum, did not have a rapid-start ballast, were not dimmable, and had a limited selection of color temperatures. Great strides have been made on all fronts. Today there are rapid-start, quiet, dimmable compact fluorescent lamps in a variety of color temperatures. There are even self-ballasted CFLs that can be dimmed with standard incandescent dimmers instead of expensive fluorescent dimmers. CFLs are a very energy-efficient source of illumination that can simply be screwed into existing household fixtures, including ceiling lights, table lamps, torchères, wall sconces, and recessed fixtures.

The electronic dimming ballasts at this point are pricey, but they will come down in cost as more manufacturers get into this emerging market. But CFLs' light output, long life, color variety, and energy efficiency make them well worth considering on any project.

Advantages of Fluorescents

Longer lamp life. A standard household A lamp has an average rated lamp life of 750 hours, while the T8 fluorescent is rated for 22,000 hours! The best that most standard reflector lamps can do is 2,000 hours. A good MR16 gets 3,500 to 6,000 hours, while compact fluorescents are rated at 10,000 hours, a huge difference. It can be especially advantageous when lamps are located where they're hard to change when they burn out, not to mention the energy savings.

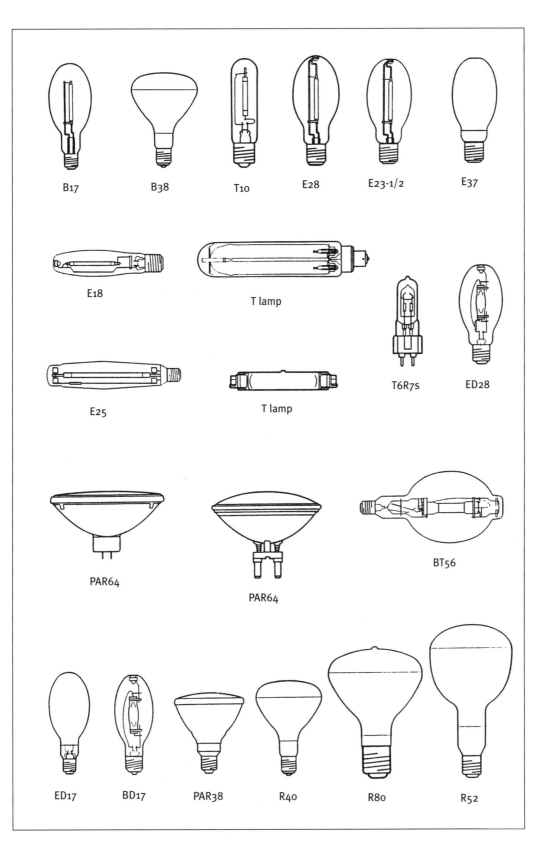

B17 B38 T10 E28 E23-1/2 E37

E18 T lamp

E25 T lamp T6R7s ED28

PAR64 PAR64 BT56

ED17 BD17 PAR38 R40 R80 R52

Figure 3.11
Here is a sampling of H.I.D.
(High Intensity Discharge)
lamp shapes.

Lower maintenance time and cost. Because fluorescent lamps last longer, they need to be replaced less often, saving time and money. Remember that "average rated lamp life" means that halfway through a test of a certain group of lamps, 50 percent of them are still working and 50 percent are burned out. Don't expect all T8 lamps to last 22,000 hours. Some will burn out sooner and some will last longer.

More lumen output. Fluorescent lamps can produce three to five times more lumens for the same wattage as a standard A lamp. For example, compare the light of a 40-watt household lamp and a 4-foot fluorescent lamp. Both are 40 watts, yet you can visibly see how much more light you get from the fluorescent (see Figure 3.7). Here again, you can see how using fluorescent lamps can produce significant energy savings, because you don't need to use such high-wattage lamps. The newer 4-foot fluorescent lamps with smaller diameters (known as T8's) provide 40 watts of light output while using only 34 watts of power.

Cooler source. Fluorescent lamps don't give off as much heat as incandescent sources. So not only will there be savings on air-conditioning, but you won't have the problems of heat damage and fire danger that you may have with high temperature sources such as halogen. With color-corrected phosphors, fluorescents make great light sources for closets. They can be installed closer to combustible material.

Color variety. There are a huge number of color temperatures available in fluorescent lamps, while incandescent lamps are available in relatively few. So if you need a certain color temperature for a special space or setting, you'll be able to find it more easily using fluorescent lamps.

Dimming. Fluorescent lamps do not change significantly in color temperature when dimmed, as incandescent sources do. When you use fluorescent lamps you don't have to worry that the whole color scheme will be altered when your client dims the lights.

Disadvantages of Fluorescents

Fluorescents, like all lamps, are not perfect. They too have their drawbacks. Here is a listing of the ones you need to be aware of:

Lamp life and Lumen output. Halfway through its life, a fluorescent may produce 20 percent less light than when new. So relamping (the lighting industry's term for changing a lightbulb) at that point may be a good practice to maximize the light output for the power consumed. Also the ballast, which is integral to fluorescent luminaires, will still use some power even if the lamp is removed. If you decide to remove half the lamps for purposes of energy efficiency then the ballast must be disconnected if the energy savings are to be fully realized.

Hum. There are many fluorescent luminaires on the market that have inferior magnetic ballasts. Be selective—make sure to specify an electronic (solid-state) ballast.

Relative inability to accent. Fluorescent lamps are relatively large light sources. Through the use of integral reflectors, manufacturers are able to achieve some success with fluorescent luminaires, such as wall washers for art. They can be very effective for uplighting trees. There are even compact fluorescents inside reflector envelopes that mimic the directional capabilities of PAR lamps and R lamps. But incandescent sources, such as MR16's, PAR36's and PAR20's, are still tops in the concentrated-beam category.

Temperature restrictions. A major disadvantage of fluorescents is their difficulty igniting in very cold temperatures. They may start out very dim and take several minutes to warm to full output. Below-freezing temperatures may keep them from igniting at all. Some manufacturers offer fluorescent fixtures that are specially made for colder climates.

Prime Uses for Fluorescents
Some situations are particularly well suited for fluorescents.

Ambient light. Fluorescent lamps can do a tremendous job of providing pleasing ambient light. Their soft, even glow of illumination is well suited to providing fill light. The right color temperature and a solid-state dimming ballast can team up for a very usable, flexible ambient source of light.

Storage areas. Fluorescent lamps are extremely useful for storage areas and garages. They are an inexpensive way of producing a good amount of illumination.

Closets and laundry rooms. A color-corrected fluorescent luminaire, mounted in the closet or under the overhead cabinets in the laundry room, can provide accurate illumination for color matching. It is like having daylight in these rooms when no natural light is available.

High-intensity Discharge (HID)
This is the third of the four lamp categories and the one that holds the most mystery for designers and architects. But high-intensity discharge lamps are relatively easy to understand and may end up being the perfect lamp selection for a specific aspect of an upcoming project. See Figure 3.11 for HID lamp shapes.

The truth is that it's going to be a while before we see HID sources being used much for residential interiors. They are better suited for exterior lighting (both residential and commercial). They are large in size, require a ballast, are not fully dimmable, and have a limited number of wattages.

What are they?
Inside the glass envelope of an HID lamp is a small cylinder (made of ceramic or quartz) called an "arc tube." It is filled with a blend of pressurized gases. A ballast directs electricity through the tube and charges the gases to produce light. These sources typically have a 10,000-hour lamp life and a very "high lumen output" (this means that for the power expended you get a whole lot of light).

Each kind of HID lamp has its own special blend of gases and produces a different colored light.

Mercury vapor has been around the longest. It produces a silvery blue-green light, which is terrible for skin tones but acceptable for lighting trees. The color can be a little surreal, making trees look ultragreen.

High pressure sodium is currently the most widely-used of the HID sources. Most of the streets in the United States and in other countries are illuminated with high-pressure sodium lamps, which emit a gold-orange light. These lamps too have poor color-rendering capabilities. Trees look dried out and dead, and people resemble the bottoms of copper cookware. Yet brick facades, sandstone walls, and even the Golden Gate Bridge look great when illuminated by high-pressure sodium.

Low pressure sodium has even worse color quality, which could be described as a gray-orange. This light source gives most colors the same value—for example, cars in a parking lot all appear to be the same color. So why is this the most commonly specified light source when it has the worst color-rendering ability? Unfortunately, it's in wide use because it happens to have the longest life and highest lumen output.

Metal Halide is the new kid on the block. It is the darling of the HID sources. It produces a light that is the whitest of the four types. It also comes in two very usable color temperatures: 3,000°K and 4,000°K. A special advantage over the other HID sources is that metal halide lamps come in some very small sizes, allowing for more compact luminaires.

Disadvantages of HID lamps

One of the main disadvantages of all HID lamps is their tendency to shift in color throughout their life. They don't all shift the same way, though. Metal halide will shift toward green or toward magenta. This shift differs not only with each manufacturer but with each lamp as well. Mass relamping (which means changing all the lamps at one time) halfway through their average rated lamp life will keep the color as constant as possible. Improved lamps, such as the Phillips Master Colorline™, have a shift that averages plus or minus 200°K over the lamp's life.

Even as you read this, lamp manufacturers are working hard to improve color quality, to reduce the size of mercury vapor and sodium sources, to minimize color shifting, and to extend lamp life. Understanding the properties of the various lamps in all three categories will also help you choose the correct luminaire.

Where to get more information

Lamp catalogs are good sources of more specific data on particular lamps. Manufacturers offer a wealth of information, specially compiled to help designers and architects choose the right lamp for a particular need. Many catalogs are available online through the Internet. They are also available through lighting showrooms and manufacturers' representatives in printed form, and sometimes on compact disc. The online information tends to be the most current. Products are discontinued or added periodically, so it's a good practice to verify information online before making a final specification.

The Bottom Line

Knowing which lamps work for what you want to create is the main building block for a successful and effective lighting design.

Chapter Four
CHOOSING THE CORRECT LUMINAIRES

Luminaires come in countless shapes and sizes. For purposes of this book, they will be divided into three categories: recessed, surface-mounted, and portable.

Being familiar with the many types of luminaires that are available is as important as knowing what lamps should go into them. Luminaire is the lighting industry's term for "light fixture." They come in countless shapes and sizes. For the purposes of this book, they will be divided into three categories: portable, surface-mounted, and recessed.

Portable Luminaires
Portable luminaires (see Figure 4.1 for some typical styles) are the ones with which we are most familiar. They include reading lights, **torchères** (floor lamps), and **uplights** (accent lights that are located on the floor behind plants to cast a shadow pattern on the ceiling). If used correctly, they can be a quick fix for a good number of lighting problems. If they are misused, they can visually dominate a room, letting everything else fall into secondary importance (see Figure 4.2). A portable luminaire has a cord and plug and can be easily moved from one location to another.

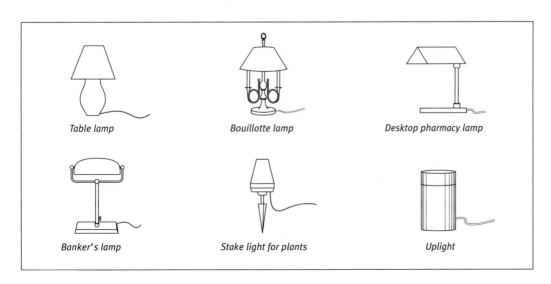

Table lamp

Bouillotte lamp

Desktop pharmacy lamp

Banker's lamp

Stake light for plants

Uplight

Figure 4.1
Typical portable luminaires

*Figure 4.2
Table lamps with
translucent shades become
the focal point of the room,
forcing everything else
to fall into secondary importance.*

*Figure 4.3
A pharmacy lamp provides
excellent task lighting without drawing attention to
itself.*

*Figure 4.4
A torchère lamp is a fast,
easy way of providing
ambient light for a room.*

Please be aware that portable luminaires are just one component of effective lighting design, and for the most part should be considered as temporary fixes unless there are no other options.

Table lamps
Table lamps (what the lighting industry wants you to call portable luminaires) are probably the most overused fixtures in residences. People want one fixture to perform all the necessary lighting functions: decorative, accent, task, and ambient. The result produces a sea of lamp shades that draw your attention away from everything else.

Humans are naturally drawn to light; it is a part of our physiological makeup. For example, when you are driving down the freeway at night, you are confronted by a steady stream of oncoming headlights. They are glaring and uncomfortable to look at, but don't you look at every pair? When you are designing a room, do you want the linen lamp shades you've selected to be the first thing that people see? Or do you want them to see their hosts, the fantastic art collection, the sumptuous colors you've chosen, and the impeccable furniture selections you've made?

Table lamps can perform valuable functions if they are selected with care. A luminaire with a translucent shade (linen, silk, rice paper, etc.) works best as a decorative source of illumination. Using a low-wattage lamp (25 watts or less), they create little islands of light that draw people to seating areas and add a comforting human scale to a room.

If their primary function is to provide reading light, as mentioned in Chapter 1, consider using an opaque shade of any color and a perforated metal lid, so that the illumination is directed downward onto the table and across the reader's lap. An opaque shade without the lid may cast a hard circle of light onto the ceiling, depending on the lamp being used (see Figures 4.7 and 4.8).

Another consideration is adding a translucent white opal glass or acrylic diffuser on the bottom of the shade. This softens the light and shields the lamps from view. This works very well for swing-arm reading lights that are mounted on a wall next to the bed.

Having these luminaires on dimmers or fitted with three-way lamps (a lamp that can be switched to 50, 100, or 150 watts) allows some flexibility in light level. This allows them to be both decorative and task sources, depending on the need at the time.

A good alternative would be a pharmacy-type luminaire (see Figure 4.9) with a metal or "cased-glass" (colored glass on the outside and white glass on the inside) shade on a portable floor or table model. Most of these luminaires have adjustable necks so that they can be easily repositioned for the particular height of the person using them (see Plate 1.24).

Selecting a luminaire with an opaque shade (normally metal) enables it to be positioned below eye level, providing shadow and glare-free illumination. The opaque shade also allows for the light level to be bumped up significantly without drawing attention to the luminaire itself (see Figure 4.3).

Torchères
Another portable luminaire that has been in demand is the torchère (a floor lamp that projects light upward (see Figure 4.4). It is a quick, easy way of providing some ambient light for a given space. Select a luminaire that has an opaque (solid) shade (see Figure 4.10). A translucent shade, such as glass, will draw too much attention to the torchère itself.

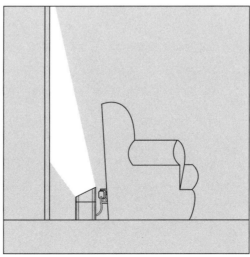

Figure 4.5 (left)
An uplight behind a plant can help add texture and shadow to a room setting.

Figure 4.6 (right)
A series of uplights could do a pretty good job of washing a screen with illumination if lighting cannot come from the ceiling.

Figure 4.7
The black opaque shade on this translucent table lamp, by Donghia, combines two geometric shapes for a positive sculptural effect.

Figure 4.8
The white opaque shade on this table lamp, manufactured by Sirmos, directs your attention to the conical forms of the base.

Figure 4.9
This fixture that combines metal and glass, is an interesting interpretation of the pharmacy lamp. The threaded collar allows the height of the fixture to be raised and lowered as needed.

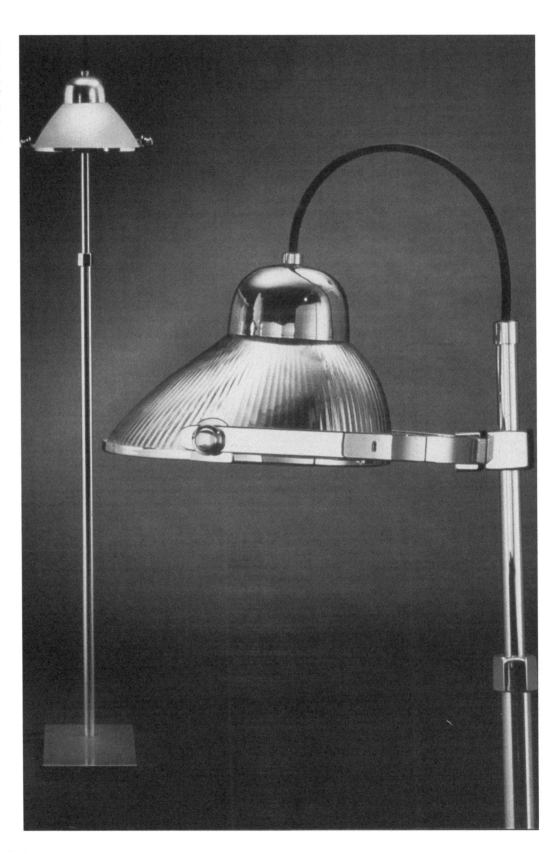

Figure 4.10
This group of torchères, man-ufactured by Boyd Lighting, can provide a good source of instant ambient light. Note that the flared tops of the torchères are opaque, allow-ing them to function solely as indirect light sources.

Figure 4.11
A portable accent light on top of a bookcase could do an adequate job of illuminating a painting when budget or ceiling inaccessibility is a problem.

Figure 4.12
A linear light source on top of a canopy bed could provide some subtle ambient light without immediately revealing the location of the luminaire.

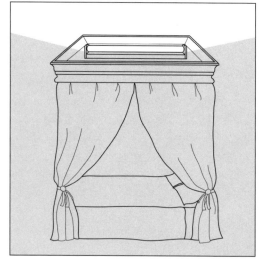

Figure 4.13
Backlighting a translucent screen is another way of getting some ambient light into a room.

Many torchères are available with halogen sources and integral dimmers, making them energy-efficient and capable of a wide range of light levels. They come in many styles to fit into most interiors, from the very traditional to ultramodern.

Uplights

Uplights are another source of illumination for rooms that need some visual texture. An uplight located behind a tall, leafy plant will cast interesting shadows on the walls and ceiling for a dramatic effect (see Figure 4.5).

Sometimes, due to existing construction constraints (such as concrete ceilings) or budget constraints, uplights could be used to wash a painted screen with illumination instead of using recessed or track lighting (see Figure 4.6).

Adjustable accent lights

Portable adjustable accent lights are another very flexible solution for highlighting objects without installing track or recessed luminaires. They can be tucked into bookcases or behind furniture to help add some focal points, giving added depth and dimension (see Figure 4.11). Many track-lighting companies make weighted bases that accept their track heads. Ready-made units are also commonly available.

Where you place your portable luminaire can be a creative endeavor in and of itself. For example, how about using one on top of a canopy bed to provide some ambient light in a bedroom (see Figure 4.12)? Or what about placing an uplight behind a translucent screen to add some visual interest to a dark corner and some soft fill light for the room (see Figure 4.13)?

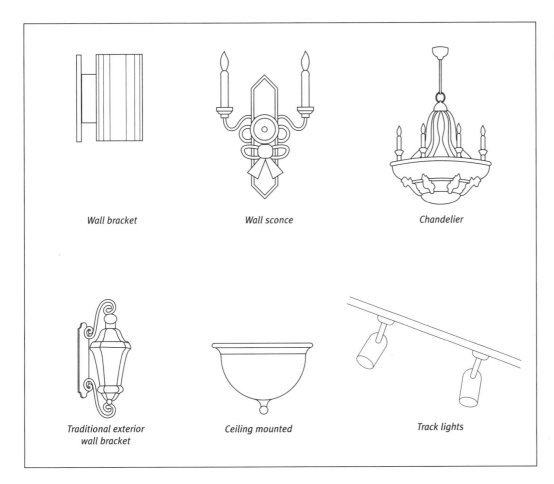

*Figure 4.14
Typical surface-mounted luminaires.*

Wall bracket   *Wall sconce*   *Chandelier*

*Traditional exterior
wall bracket*   *Ceiling mounted*   *Track lights*

Picture lights

Portable picture lights are available in a variety of sizes to do an adequate job of lighting most pieces of flat art. If you are going to use this type of luminaire remember to look for the kind that is adjustable from front to back in order to accommodate different frame depths. The battery-operated variety of picture lights, while appealing because they do not require a cord and plug, have a very short life due to the battery. This becomes a maintenance nightmare.

Be aware, though, that picture lights can be harmful to artwork. They project heat and ultraviolet light toward the surface of the art. This will cause paintings and works on paper to yellow and become brittle.

Swags

Hanging fixtures that plug in and are portable are often called swags. They utilize two hooks in the ceiling, and the cord is woven through the chain. These were popular from the mid '60s through the late '70s and may still be an option if a junction box is not feasible or is placed incorrectly. Stores such as Ikea and Pier One Imports have many inexpensive varieties of swag-type luminaires in stock.

Please note that track lighting is almost exclusively a source of accent light — not ambient or task.

Surface-Mounted Luminaires

Types of Surface-Mounted Fixtures

Surface-mounted luminaires are fixtures that are hardwired to a wall, ceiling, column, or even a tree. They normally require a junction box, to which they are attached. These luminaires project out from (as opposed to being recessed into) the surface on which they are mounted. These include wall sconces (see Figure 4.15), chandeliers, under-cabinet lights, and track lighting. (See Figure 4.14 for some typical surface-mounted luminaire types).

In older homes the only source of illumination is often a surface-mounted fixture in the center of the room. Too often such a luminaire is called upon to perform all the lighting functions for that room. It can be an uncomfortable glaring light, often referred to in the industry as a "glare bomb."

Replacing the existing ceiling-mounted luminaire with a pendant-hung indirect variety of luminaire (as mentioned in Chapter 1's section on ambient light) will fill the room with soft, flattering illumination (see Figure 4.17). Sometimes simply replacing one surface-mounted luminaire for another can make a world of difference in the quality of light in that space.

Chandeliers are also surface-mounted luminaires. The most common mistake is to let them be the sole source of illumination in an entry, living room or dining room. Use additional light sources in the room for ambient and accent light, so that the chandelier gives only the illusion of providing the room's illumination (see Plate 2.23).

Track lighting

Somewhere along the line, track lighting became the easy answer to all lighting design problems. Since it falls into the surface-mounted category, we can address that misconception here.

Track lighting is the solution for accent lighting in some situations, such as where there is not enough ceiling depth to install recessed units and in rental spaces, where the clients would like to be able to take it with them. Also they are appropriate for spaces such as artist's studios where the lighting must be highly flexible.

Ordinarily, track lighting cannot be a good source of ambient illumination, because it is normally mounted on the ceiling. The track heads are too close to the ceiling to produce any adequate indirect lighting. Track lighting, due to the usual configuration of the fixtures, is typically very directional. Care must be taken not to position the fixtures so that the light beam hits people in the eyes.

If the track run is suspended from a series of stems or is wall-mounted, it is possible for it to provide some adequate ambient illumination. Should this be the case, use a track luminaire with a lamp that has a wide beam spread to keep the fill light as even as possible.

Figure 4.15
A translucent wall sconce such as this alabaster version, by Boyd Lighting, should be used mainly as a decorative element. Fixtures like these can help make a room with very high ceilings appear more human in scale, by creating a perceived secondary ceiling line.

Track lighting is also a poor choice for task lighting. The main reason for this is that the beam of light produced by the track luminaire is above your client's head, so it will cast a dark shadow onto their book or racing form. The track lighting fixtures are also visually intrusive. If there is another way to go (such as recessed lighting), consider taking that approach.

If not, there is a technique to minimize the track's presence. If the space has open beam construction (a flat or sloped ceiling where the beams are exposed), try to mount the track on the back side of the beams, so that as people enter the room the beams act as a natural baffle for the track runs (see Figure 4.16).

Selecting a color for the track and the track fixtures that is as close as possible to that of the mounting surface will minimize its visibility. Then people will tend to look at what is being illuminated rather than conspicuous fixtures on the ceiling.

Often designers specify track lighting because they fear that recessed lighting will be more expensive and wreck the ceiling.

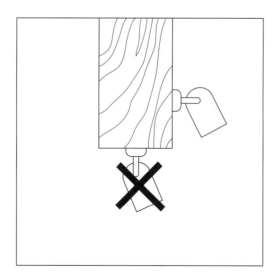

Figure 4.16
Mounting the track run on the side of the beam instead of on the bottom allows the beam itself to screen the luminaires from view when people enter the room.

Figure 4.17
This plaster fixture, by Boyd Lighting, offers a good source of ambient illumination for this entry foyer because it projects light upward without drawing attention to the luminaire itself.

Remodel Versus New Construction

Today people tend to stay in their present homes and upgrade them instead of moving to larger homes or building new ones. Designers are now finding themselves involved with remodel projects more than ever (see Plates 1.5, 1.6, 1.7, and 1.8). The more of these you do, the more you become accustomed to the problems that are inherent in this kind of work. What designers may forget is how traumatizing remodeling can be for the homeowners themselves, especially if this is their first remodeling experience (see Plates 1.9, 1.10, 1.11, 1.12, 1.13, 1.14 and 1.15).

There's no avoiding the sense of invasion that the clients feel and how things like plaster dust can literally touch every aspect of their lives. The main thing they feel is loss of control. All of a sudden, they have less power over what is happening around them. This powerlessness, no matter how subconsciously felt, can make them edgy, nervous, and irritable.

Your job is to give them some sense of control over the process, such as letting them designate which doors the workers should use, what time they can begin work, what time they must stop, where they can park, which bathroom should be used, and whether workers should answer the telephone.

You may even go as far as suggesting a private job site phone/fax line and a rented portable toilet to save wear and tear on your clients. This is a minor investment that could help offset the problems that inevitably arise on every job.

As a designer, you will come to know how much psychology can be an integral part of your day to-day dealings with your clients. We are all fearful of the unknown and dislike unwelcome surprises. Informing your clients ahead of time about what to expect and how they can involve themselves will allow the remodel process to proceed as smoothly as possible. In reality, no project is problem-free.

It's helpful to go through through the remodel process in your own home, to learn firsthand how awful it can be. More than a few relationships have crumbled under the weight of a remodel.

Recommend that your clients move out of the space to be remodeled, if it's at all feasible for them to do so. Moving in with other family members, or better yet, finding a short-term rental, will allow them to create an environment free from dust, noise, chaos, workers, and general chaos. The added cost will be well worth it—in the end, your clients will thank you. Plus, you won't have to deal with them while they're spinning out of control emotionally.

The following pages contain a checklist of the remodel process, which you can copy and give to your clients at the beginning of the project. Giving it to them in writing is important, because we all have selective memory. Let them ask their questions up front, then help them prepare for the onslaught.

What designers may forget is how traumatizing remodeling can be for home owners.

Client Handout: The Realities of Remodeling for the Homeowner

At some point you looked around your home and realized it was time for some changes. It's almost inevitable, because most residences require updating as people's needs change.

Remodeling can strike fear into the heart of the most intrepid person. Remodeling has its inherent problems, but most difficulties can be greatly minimized with proper planning and by having the appropriate expectations.

Many of our clients have been through remodeling projects before, but for those of you who have not; we have put together this list of things to expect:

1. *References*—It is my job as your designer to recommend reputable tradespeople. If you have other recommendations or suggestions, I will be happy to contact them.

2. *Contracts*—It is always a good idea to have a contract, spelling out what is expected from the contractor or tradesperson, what that person will receive in return, and a completion date. This protects you legally but also, more importantly, serves as a reference to remind the contractor what has been promised.

3. *Scheduling*—Since light fixture delivery can be from six to eight weeks, the fixtures need to be selected and ordered before scheduling the electrician. Sometimes delivery is delayed. The best option may be to schedule the installation after all the fixtures and related components have arrived.

4. *Keep on top of things*—Whether you have contracted with me, as your designer, to oversee the remodeling or have hired a general contractor, it is important that you understand the timetables and check that the work is proceeding as planned.

5. *Problems will come up*—Don't let this scare you. It is the nature of remodel projects. If you haven't hired someone to work out the problems as they come up, you will need to deal with them yourself. Some people will have no difficulty with that, while others would prefer to have someone else oversee the project. A deciding factor might be to look at what you feel your own time is worth. Either way, just be prepared to answer questions and you will be able to get through your remodel with a minimum of hassle.

6. *Recessed light fixtures made for remodel*—There are many recessed luminaires that are now made to fit into holes cut into the ceiling that are the same diameter as the luminaire itself. These round openings can made with a hole saw, which creates a very clean opening in the ceiling. Using this technique, you can eliminate a lot of replastering and repainting. Another special tool called a right-angle drill enables an electri-

cian to feed wires from luminaire to luminaire above the ceiling line, so the ceiling can remain intact. The more difficult part is to get from the luminaires to the switch locations. That usually involves opening up parts of the wall and ceiling in order to feed the wires through the fire blocking or other obstacles. An electrician specializing in remodel work will keep this opening-up to a minimum. A newer technique electricians have been using is to run the wiring under the joists through a channel cut into the plaster or drywall. This wire is then covered with a narrow metal plate that is the same width as the joist. This covers the wire and passes code requirements. Please note that when necessary holes are made, a plasterer or drywall installer and painter will be needed to follow up the electrician's work.

7. *Hidden challenges*—No contractor can detect everything that's behind a wall or ceiling prior to starting a project. Sometimes there are factors that necessitate changing luminaire and switch locations, such as additional brace beams, shallow ceiling depths, or ductwork. These occurrences are a normal part of a remodel project and a certain amount of change should be expected.

8. *Plaster dust*—There are few things more invasive in this world than plaster or drywall dust. Even if the rooms being remodeled are sealed off with plastic sheeting, the dust still penetrates other parts of the house. It is a problem that can be minimized but never eliminated.

9. *Tradespeople in the house*—During the remodel process, you will have a number of people working in your home. It is a good idea to establish house rules that will keep things comfortable. For example, you should designate which one door should be used, which one bathroom to use, and if and when the workers should answer the phone. Remember that they are people too, and sometimes a cup of coffee or a soda is greatly appreciated.

10. *Escape the chaos*—If at all possible, find a temporary housing situation that takes you out of the center of the remodel storm. The investment you make in alternative housing will be worth every cent.

With these things in mind, we are sure your remodeling project will go more smoothly. Please feel free to contact your general contractor, your electrician, or me at any time. Communication is important in any project.

New Construction

Those designers lucky enough to be doing a project from the ground up can still benefit from some prior knowledge as well. First of all, incorporate the lighting design into the project right at the beginning—the earlier the better, preferably before the architect has finalized the plans.

Often you receive the project after the drawings have been submitted to the planning department for approval and necessary permits. Normally the architect has drawn in a lighting plan in order to make his or her submissions.

In most cases these are specifications that are called out generically, such as "recessed luminaire," "surface-mounted luminaire," or "switch," without any manufacturer's names or catalog numbers. Where they are located apply very little to what you will be doing because you haven't yet designed the space. Put together a furniture layout before trying to lay out the lighting. Knowing the color and reflectivity of the surfaces you are lighting is also very helpful in selecting the right luminaire and lamp combination.

Changes in electrical plans can be made after permit approval without resubmitting the plans. The electrical inspector will simply refigure the permit fee based on the number of luminaires and outlets installed in the final design. It is important, though, to keep local codes in mind when making these changes. If you have any questions, ask the electrician.

Tools of the Trade

Lighting components and related installation tools for remodel projects have greatly improved to meet the needs of the remodel industry. It used to be that in order for recessed luminaires to be installed into a ceiling, the contractor had to cut a 12-inch square opening in the drywall or plaster and lath, then install bar hangers (metal collars) to attach the housing to the joists. Next, the contractor would cut a series of holes or channels in the ceiling to run wire from unit to unit and down to the switch. Then a plasterer or drywall contractor had to come in and patch and sand all the holes, followed by a painter.

Figure 4.18
Remodel cans allow for installation from below the ceiling, often without making a hole larger than the diameter of the luminaire itself.

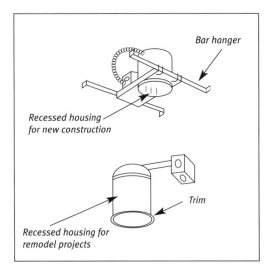

Bar hanger

Recessed housing for new construction

Trim

Recessed housing for remodel projects

Presently, many remodel projects can be installed with minimal patching or painting. Here are the components and tools of which one should be aware. Some of these were touched on earlier in this chapter.

Remodel cans. There are housings for recessed luminaires that are specifically made to be installed into existing ceilings. They can fit into a hole that is the same diameter as the housing itself. These housings are held in place by using metal clips to attach to the ceiling material, instead of the joists. these cans come in different diameters. It's best to stay with oversize.

The series of trims that fit into these housings have lips that are slightly wider than the housings so that they create a finished edge for the opening (see Figure 4.18). In any area where insulation might come in contact with the luminaire, the housing code requires the use of an IC-rated housing. These housings are rated for direct contact with insulation and are large. They are not yet made in remodel versions, but it will be happening soon.

Hole saw. When remodel cans first came into the market, the contractors were still using a hand-held saw, often called a Skilsaw to make the rounded openings. This was a less-than-perfect method that wreaked havoc with plaster-and-lath ceilings. They would crack and crumble as the saw moved up and down.

Then a hole saw (originally designed to bore holes in doors in order to install hardware) was retooled to cut near-perfect holes in ceilings for remodel cans. It also does a great job of cutting holes in walls for junction boxes (see Figure 4.19).

The hole saw is actually a special bit that attaches to a power drill. Good electricians will have various diameters as part of their equipment. Ask bidding electricians if they use them. Those who say they don't could cost your clients plenty in replastering and repainting down the line.

Right-angle drill. Another great twentieth century invention. It allows the electrician to drill holes through joists above the ceiling line to wire from luminaire to luminaire with little or no opening of the ceiling beyond the holes cut for the remodel cans (see Figure 4.20). This drill comes with a series of 12-inch bits that can be linked together, allowing the electrician to drill up to 4 feet away from the starting position. This can be done from two directions, allowing the luminaires to be spaced up to 8 feet apart without disturbing the ceiling between them.

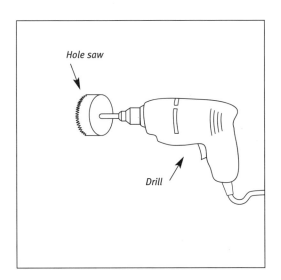

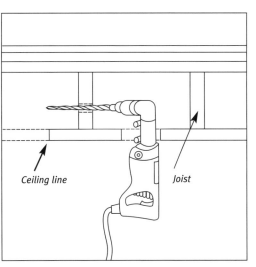

Figure 4.19 (left)
A hole saw can make nearly perfect holes in walls and ceilings, even those made of plaster and lath.

Figure 4.20 (right)
A right-angle drill can make holes in joists above the ceiling line.

There are longer flexible drill bits on the market, but the extra length could cause the end of the bit to end up poking through the new carpeting upstairs, or through the tile floor in the guest bath—just the type of little surprises that should be avoided.

The right-angle drill should be a part of a good electrician's tool collection, but it can be obtained from a tool rental place for a nominal fee of $12–$15 a day. This is the electrician's responsibility. Again, before you hire them, ask the bidding electricians if they have used right-angle drills. The newer method of running the wiring below the joists, which was mentioned earlier, has eliminated much of the need for right-angle drills.

Stud finder. Calm down—it's not as exciting as you may think. The simple truth is that nobody has X-ray vision. So how does the electrician know where to put a recessed luminaire if he doesn't know where the joists are located or how they are spaced? Not all joists run on perfect 16-inch centers. Sometimes there is additional blocking to support an upstairs fireplace, bathroom, or heart-shaped waterbed. A stud finder is an electronic device (that senses the density changes in the ceiling) or a magnetic device (that detects nails or screws in the ceiling) to help determine how the joists are laid out (see Figure 4.21). Using a chalk line or tape, the joist pattern can then be laid out. If the ceiling has acoustical tile over dense plaster, locating joists will be more difficult.

Wire probe. Once the joists have been charted, the next step is to see if there are any other obstructions that the stud finder didn't pick up (see Figure 4.22). What the electrician should do is drill a tiny hole and insert a wire probe (also called a fish tape), which is simply a flexible 1/8-inch diameter length of wire. The electrician feels around to see if there are any obstructions and to verify that there is adequate depth for the particular recessed luminaire specified. Sometimes ceilings change in depth depending on what the floor above is supporting.

Understanding how these tools and components work will make you a better director of the

Figure 4.21 (left)
A stud finder helps determine the joist spacing and obstructions by sensing changes in density above the ceiling line.

Figure 4.22 (right)
A wire probe allows the electrician to check if any nonmetal obstructions are in the way of a proposed recessed luminaire location.

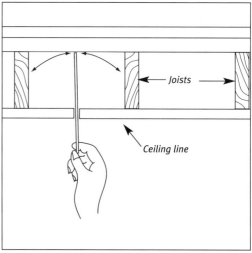

work. You'll be amazed at the respect you get from an electrician when you use buzzwords like "hole saw" and "right-angle drill." It's like asking your auto mechanic, "Can you check the timing because the engine is 'dieseling'?" instead of, "My car continues to run when I turn off the engine. Can you fix it?"

Low-voltage Lighting

Many people, including electricians, are confused or intimidated by low-voltage lighting. There are many common misconceptions, which will be clarified in this section.

The National Electrical Code labels anything under 50 volts as low voltage. The most widely used systems are 12 volts (fixtures and transformers), while 6-volt and 24-volt systems are the next most common. By comparison, line voltage (house current) is 120 volts.

 There are two kinds of transformers, just like there are for fluorescents: magnetic and electronic. Magnetic transformers have a lower failure rate but tend to be a little larger than electronic transformers, which are more compact and are used in small fixtures. A transformer is used to convert line voltage to low voltage. These transformers can be located within the luminaire (integral) or located elsewhere (remote).

Advantages to Low-voltage

Size. Some low-voltage lamps can come in very compact sizes. These tiny lamps allow for fairly small luminaires. These luminaires are easier to tuck out of the way and allow for minimal openings in ceilings. Landscape, track, and recessed luminaires include examples of small fixtures using low-voltage lamps for size advantage.

Beam Spread. Low-voltage lamps come in a great variety of beam spreads, from very tight spots of light to wide floods of illumination. Matching a beam spread to the proportions of a particular painting, tabletop, or plant will make it stand out dramatically and help add dimensionality to a room.

Disadvantages of Low Voltage

Transformers and Voltage Drop. If you choose a remote transformer system, you will experience more voltage drop in the wire from the transformer to the housing, as the distance between them increases. The farther away the luminaires are from the transformer, the dimmer they become. If the distance between luminaires and the transformers is too great, it's best to use an additional transformer so that each luminaire is near a transformer.

The magnitude of the voltage drop is directly proportional to the distance from the transformer and to the current, but increasing the size of the cable can mitigate this. If each luminaire has its own transformer, then there is no danger of voltage drop. However, this does increase the materials cost.

Also, remember that code requires that transformers be accessible. This is so that if one malfunctions an electrician can easily reach the problem unit.

Louvers are designed to help cut glare at its source by shielding the light.

Limited Wattage. Most low-voltage lamps are available in 75 watts maximum, with a few at 100 watts. This amount of wattage may not be enough to adequately illuminate larger objects, such as tall trees or long walls.

Hum. All low-voltage systems have some inherent noise. The greater the number of transformers, the greater the cumulative noise. Locating the transformer remotely puts that noise in a more out-of-the-way spot. For some people, the hum is barely perceptible; for others, it's a constant annoyance. Transformers are not the only potential source of noise. Particular lamps, such as many of the PAR36's, as mentioned in Chapter 3, have their own audible sound. Some dimmers also hum. Choosing components that are compatible will produce the quietest system. Inform your client about potential hum or noise before, not after, installation.

Helpful Hints to Minimize Hum

1. Match the transformers and the dimmers. If you use luminaires that have electronic transformers, specify an electronic low-voltage dimmer. If you have magnetic transformers, use a low-voltage dimmer designed for magnetic loads. This helps keep the system from humming.

2. Use a remote transformer system so that the noise is located in the basement, attic, garage, or closet.

3. Specify luminaires that use MR16 or MR11 lamps, to avoid the vibration of PAR 36 lamps. The MR lamps tend to be much quieter. Lamp filaments can be a component in the amount of noise produced by a lamp.

4. In using recessed luminaires, make sure to specify a luminaire that has the transformer separate from the housing or with some type of flexible mounting between the housing and the transformer. Otherwise, the vibrations of the transformer may create a resonance in the housing that amplifies the sound.

5. In a room that has hard surfaces, add sound-dampening materials, such as curtains, plants, carpeting, or acoustical tile.

Figure 4.23
The best of the three louver types available is the honeycomb.

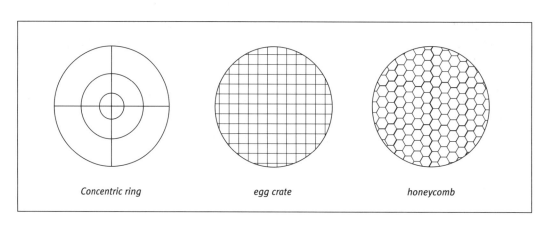

Concentric ring   egg crate   honeycomb

Accessories

There are many optional accessories for basic luminaires. Some that can help a particular luminaire do the best possible job of illumination are listed below.

Louvers

Louvers are designed to help cut glare at its source by shielding the light. There are three basic types available: concentric ring, egg crate, and honeycomb (see Figure 4.23). Check with the luminaire manufacturer for the appropriate louver holder to specify. Some louvers are held in place by pressure.

The concentric ring louver, which looks like a gun sight, was the first one developed and is, for the most part, useless. The egg crate louver is an improvement over the concentric ring but is not the best. The ultimate is the honeycomb louver. They can be made for tiny MR11 fixtures or huge HID luminaires.

Filters

There are color filters available for a majority of the luminaires on the market today. One of the most popular is the color-correcting daylight-blue filter mentioned in Chapter 2. This filter helps minimize the amber hue of incandescent light and produces a whiter light. This whiter light renders art and plantings in a more natural color. Remember, though, that people do not look good under a whiter light, so use this color-corrected filter for objects only, not your clients or their guests.

There are also peach-colored filters, sometimes known as "cosmetic filters", that are very complimentary to skin tones. Many other filter colors are available as well. These tend to make a strong statement and should be used judiciously. They also tend to cut down on the amount of light a luminaire can produce, depending on intensity of the color. Blue, green, red, and amber are industry standards.

There are also MR16 lamps on the market that have a coated fixed lens to produce specific colors. The advantage is that you don't have to buy a separate filter. The disadvantage is that you are committed to that one color. A clear lamp can be adapted to project many colors simply by changing the filter. Try to select dichroic colored lenses; they hold up best and give truer colors. Be aware that you may get a rainbow effect at the edges when an MR flood lamp is used.

Lenses

As opposed to filters, lenses are not colored. Instead, they are etched, formed, or sandblasted in various ways to alter the beam spread of a given lamp. Here are some examples:

Spread lenses are pieces of glass that are sandblasted or patterned to widen the overall circle of light produced by a particular lamp. They also help soften the edges of a spread of light. Use these to avoid a sharp cutoff of light.

Rule of Thumb: Try to get the louver as close to the face of the lamp as possible. This will allow for the greatest amount of illumination. The further away the louver is, the more illumination you would be blocking.

Today people move their furniture around more. A fixed recessed downlight has no flexibility.

Linear spread lenses stretch a beam spread either vertically or horizontally, depending on how the lens is positioned in front of the lamp. These work particularly well for a rectangular painting or tall sculpture.

Fresnel lenses are holdovers from theatrical lighting. They too help diffuse the light patterns, as does a spread lens. Fresnel lenses are used primarily with recessed luminaires and some track systems.

The Steps to Effective Lighting Design

Furniture Layout

Your first step, as hard as it may be, is to come up with a furniture layout. Even if the exact design of the sofa or the finish of the dining room table hasn't been finalized, the location is important and greatly affects how your lighting is placed.

This is difficult, but without a semblance of a furniture plan, the lighting will neither complement your design nor be successfully integrated into it. For example, if you are floating a seating arrangement in the center of the living room and plan on table or reading lamps, you must know the location of the furniture and the type of floor covering in order to place the floor plugs in the correct location.

If a client cannot decide on one of your layouts, draw in the floor plugs with a note right on the plan that states "Floor plug locations to be designated upon finalized layout of furniture. See owners or interior designer prior to installation." (see Figure 4.24).

Another example would be the placement of wall sconces as the ambient light source in a dining room. Their location will affect the placement of art or tall furniture. Will they be placed on either side of the mirror over the sideboard, or will they flank the china hutch? Having a good idea of the size of the mirror or the furniture piece will determine the mounting location of the wall sconces.

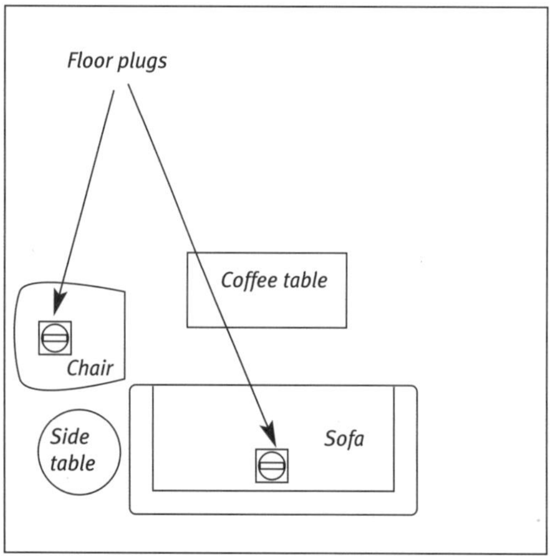

*Figure 4.24
The location of floor plugs is determined by the furniture plan and the type of floor covering to be used. This is why it's important to have a furniture layout before implementing a lighting plan.*

Floor plugs

Coffee table

Chair

Side table

Sofa

Also, will the dining room table be centered in the room or centered in the space left after the sideboard is placed? This will determine the optimal location of the chandelier.

As you will soon understand, every design decision is based on a previous design aspect that has been addressed. Help your clients see how integral the furniture arrangement is to the lighting design. Color and style can be decided later; placement is the key.

Elevations

Another important factor is to study the elevations. Check which ceilings are sloped and how high they are. This will help determine which luminaires you use and where to place them. The higher the ceiling, the further out from the wall the recessed adjustable luminaires need to be placed in order to illuminate the center of the wall, where the art will be displayed.

If the art is tall, the luminaires need to be closer to the walls in order to let some illumination reach the top of the piece. If, for example, you have a long tapestry that hangs from the ceiling line, you should use a wall-wash luminaire that more evenly illuminates the full length of the weaving. Manufacturer's catalogs show spacing recommendations based on ceiling heights. Get comfortable using these charts, as they provide very useful information.

Ask Questions

There are no hard-and-fast rules to luminaire placement. It is entirely dependent on what is in the space. The answer to the question "How many recessed lights do I need for a 12-foot x 18-foot room?" requires a series of questions:

What is the room to be used for? *(Some functions require more light than others).*

What is the age of the people living in the house? *(The older we get, the more we are adversely affected by glare).*

How high are the ceilings? *(Tall ceilings allow wall sconces to be mounted higher, so art can be mounted below them).*

Are the ceilings flat or sloped? *(If a ceiling slopes away from the wall you want to light, then a luminaire that compensates for that slope needs to be specified. Numerous manufacturers make them. They are recessed luminaires that have an integral mirror to allow for 90 degrees of adjustment. They are often referred to as a "mirror reflector").*

What colors are the walls, ceiling, and floors? *(Darker colors absorb more light, requiring higher levels of illumination).*

Where will the art be? *(Determining the location of art pieces helps determine the number of accent lights needed).*

Be Aware of Door Swings

Check the architectural plans to see which way the doors swing. This determines where your switches and dimmers should be located. Don't end up placing them behind the door. This is a common mistake that can be very irritating to the clients once they have moved into their new home. Make sure to have the general contractor or architect let you know if a door swing is going to change.

Door swings will affect your furniture placement as well. Double doors that open into the dining room will take up wall space (unless they are pocket doors). This will determine the visual centerline of the wall on which you place furniture and art, which will in turn affect the location of the wall sconces.

Reflected Ceiling Plan

Study the reflected ceiling plan. It will show how the joists run, where the ductwork will go for heating and ventilation, skylight locations, coffered ceilings, exposed beams, and all the other physical aspects that dictate where lighting can be placed. Specifying recessed adjustable luminaires allows some leeway in placement. You may want a tight spot of light in the middle of a coffee table. A recessed adjustable luminaire can do that without having to be dead center over the table.

Also, as mentioned earlier, people move their furniture and art around more today. A fixed recessed downlight has no flexibility, whereas recessed adjustable luminaires can be redirected to illuminate these components in their new locations.

Maintenance

Take into account the accessibility of the luminaire locations you choose. If the owners cannot easily reach a luminaire to change a burned-out lamp, they are much less likely to do it. For example, if you have a 20-foot ceiling in the entryway, don't put a recessed downlight in the center of the ceiling in order to illuminate the foyer table. Use a recessed adjustable luminaire, installed above the balcony railing on the second floor, to facilitate relamping (see Figure 4.25). A long-life lamp is also advantageous in this situation.

You can also put together a relamping guide for your clients, or the people who will change the lamps for your clients. A binder that shows photographs of specific luminaires and the lamps that go in them will save a lot of trial-and-error time.

Figure 4.25
It's better to locate a recessed adjustable luminaire over the balcony to facilitate relamping than in the center of a 20' high ceiling.

Also, get your clients to buy an extra dozen of each type of lamp to have on hand, and put a snapshot of the fixtures that the lamps go in on the front of the lamp carton or storage box. Using clear or translucent containers will let people know when they are running low on a specific lamp type.

Understanding how a lighting system will be maintained, and using a little foresight in helping your clients to maintain it, will improve your design and your client's long-term appreciation of it.

Getting More Information on Luminaires

(see Appendix One for more detailed resource information)

Now you have a good base of information on which to make your luminaire selections. Try to build your luminaire catalog library and keep it updated. Lighting showrooms are good places to get catalogs and see new fixtures, and many conduct seminars on new lighting products. Build a rapport with the regional manufacturers' representatives. They are eager to keep you up to date on the latest offerings from the companies they represent, and can get you samples to show your clients for approval.

Join organizations such as: the International Association of Lighting Designers (IALD), www.iald.org; the Illuminating Engineering Society (IES), www.iesna.org; or the American Lighting Association (ALA), www.americanlightingassoc.com.

These professional organizations give classes and seminars on lighting-related topics. Attending these functions will help broaden your understanding of lighting design and keep your education current.

Subscribe to industry-related magazines, such as: *Lighting Design and Application* (LD&A), www.iesna.org; *Professional Lighting Design North America* (PLD), www.pldplus.com; *Architectural Lighting*, www.lightforum.com; and *Lighting Dimensions*, www.lightingdimensions.com. These are all excellent sources for technical and aesthetic information.

The Bottom Line

Along with a working knowledge of lamps, a good grasp of what certain luminaires can do will give you the tools you need to create outstanding lighting designs for your clients.

Chapter Five

DAYLIGHTING—INTEGRATION OF NATURAL LIGHT

Natural light is a wonderful source of illumination. Used correctly it can transform a dark dreary house into a bright, inviting sanctuary.

Daylighting is an all-natural source of illumination that is available to everyone. Making optimal use of daylight can certainly brighten and open up a room or area. Designers should explore the options of daylight. Here are some considerations.

Using Windows and Window Coverings

Windows are the first option when thinking about getting natural light into a room. Windows do a fine job of providing daylight for rooms that run along the perimeter of the house. There is however, the problem of sun damage (permanent fading and disintegration of natural fibers and woods). The sun's ultraviolet (UV) rays eventually harm the furnishings and surfaces within the home. Almost all sources of light damage photosensitive materials, but natural daylight does the most damage.

Window treatments, such as shades, drapes, sheers, and miniblinds, do a good job of diffusing the light and slowing down the process of ultraviolet damage. Shutters and blackout shades do a better job of blocking light that is not needed, such as when the homeowners are on vacation. Quantitative information on recommended maximum exposure to UV light is available in the IES Handbook, which is a great source of technical information on industry standards.

Some companies offer a ready-made ultraviolet film that's applied directly to windows or sandwiched between two panes of glass. These companies claim to cut 99 percent of the sun's harmful rays. What they don't tell you is that any standard glass or Plexiglas® will filter out 98 percent of the ultraviolet light. This is just an additional 1 percent over what standard glass already accomplishes.

If it would normally take 5 years for the sun to take its toll, the extra 1 percent of UV protection in the film would double the life of your furniture, rugs, and other furnishings. That's a pretty good deal. Remember, though, not only daylight, but almost all sources of light also contribute to the damage. LEDs and light traveling through fiber optics do not contain UV rays. These two sources are now being used to illuminate light-sensitive materials.

You can't eliminate the damage caused by natural light unless you use blackout shades all day, which could be somewhat depressing for your clients. But at least you can slow down the process. There are manufacturers of motorized shades that can help control natural light to the amount needed. Different types of shade materials can be scrolled together to offer a variety of options. There is even one that allows the shade to come up from the bottom for privacy and create a kind of "clerestory" (a long, narrow window extending along the top part of a wall) allowing natural light to come in without loss of privacy (see Figure 5.1).

At night windows are also wonderful visual portals to exterior spaces, making the inside rooms appear larger. Making good use of windows and exterior lighting can also work wonders in making the exterior landscaping and view a part of the interior spaces. How often have we entered a wonderfully designed interior only to find that the windows are all **black mirrors** at night, where you see your own reflection instead of the view beyond the glass? Exterior lighting will help minimize those reflective surfaces and enlarge the interior at night by visually extending your view out into the landscape (see Color Plate 1.31). Exterior lighting techniques will be addressed extensively in Chapter 15.

Using Doors

Doors, especially interior doors, do not have to be solid. French doors (they come in many styles), fitted with clear or frosted glass, allow light to travel into the room beyond and though the space, so the natural light is shared with the inner rooms.

Using Clear Skylights

Skylights are a great source of natural light but should be used with a few precautions. They come in three standard varieties: clear, bronze, or white. All three varieties can come standard with an ultraviolet inhibitor, or it can be ordered as an option. Although the most popular, the clear skylights cause the most problems, and result in the most severe sun damage.

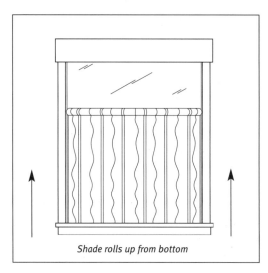

Figure 5.1
A shade that raises and lowers from the bottom allows light to come in without loss of privacy

Shade rolls up from bottom

1. The daylight coming through the skylight will be projected in the shape of the skylight. Your clients will be confronted by an intense square, circle, or rectangle of light. The pattern of the sun will eventually be traced on the surfaces of the furniture, floors and wall coverings.

2. The light coming through a clear skylight will be a hard, harsh light that casts unattractive shadows on people's faces.

3. Clear skylights show dust and dirt immediately—maintenance is a constant problem.

In the case of an existing clear skylight, one solution is to get a pleated or Roman-style shade to help diffuse the light. This is especially good for operable skylights, as the shade can be pulled back to allow for ventilation when needed (see Figure 5.2).

If the skylight is nonoperable, you can install a white acrylic or glass diffuser within the light well to help spread out the sun's illumination. If there is enough room in the light well above the shade or diffuser, luminaires can be installed to keep the skylight from becoming a negative space at night (see Figure 5.3).

Using Bronze Skylights

The same considerations listed for clear skylights also apply to bronze-tinted skylights, which cut down tremendously on the amount of light allowed through. The main concern, though, is not reducing the amount of light, but diffusing the light for a more user-friendly illumination.

Using White Skylights

In new construction or a remodel project that will include installing skylights, you should consider using white (also known as opal or frosted) skylights for several reasons:

1. They distribute the light more evenly in a room.

2. They don't project a light pattern.

3. They don't become **black holes** at night.

4. They minimize maintenance.

> In a project that will include skylights, consider using the white variety instead of clear or bronze.

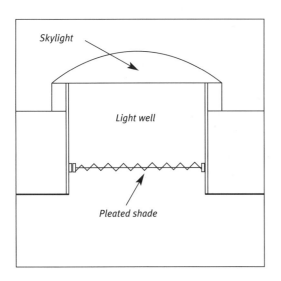

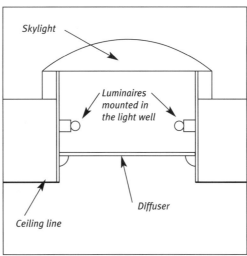

Figure 5.2 (left)
A pleated or Roman-type shade fitted into the light well will help diffuse the daylight flooding into the room

Figure 5.3 (right)
Lighting in the light well above the diffuser keeps the skylight from becoming a "black hole" at night

Don't try to light a glass block wall. It is a translucent product, so light passes through it. At best, you would highlight the grout in between the blocks, which is not the most visually ornate aspect. If the blocks are frosted, then the wall can be directly illuminated.

Using Glass Block

Glass block (also known as glass brick) is a building material that was popular in between 1930s and the 1950s and then fell out of popularity. The postmodern influence of the 1980s brought about a resurgence of its use. Succinctly put, glass block turns walls into windows. They come in clear, patterned, curved, frosted, colored, solid, or hollow varieties. This allows for varying degrees of light transference and varying degrees of privacy. Rooms with little or no natural light could benefit greatly from the installation of a glass block wall, which allows them to borrow light from adjoining rooms with windows or skylights.

Don't try to light a transparent glass block wall. At best, you would highlight the grout between the blocks, which is not the most visually attractive aspect. The trick is to light the opposite wall. What you end up seeing is the illuminated wall through the glass block. This creates the illusion that the block itself is illuminated (see Figure 5.4). If the blocks are frosted, then the wall can be directly illuminated.

Using Mirrors

The use of mirrors can be another tool to help make the most of natural light in a space. You can greatly increase the perceived amount of daylight in a room with windows on one side by installing mirrors on the opposite wall. Mirrors can also greatly increase the apparent depth of an area by giving the illusion that the interior extends much farther than it actually does. Cramped areas can become brighter and feel more open.

Working with Natural Light

Areas such as kitchens and family rooms that are used frequently during the day are prime candidates for maximizing natural light. Closets and laundry rooms that have some source of natural light make it easier to color-match blouses to skirts, ties to suits, and high heels to slacks. Be sure to take precautions to block the natural light when it's not required, as many fabrics, especially silk and wool, are quickly damaged by light.

Figure 5.4
Glass block appears to be illuminated if the wall behind it is washed with light

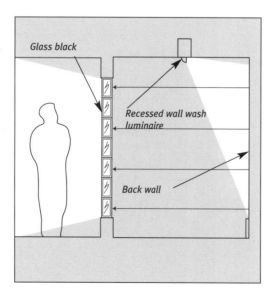

Glass black

Recessed wall wash luminaire

Back wall

Don't forget that light colors reflect more light than dark colors. A Navajo White room will make better use of the natural light than one painted a Hunter Green.

The Bottom Line

Natural light is a wonderful source of illumination. Used correctly, it can transform a dark, dreary house into a bright, inviting sanctuary during the day.

Chapter Six

CONTROLS—DIMMING, SWITCHING, TIMERS, PHOTOSENSORS, MOTION DETECTORS

Every room is capable of being viewed and used in multiple ways. Clients may want subtle mood lighting for entertaining, yet also want the ability to increase light levels for cleaning. Multiple scene controllers can do this at the push of a button.

Once you have formulated a lighting design, the next step is to decide how to regulate the system or control the lighting design to achieve the desired effect.

There are many options, from simple switches to preset multiple-zone/multiple-scene controllers and even being able to turn on lights from a car phone. Every room is capable of being viewed and used in numerous ways. A multiple-scene controller allows the same lights to be illuminated at various levels by a single control unit (see Figure 6.8). Clients may want subtle mood lighting for entertaining yet also want the ability to increase light levels for cleaning. Multiple scene controllers can do this at the push of a button.

The options may be almost limitless, but they need to be matched to the wants and capabilities of your clients. Designing a dimming system that is too complicated leaves the clients intimidated and ultimately frustrated. Try to meet their needs with a simple-to-operate control system. Also remember that they are the ones who will be living in the house, so the controls must be logically placed to match their traffic patterns.

A common mistake is to locate a majority of the controls at the front door. Most people living in single-family houses in the U.S. don't enter through the front door. They park in the garage and enter through the garage. This spot should be your starting point. On the other hand, people who live in condominiums do enter through the front door. Each project is different, as are the needs of your various clients. Give them options and let them tell you what they want.

Switch Controls

Today, people can put dimmers on most everything, but there are some instances where simple switching is the best choice. Low-activity rooms, such as closets, storage rooms, attics, and pantries don't need varying light levels and don't require dimmers. These rooms. If your clients have children or are on the forgetful side, you might recommend the following alternatives to simple toggle switches.

Momentary Contact Switches

Momentary contact switches (door jam switches) are devices that turn on the light when the door is opened. It's the same way the light in your refrigerator operates. When the door is shut, the light automatically goes out. This works only if the clients, their children, and other household members remember to shut the door completely. Bi-fold doors don't work well with momentary contact switches because they need to be fully closed to make a good connection.

Motion Sensors

Motion Sensors turn the lights on as someone enters the room or closet and keeps them on as long as there is movement or for a certain length of time, as preset in the sensor. Some companies make motion sensors with a manual override for clients who plan to spend a great deal of time in a particular room without moving around. For example, if there is a safe in the master-bedroom closet and your clients occasionally review important papers or sort through jewelry there, an override on the motion sensor in this location would be advisable.

Panic Switches

Panic Switches are switches normally located in the master bedroom that turn on exterior perimeter lights. Nobody wants to run downstairs to the front door when there is a suspicious noise outside at night—most people don't even want to get out of bed. This will also allow the occupants to turn off the outside or entry lights if they are left on inadvertently.

Half-Switched Receptacles

Half-switched receptacles, also known as "half-hot" plugs, can be a terrific labor-saving device in houses that use a lot of portable luminaires. In a half-switched receptacle, a wall switch activates one of the two outlets and the other outlet is continuously live.

This allows the clients to plug their table lamps, torchères, reading lights, china hutch lighting, or uplights into the switched receptacles. So instead of going from luminaire to lumi-

Figure 6.1 (left)
Half-switched receptacles help combine a number of portable luminaires into one switching group.

Figure 6.2 (right)
A socket dimmer is a very easy way to make an existing table lamp dimmable.

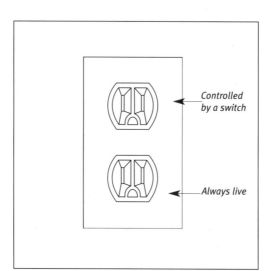

Controlled by a switch

Always live

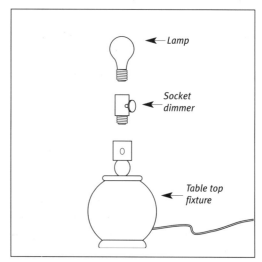

Lamp

Socket dimmer

Table top fixture

naire to turn them all on or off, they would all come on at the flick of one switch (see Figure 6.1). Items they don't want to be turned on and off, such as clocks, televisions, or stereo equipment, would be plugged into the non-switched receptacles.

Caution: Do not put the half-switched receptacles on a dimmer, because if someone plugged a television or vacuum cleaner into a dimmed receptacle, it could damage the appliance or be a possible fire hazard. This is also a code violation. If your clients want to dim their table lamps, have them purchase ones with integral dimmers. If they already have the table lamps, they can be retrofitted with screw-in type **socket dimmers** (see Figure 6.2) or cord dimmers (see Figure 6.3).

Sound-Actuated Switches

Sound-actuated switches are devices that turn on lights when a noise is made. They are a low-end solution to half-switched receptacles with one inherent problem: If your clients or their guests make noises that are as loud as clapping, they may find the lights turning on and off at an inopportune moment!

Three-way Switching

Three-way switching is a term that confuses homeowners and designers alike. The natural impression is that a light or group of lights can be turned on from three locations, which is incorrect. The correct answer is two locations. Why? Because a single-location switch has two terminals and a three-way switch has three terminals. It does not refer to the number of control spots. The actual luminaire counts as one leg in the switching chain.

A four-way switching system allows three or more locations to turn a light or groups of lights on and off (see Figure 6.5). For example, if you have a hallway with a switch at both ends, one of these switches can be replaced with a three-way dimmer to allow for a variety of light levels. The three-way switch at one end of the hall will turn on the lights at whatever level the dimmer at the other end of the hall has been set to (see Figure 6.4). In simple

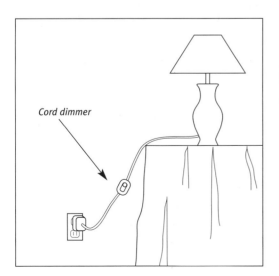

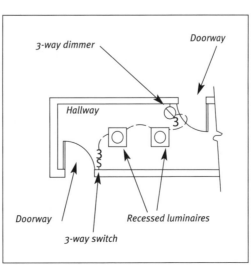

Figure 6.3 (left)
A cord dimmer is a quick way of obtaining a full range of light levels from an existing luminaire.

Figure 6.4 (right)
A three-way set-up means that the lights are controlled from two locations (not three.)

three-way setups, you can't put a dimmer at both ends. More sophisticated (and more expensive) systems would allow dimming at both ends.

Timers

Timers are another option for turning lights on and off. Clients who travel or are cautious about security will want their home to look occupied at night. Lights controlled by timers that go on or off at staggered times makes it feel like someone is home. Here are your options.

Plug-In Timers

Plug-in timers are readily available at hardware stores and home improvement centers. You plug them into a live receptacle, then plug a portable luminaire such as a table lamp into it. Then the device is manually set to switch on and off at specific times. Use a few in the living room that are set to come on at dusk and go off around 11:00 p.m. Then have one go on in the bedroom at 11:05 p.m. and stay on until midnight. This gives the impression of people being in a gathering spot then going off to bed in a natural progression.

24-Hour Programmable Timers

This type of programmable timer simply turns specific lights on and off at the same time each day. They are available in hardwired (permanently installed) varieties as well as plug-in units. The timer is normally located in the garage. These devices have an override switch, located inside the control box, that allows the homeowner to turn the lights on or off if needed. When these units turn the lights on and off at the same time every day, it is more evident to anyone casing the house that no one is home and that timers are being used.

24-Hour/ 7 Day Programmable Timers

Another kind of programmable timer allows for different settings each day and gives the option to skip days, for an appearance that seems to be controlled by a person instead of a device. For example, on Monday the lights come on at 7:17 p.m. and go off at 11:33 p.m. On Tuesday the lights come on at 6:50 p.m. and go off at 11:57 p.m.. Each day can be a little different. This is great for weekend residences and for clients who travel frequently.

Figure 6.5
A four-way set-up indicates that there are three or more switches that can turn on a specific light or group of lights.

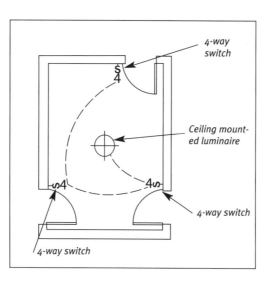

Photosensors

Photosensors (also known as photocells or photoelectric cells) are activated by the absence of light. The luminaires come on at dusk and turn off at dawn. Cleaning the photosensor itself regularly is a priority. Otherwise, as it gets dirtier, the cell reads dusk as coming sooner, and eventually the lights may stay on all the time. Be sure to locate the sensor in a spot that is free of shade, so that it can detect true dawn and dusk, yet not in the direct path of another light, such as a streetlight, which would cause the unit to "see" daylight all night long and never come on.

Dimmers

Dimmers are a form of control that allows a variable adjustment of light levels (see Figure 6.6). Dimmers come in many varieties, such as rotary, toggle, glider, touch, low voltage, and line voltage.

Here are some points that will help you and your clients make an informed decision.

1. Choose a dimmer that is specifically made for the luminaire type that you are dimming. As was mentioned in Chapter 3, use a low-voltage dimmer when dimming a low-voltage system. If the low-voltage luminaire uses an electronic (solid-state) transformer, the dimmer

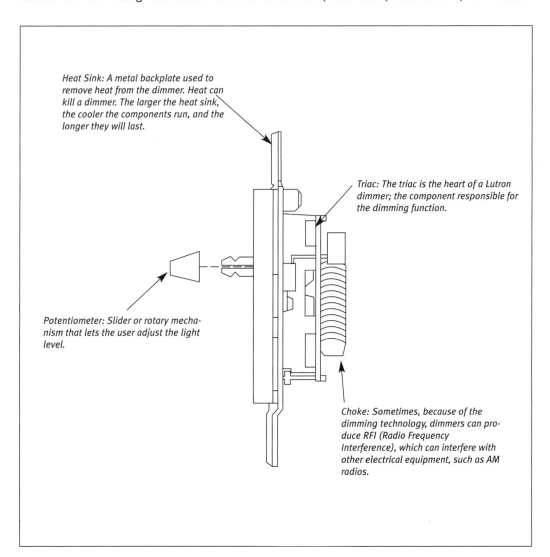

Figure 6.6
The components of a typical dimmer switch.

Courtesy of Lutron.

Heat Sink: A metal backplate used to remove heat from the dimmer. Heat can kill a dimmer. The larger the heat sink, the cooler the components run, and the longer they will last.

Triac: The triac is the heart of a Lutron dimmer; the component responsible for the dimming function.

Potentiometer: Slider or rotary mechanism that lets the user adjust the light level.

Choke: Sometimes, because of the dimming technology, dimmers can produce RFI (Radio Frequency Interference), which can interfere with other electrical equipment, such as AM radios.

The mounting of two or more controls side by side within one enclosure is called ganging. De-rating is the reduction of the maximum capacity (hood) a dimmer can reliably handle when the side sections (fins) are removed.

must be electronic as well or there will be an audible humming noise and possible damage to the dimmer or fixture. If the low-voltage luminaires use magnetic transformers, then the dimmer must be magnetic as well.

Note: Some low-voltage electronic dimmers have only a 300-watt capacity, as compared to a standard 600-watt low-voltage or line-voltage dimmer. Consequently, you should pay special attention to the number of total watts each dimmer can handle.

2. Be aware of the dimmer's maximum wattage. A normal dimmer is rated for 600 watts. Putting 600 watts on that dimmer requires it to work its hardest. Most manufacturers will provide guidelines for load limits. For example, a Lutron low-voltage dimmer, such as the Skylark SLV600P, can optimally handle 450 watts of luminaires. The mounting of two or more controls side-by-side within one enclosure is called **ganging**. Ganging dimmers decreases their load capacities.

3. **De-rating** is the reduction of the maximum capacity (load) a dimmer can reliably handle when the side sections (fins) are removed. Allow for de-rating when banking dimmers. Dimmers' wattage capacities are reduced when put together in a single box. Dimmers produce heat and need airspace around them in order to work properly. If too many dimmers are put too close together, they will overheat and cause problems down the line. Manufacturers' guidelines will tell you how much load (wattage) a dimmer can handle when two or more dimmers are ganged together. A scored section along each side of the mounting plate or fin is designed to be snapped off for ease of mounting multiple controls in one enclosure.

4. Choose well-made dimmers. The rotary and toggle-style dimmers commonly available in hardware stores are poorly made. Don't expect much from a $4.95 dimmer; chances are that in six months they will fail.

Figure 6.7
Dimmer switches come in many varieties. Here are a few for you and your clients to consider.

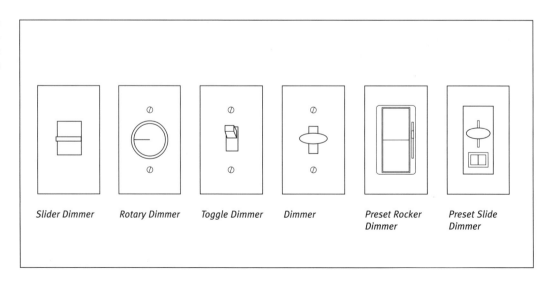

Slider Dimmer   *Rotary Dimmer*   *Toggle Dimmer*   *Dimmer*   *Preset Rocker Dimmer*   *Preset Slide Dimmer*

5. Choose a dimmer style that matches the switch plates being used throughout the house. Some dimmers require special plates that aren't compatible with standard plates for toggle switches or receptacles. Different plate styles in the same house may draw too much attention to an element that should be as low-key as possible. Show your clients the choices available and let them select the style they like (see Figure 6.7).

Preset Dimming Systems

Beyond standard dimmers are multiple-zone/multiple-scene controllers that allow for a great variety of predetermined light level combinations (see Figure 6.8). These systems, initially very expensive, have come down to a price range than can work within the budget of many projects.

Usually, these controllers are used only for entertaining spaces, such as living rooms, dining rooms, entries, and kitchens. Sometimes the master bedroom is included as well. For loads up to 1,950 watts total in a room, there are a good number of three-to-six channel controllers that fit into a standard four-gang box and use standard wiring. For loads beyond 2,000 watts, a remote dimmer panel is required. Then the loads are virtually limitless. The cost goes up significantly as more sophisticated components are added.

Most of these preset controllers have adjustable fade rates that help soften the transition from one scene to the next. This is like the lights dimming in a theater as the play is about to begin.

There are also computer-terminal-managed controllers, allowing people to turn on lights and even the hot tub from their car phones. For some, this is the ultimate dream package, but it certainly could scare the au pair if she's home alone.

Again, don't overdesign the control system. A young, hip couple may love these bells and whistles, but older clients or young children may never get the hang of a sophisticated system.

Note: Some low-voltage electronic dimmers have only a 300-watt capacity, compared to a standard 600-watt low-voltage or line-voltage dimmer. So pay special attention to the number of total watts each dimmer can handle.

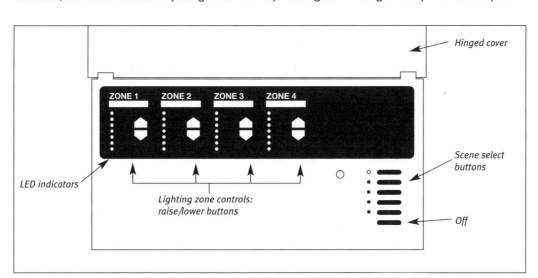

Figure 6.8
A preset controller allows lights in a room to come on together at different levels called "scenes."

It is an industry recommendation that fluorescent luminaires with dimming ballasts should be operated at full capacity for 100 hours before dimming them, in order to break in the system. Some dimming ballasts are pre-cured by the manufacturer prior to being sold.

Commonly asked questions about dimming:

Do dimmers save energy?
Yes, a fixture on a dimmer uses only the energy consumed.

Does using a dimmer shorten the life of the lamp?
No, heat decreases the life of the lamp. Lower wattage consumption means less heat and longer lamp life. With halogen lamps, it may be necessary to operate them at maximum illumination periodically in order to to burn off any black residue, which results from the tungsten evaporation.

Why does the dimmer feel warm to the touch?
This is normal. It is the result of dissipated heat transferred to the fins (a heat sink system) located on the back of the device.

What about feedback from radios or stereos? With magnetic dimmers some buzzing may occur. Filters are usually installed in the better grade of dimmers. Remote debuzzing coils may be installed.

Low-Voltage Dimming
Low-voltage dimmer selection is crucial. Noise from the dimmer and transformer can be greatly reduced if these components are designed to work with each other. The manufacturer's specifications will help you make the correct choice.

As was mentioned before, a common mistake is the specification of a low-voltage dimmer that is not compatible with the type of transformer used in the low-voltage luminaire that it is controlling. Find out the type of transformer before specifying the dimmer. If the information isn't readily apparent in the catalog, call your distributor or manufacturer's representative to find the information you need.

Fluorescent Dimming
Dimming of fluorescents has come a long way. As people become more comfortable with fluorescent lighting, their demand for control of the light levels will increase as well. First of all, in order to dim fluorescents, a special dimming ballast in the luminaire must be used. Standard ballasts will not work.

One of the recurring complaints about early fluorescent luminaires was the incessant hum. Most of this came from magnetic ballasts that vibrate. This vibration may resonate against the metal luminaire housing, increasing the level of the hum.

However, the newer electronic ballasts are extremely quiet. When you add a dimmer for a fluorescent luminaire, the electrician will need to run one or two additional wires from the dimmer to the ballast, and from there to the luminaire. Fluorescent dimmers require that there be additional wires to carry the dimmed current.

For new construction, this would not be a problem. It is a bit more complicated for a remodeling project—not impossible, just a little more difficult. It's no more involved than adding the additional wiring for a three-way switch.

Here are some comparisons between dimming fluorescent luminaires with magnetic ballasts and dimming them with electronic ballasts:

1. Hum is more evident in magnetic ballasts.

2. Both electronic and magnetic ballasts in the moderate price range are dimmable down to 10–20 percent of the light output. Magnetic fluorescent dimmers usually have stops that keep users from dimming beyond the 20 percent mark.

3. High-end electronic ballasts can have full-range dimming capabilities; in some instances, such as the Hi-Lume electronic dimming ballast by Lutron, they allow for the dimming of unlike lamp lengths together.

4. There are now magnetic ballasts on the market that offer full-range dimming as well. Both Bash Theatrical Lighting and Lighting & Electronics offer a wide selection of ballasts.

5. Fluorescent dimming can be pricey. But, considering the savings in electricity, the payback period can be very rapid—usually only two or three years in a typical household. The quality of the components is also a factor. Inexpensive fluorescent sockets can make dimming at low levels inconsistent and cause the light to flutter. Some more reasonably priced fluorescent dimming systems allow for dimming down to 50 percent. For some clients with budget constraints, this may be adequate.

6. Both magnetically and electronically ballasted fluorescent luminaires can be dimmed automatically when tied to a photosensor. This helps balance the need for artificial light with available daylight, or with use frequency. A home office would be a good candidate for this type of control system.

7. As mentioned in Chapter 3, there are now self-ballasted compact fluorescent sources that can be dimmed with a standard incandescent dimmer. This is the new wave of fluorescent dimming.

HID Dimming
Dimming technology for high-intensity discharge lamps is still in early development stages. At best, these sources can be dimmed only to 40 percent without shortening lamp or ballast life. There is another system that dims the lamps down to 12–15 percent, but this shortens the life of both lamp and ballast. The color shift of dimmed HID sources is generally undesirable.

As with much lighting technology, improvements in HID dimming should arrive in the next three to five years. Like all aspects of your lighting design, involve the clients. Give them their options and help them make an informed decision on how they want to (and can afford to) control the lighting system in their house.

Central Home Lighting Control Systems

A logical step in central design was a system that allowed for remote control of the entire house from a few choice locations, such as the master bedroom, the front door, and the door into the house from the garage. Options include turning all the lights in the house on or off, activating pathways of illumination, or turning on exterior **security lighting** (see Figure 6.9).

A controller can override other switching and dimming devices in the house and change your clients' preset light levels. These systems involve complex wiring, so they may be cost-effective only in new construction. Remodel projects may require too much opening of walls and ceilings to justify the total expense. Newer radio-controlled components are making "smart house" systems a possibility for existing homes, because little hardwiring is needed. The controls are activated by radio signals instead of electricity running through the walls.

The Bottom Line

Designers should review material and installation costs prior to starting the project. Gathering this information will help the clients make informed decisions. A lighting designer, lighting showroom or electrical distributor can work with you and the contractor to determine the components required and helps put the package together. You and your clients will greatly benefit from taking advantage of this type of service.

Remember not to overdesign the controls. They must be user-friendly for the specific client. Each client has a certain comfort level with technology that must be taken into account.

Figure 6.9
A master control allows for activating any of the lights in the house from a central location.

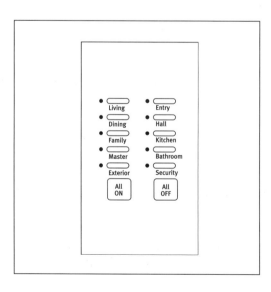

Understanding Light

COLOR SECTION ONE

Lighting can make a huge difference in how a space is perceived. The purpose of this section is to get a feel for what lighting can do to a given space, especially the color. The difference is as clear as day and night.

Plate 1.1 - This living room is hardly conducive to conversation or comfort. Visitors would practically have to yell across the room to be heard by the people sitting on the opposite sofa. This space not only needs better lighting, but begs for the confident hand of a good interior designer.

Plate 1.2 - The room takes on a whole new personality when good interior and lighting design are blended. Three recessed adjustable fixtures highlight paintings, plants, art objects, and tabletops, adding a dramatic layer of accent lighting. The center fixture illuminates the coffee table, while the other two cross-illuminate the large painting and offer some fore-lighting of the two ficus trees. The potted plants are back-illuminated with two uplights positioned on the floors behind the containers. A can-tilevered ledge, off to the right, hides a linear strip of xenon indirect illumination to help soften shadows on people's faces.

Plate 1.3 - The "before" shot of the dining room offers little in the way of any redeeming lighting or interior design. It's as if 1972 had come and gone without the former owners ever noticing.

Plate 1.4 - The dining area is located on the opposite side of the large main room. An enormous hanging fixture, designed by Ingo Maurer, draws guests to the table. This luminaire has five sockets inside. Four are fitted with 100-watt A lamps to provide both ambient and decorative light. The fifth lamp is a 75-watt PAR30 spot, directed though a bottom opening to add visual punch to the yellow art glass bowl in the center of the table. Two recessed adjustable luminaires, using 50-watt MR16 lamps, offer accent light for the painting and the red metal sculpture in the foreground.

Plate 1.5 - The "before" picture of the wet bar shows a single square recessed fixture that was used to provide the only illumination for the space. This downlighting made the person serving drinks appear as frightening as the wallpaper behind them.

Plate 1.6 - The wet bar area has been transformed into an inviting spot in the main room using a series of three pendant lights that cast a bright red glow. A pair of recessed adjustable low-voltage fixtures highlight the Japanese block prints. Above the cantilever, a run of linear low-voltage lighting, using xenon lamps, provides much-needed ambient light.

Plate 1.7 - This master bedroom has become an inviting retreat through good interior design, color selection, and lighting. The ceiling glow comes from one of a pair of torchères flanking the armoire holding the television. The two reading lights above the bed are individually controlled, recessed, adjustable, low-voltage fixtures. The fixture above the left side of the bed illuminates reading material for the person on the right side of the bed, a positioning that directs light away from the person who is trying to sleep. Each of these fixtures uses a 20-watt MR16 spot to provide a controlled beam of illumination. The backyard area is also illuminated, so that the sliding doors don't become black mirrors at night.

Plate 1.8 - The "before" picture of the bedroom shows that the former owners were in a bit of a rush to leave the property. Beyond the sliding glass doors, a frightening glimpse of the Astrourf - covered patio can be seen.

Plate 1.9 - During the day this stone Fu dog draws little attention to itself.

Plate 1.10 - In the evening, he has a yellowish cast when lit with a single 50-watt MR16 spot.

Plate 1.11 - Adding a daylight blue filter to the fixture brings out the piece's cool stone quality.

Plate 1.12 - Before: The façade of this 1970s-era home has the feel of a bunker. Although the bones of the house are good, anyone can see that this project is ripe for an upgrade.

Plate 1.13 - After: The front yard of the home has been greatly improved with the addition of specimen cacti, succulents, and a new slate façade. But the exterior fixtures, which illuminate the plants and the building, have an amber cast that makes the plants look unhealthy.

Plate 1.14 - The same house with the same fixtures. The one difference is that all of the exterior directional fixtures have been fitted with daylight blue filters to correct the color of light to a more naturalistic hue.

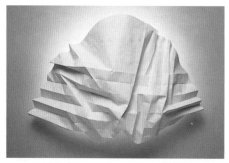

Plate 1.15 - It's not always just the color of the light source that affects our perception of an object or a space. Here an opaque wall sconce is mounted on a light blue wall. The fixture appears to fade into the wall because they are close in color value.

Plate 1.16 - Here the same opaque fixture is mounted on a wall covered in richly colored red wallpaper. The incandescent light mixes with the red color to create an interesting orange corona of illumination. Even though the fixture is white, it becomes a striking contrast against the vibrant wall color.

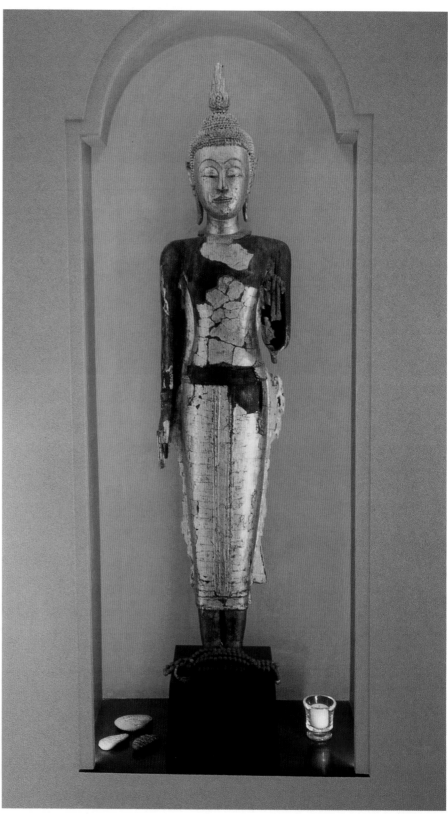

Plate 1.17 - This art niche is illuminated with a series of LEDs that follow the perimeter of the opening. The color of these diodes is yellow, while the niche itself is painted a crimson red. The combination of these two colors creates a vivid orange-red background for the Buddha figure.

Plate 1.18 - This entryway has a decidedly 1980s feel. The center fixture is an Art Deco-inspired metal and glass pendant.

Plate 1.19 - The same entryway redone twenty-two years later. Architecturally nothing has changed. The dramatic look results from the introduction of supersaturated color on the walls, new furniture, and lighting. The center fixture has been replaced with a traditional transitional pendant with opaque shades. The new mirror on the far wall is flanked with a pair of candlestick wall sconces. Two recessed adjustable low-voltage fixtures are illuminating the face of the console and the Roman bust off to the left. Even in this very traditional space, a little bit of modern lighting can make all the difference.

Plate 1.20 - This entryway is totally dedicated to drama. The tabletop and artwork take center stage in the space. A layer of ambient light would have helped make family and friends as important as the art.

Plate 1.21 - Here a low-tech solution to produce an interesting effect. A small mirrored ball has been placed on the top of the Indian chest. A single recessed adjustable low-voltage fixture is directed toward the ball to create the starlike pattern on the ceiling. A pair of opaque wall sconces guides visitors from the entryway to the living room.

Plate 1.22 - The entryway to this rustic home is delineated with a pair of low-wattage wall sconces, which help create a sense of separation between the foyer and the soaring two-story living room. These sconces also create a secondary ceiling line to help people feel more comfortable in the room. In the center of the living room, a custom luminaire made of copper tubing and cone-shaped light fixtures provides both accent light and a decorative element. The rear door leading to the backyard is punctuated with a perforated metal star.

Plate 1.24 - A close-up of the chair located next to the fireplace shows a reading light with an opaque copper shade. This fixture provides task light without drawing attention to itself.

Plate 1.25 - This close-up of one of the niches that flank the fireplace shows a single recessed adjustable low-voltage fixture being used to illuminate the primitive art pieces. The glass shelf allows the light to travel down to the lower objects. Note how the objects have been positioned on the upper shelf to allow light to pass beyond them.

Plate 1.23 - This intimate seating area, centered on the fireplace, is a good example of light layering at work. The reveal in the ceiling is uplighted with two continuous runs of low-voltage linear light. The pendant fixture that is centered in the reveal offers the decorative element for the space, creating the illusion that it is providing the room's illumination. Recessed adjustable low-voltage fixtures illuminate the tabletop, fireplace façade, and niches, while a single floor lamp provides task light next to the chair.

Plate 1.26 - Here we have a daylight shot of a modern-styled living room. The natural light that you see comes from a bank of floor-to-ceiling windows and a white opal skylight.

Plate 1.27 - At night the same space takes on a warm inviting personality. Track runs, mounted on the side of the beams, provide accent light without drawing attention to themselves.

Plate 1.28 - Here a daylight shot shows an intimate dining space next to a bank of floor-to-ceiling windows. The view is magnificent when the sun is out, but without exterior lighting the room would feel quite small at night, because people would see their own reflection instead of the view beyond.

Plate 1.29 - As evening falls, subtly placed exterior accent lights help to keep the windows transparent at night. low-voltage directional exterior fixtures are mounted on the underside of the eave to illuminate the nearby plantings. A freeform art glass piece over the dining room table provides the decorative element for the dining room. This piece is not illuminated from within, but gets its light from a surface-mounted directional fixture installed on the ceiling.

Plate 1.30 - This entryway is trying to use a series of pagoda lights up to the front door. The effect they create is similar to an airport runway. This installation would have benefited greatly by a pair of lanterns flanking the front door and additional landscape lighting to highlight the mature plantings and the façade of the house.

Plate 1.31 - The rear portion of this two-story live/work space has the look of a giant glowing lantern at night. The warm ambient interior light contrasts nicely with the cooler-colored accent light for the garden plantings.

Plate 1.32 - During the day, this small garden falls mostly into shadow due to the tall buildings that surround it.

Plate 1.33 - At dusk the garden takes on a decided fantasy-like quality. Here the moonlighting effect comes into play. Shielded low-voltage adjustable exterior fixtures are mounted in the taller trees. The illumination is directed downward through the lower branches to create a dappled pattern of light and shadow.

Plate 1.34 - During the day the corner of this upper deck falls mostly into shadow.

Plate 1.35 - At night this same corner becomes a delightful focal point. At first viewing it appears that the three candles are providing the illumination. In reality. a pair of shielded directional exterior fixtures provide illumination for the plants and the gargoyle.

Plate 1.36 - Here in the daylight the water feature is mostly lost among the lush foliage.

Plate 1.37 - In the evening this same space becomes the main attraction of the backyard. Two exterior directional fixtures, using 50-watt MR16 narrow floods (EXN), are mounted in the fig tree to provide the accent lighting.

Plate 1.38 - This tropical backyard benefits from uninterrupted sunlight during the day.

Plate 1.39 - The owners, wanting to enjoy the same quality of light at night, use three flood-lights mounted above the window line on the back of the house. These fixtures offer an overall ambient light source that is paired with carefully concealed uplights for the Australian tree ferns.

Plate 1.40 - During the day-light hours this stucco retaining wall adds little to the feel of the backyard.

Plate 1.41 - At night this same wall takes on a wonderful textural quality when illuminated by a single fixture mounted on a staircase to the left of the dracaena. The shoji panels create an artful background when the silhouettes of banana plants are projected onto the rice paper. A single 100-watt halogen floodlight mounted on the back of the house projects the shape of the banana plants onto the rice paper.

Plate 1.42 - In daytime this black-bottomed pool is heated using the passive solar energy created when the dark color absorbs the energy of the sun.

Plate 1.43 - After nightfall the water takes on a lagoon-like quality when the pool lights are fitted with blue lenses. Normally pools are illuminated with incandescent sources, which turn the water yellow. Yellow water looks uninviting.

Plate 1.44 - In this shot the "black mirror" effect is used to create this interesting vignette. The Romanesque columns are reflected in the water's surface when the pool lights are turned off. Hidden low-voltage accent lights illuminate the columns and the surrounding oak trees.

Plate 1.45 - As dusk begins to fall, this sensational colonnade gleams against the azure sky. A recessed well light is located at the base of each of the columns to create this impressive effect.

Chapter Seven

SPECIAL EFFECTS

Don't let visually powerful lighting cause other aspects of the design to suffer loss of impact, unless the lighting is to be the central focus.

Now that you have worked your way through the basics of lighting design, this chapter will describe some relatively new products and lighting design techniques.

Homeowners might consider using special lighting treatments that are subtle or controllable enough to be experienced every day. Day-to-day use of specialized lighting, such as **neon**, fiber optics, LEDs, and **framing projectors** in residential applications may be too intense for your clients. Commercial spaces can be more adventurous, because people want to be visually transported to a space that has a bit of fantasy to it.

This approach is similar to choosing art that you can live with. A particular painting or sculpture may have an impact initially, but will your clients love it enough to have it as a constant part of their daily existence? Just as in film, music, and computer graphics, people can get too creative, allowing their creation to outshine the main event. Lighting special effects can divert attention away from the rest of the space and the people in it. Still, working with your client to make a strong statement is certainly a design option. Some people want a living space that makes guests say, "Wow!"

Usually, lighting works best as part of the background, bringing people's attention to the environment, but rarely to the lighting itself. Designers put together many elements to create an overall effect, including color, furniture, art, plant material, window treatments, and floor coverings. Don't let strong lighting cause other aspects of the design to suffer or take a secondary role in terms of visual inclusion, unless the lighting is to be the central focus.

As has been said in real estate, there are three important things to consider: location, location, location. Since these special lighting effects can have such a strong presence, picking the right placement is a major factor. A glowing visual treat at the end of a long hallway pulls people toward it. These special uses of lighting can help give subtle direction to guests. Art glass is making an appearance as a luminous presence in upscale homes. Take a look at Figure 7.1 to see how light and glass can combine to make quite a statement.

Figure 7.1
This large-scale art glass sculpture casts an amazing refracted shadow pattern on the wall behind, when illuminated with a single low voltage spot.

The interior entrance gives a first impression of the owners and of what the rest of the house is like. A special effect here can give a great visual clue as to what's in store. Since the entry foyer is not a place where family and guests linger, it is a good spot to consider using lighting with some pizzazz. Look at Plates 7.2 and 7.3 to see how different an art glass sculpture can appear when illuminated from within.

Another property of special-effects lighting is that it can give the designer an ability to add dimension to a space. Since the effect is often the strongest visual presence in the room, balancing its light level with the other lighting in a room will help add an intriguing 3-D feel (see Plates 2.30, 2.31 and 2.32).

Additionally, a visually strong special effect can draw people's attention away from the less desirable elements of a structure, or possibly turn those undesirable elements into a fascinating design look. A room with a jumble of architectural features might benefit from the eye-catching characteristics of a special lighting effect, such as a neon sculpture.

Apply this concept to an outside situation: An illuminated sculpture could visually allow your client's neighbor's scruffy backyard to fall into the shadows. This involves using the **glare factor** as a positive aspect of a special effect. As your eyes adjust to the brightness of a neon sculpture, for example, your irises contract to accommodate that brightness. The surrounding area appears to darken considerably, at least as you perceive it. This helps the less-than-pleasant aspects of the neighbor's property to fade away into the darkness.

Framing Projectors

Also known as "optical framing projectors," these luminaires can focus light to match the shape of the art or table it illuminates. The simpler models on the market use a series of shutters to make the beam of light approximate the size of the art. The more sophisticated units use a custom-cut metal template to match the shape of the art (see Figure 7.2). Ready-made templates are also available for both high-end and low-end optical projectors.

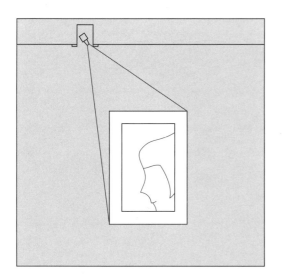
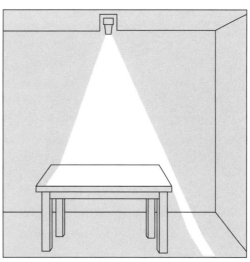

Figure 7.2 (left)
A framing projector uses a template or series of shutters to "cut" the light to the shape of the art.

Figure 7.3 (right)
A table that is lighted with a framing projector must stay in its exact position or a disturbing rim of light appears on the floor.

*Figure 7.4 (left)
During the day this cast glass
sculpture creates a strong silhouette against the lightly
colored wall.*

*Figure 7.5(right)
At night this same sculpture
takes on a very different look
when uplighted through the
base.*

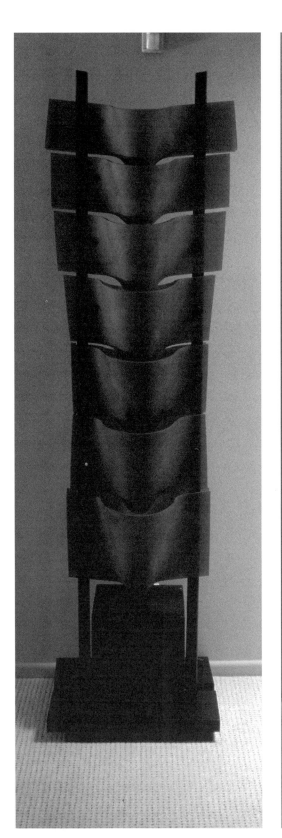

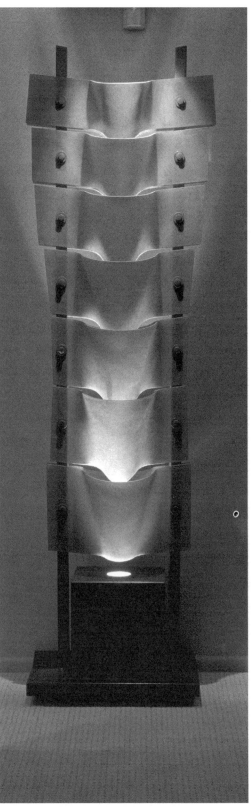

Before MR16s, MR11s, and PAR36s came along, framing projectors were the only way to get a controlled beam spread. Theatrical luminaires gained that ability decades ago but were simply too bulky for residential use.

Like everything else that's discussed in this book, framing projectors have their pros and cons. The expensive models do an excellent job of framing the art or sculpture. Inexpensive models have less precise optics, so the horizontal and vertical lines tend to be slightly convex.

The projectors can cause the art to predominate in the room. A recessed adjustable luminaire without an optical lens, using an MR16 lamp, would allow for some light spillage beyond the art piece itself. This actually helps integrate it into the overall design. Framing projectors can be adjusted to soften their focus to create the same effect. If this is the design goal, then using the much less expensive luminaire with the MR16 is the way to go.

Framing projectors may need regular adjustments if there is much movement in the building itself, such as kids running around, or if the house is built near a major thoroughfare. An out-of-adjustment framing projector pointed down onto a table can create a disconcerting corona of light on the floor (see Figure 7.3).

The housing for the framing projector needs to be accessible. That means having a 12-inch-diameter cover plate in the ceiling or installing a trap door in the floor of the room above. If the room upstairs is an accessible attic space, there is no problem, but if it's a bedroom, then carpeting cannot be permanently installed there.

If your clients have a very valuable, prestigious piece of art with which they want to dazzle their family and friends, a framing projector would certainly do the trick. Sometimes it's money that helps your client make the final decision. A good recessed framing projector by such companies as Wendelighting can cost around $1,500, plus the cost of installation.

A simpler recessed adjustable MR16 luminaire would cost around $165 plus installation. Surface-mounted framing projectors can cost from $350 on up and are less expensive to install than a recessed luminaire but are visually intrusive in the space.

The recessed framing projectors are not very flexible. The lower-price units do an acceptable job of making a square, rectangle, or circle but usually cannot make irregular shapes. Higher-priced framing projectors can mimic almost any shape but must be refitted with a new template if the art is changed.

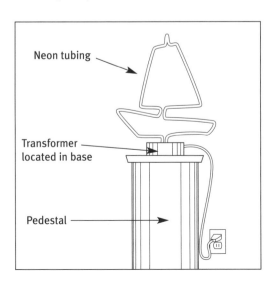

Neon tubing

Transformer located in base

Pedestal

Figure 7.6
A neon sculpture with a plug-in type transformer creates a strong visual statement.

Neon

Neon has been around for a long time. It was very popular from the 1930s to the 1950s and then began a decline in the 1960s and 1970s. It is enjoying a resurgence of popularity, due mostly to craftspeople's refining the art of neon and the more widespread acceptance by architects and designers. Also, the availability of improved transformers allows for a reduction in the noise levels. Plus easier dimming systems have made dimming more user-friendly (see Plates 2.39, 2.40, 2.41, 2.42 and 2.43).

Officially, neon in hardwired installations has not been allowed in residences for over forty years. The **National Electric Code** does not allow systems of 1,000 volts or more to be installed in homes. Neon normally runs in the 3,000 to 15,000 volt range. This is for the issue of safety. Remember when, as a kid, you stuck a fork in the wall plug and got a nasty shock? Or was it your buddy in college? Well, that was 120 volts of electricity. Imagine 15,000 volts coursing through your body. You would be one crispy critter.

Portable neon sculpture is legal and **UL**-listed (Underwriters Laboratories—they test stuff out to make sure that it's safe). The main precaution is to make sure that the connections are secure and covered to protect people from the possibility of getting shocked. There is some really great neon sculpture out there in museums and private collections (see Figure 7.6).

Neon is a glass vacuum tube filled with neon gas. When electricity is passed through the tube, the gas is excited to produce an orange-red glow. The addition of other gases or phosphors, as well as the use of different-colored tubing, produces a variety of colors. The glass tubing is heated and formed into letters or designs. The overall length and diameter of the tubing determines the size transformer that is needed. Systems with multiple tubes wired in series require more voltage.

Full-brightness neon, installed in a commercial setting, may be too strong to work comfortably within a residential design. Advanced dimming capabilities now offer a wide range of light levels so that the neon may be more easily integrated into a particular setting.

For an added special effect, helium and neon can be combined in a tube to create a curious luminous bubbling effect by using radio-frequency transformers. The bubbling effect is created as radio waves vary (see this type of neon used to visually extend a small dining room at night in Plates 2.52 and 2.53).

Cold Cathode

Cold cathode is a close relative of neon. The tubing is slightly larger (25mm) in diameter than neon (20mm or smaller). Basically, cold cathode is used for illumination purposes, whereas neon is used for signage and as an art form, although there is some crossover. Cold cathode, like neon, comes in more than thirty colors. With cold cathode installations, there are transformers that operate at less than 1,000 volts, which allows them to be permanently installed in residences. Inspectors will want to see a UL label or the label of some other nationally recognized testing laboratory.

In homes, cold cathode can do a wonderful job of indirect light behind cove or crown molding. Its small diameter, compared to standard fluorescent lamps, allows a less bulky architectural detail to conceal it (see Figure 7.7). The transformer does have an inherent hum, so it should be located remotely within a soundproof space. The inside of a niche detail could also use cold cathode as its light source (see Figure 7.8). Or it could be used to outline the inside perimeter of a skylight (see Figure 7.9).

Think of cold cathode as a source of light that isn't seen but experienced, while neon is meant to be seen.

Fiber Optics

Fiber optics have come a long way in their application possibilities. Illuminated from one end, the light travels through the fiber-optic filament or bundle of filaments in a tube or casing. One variety, called "end-lit" fiber optics, projects an intense light from the end of the fiber-optic run opposite the light source (see Plates 2.50 and 2.51). The other variety, called "edge-lit," illuminates the length of the fiber-optic run. Presently, most fiber-optic runs are illuminated by halogen or metal halide sources.

A fiber-optic package usually contains two components: the fiber-optic material itself and its source of light, usually called an "illuminator." The illuminator is a remotely located shielded box that houses a lamp, a ballast (if an HID source is being used), and a fan (to keep the lamp cool and to help lengthen its life). It can also house an optional color wheel or filter holder that allows the owner to change the color of the

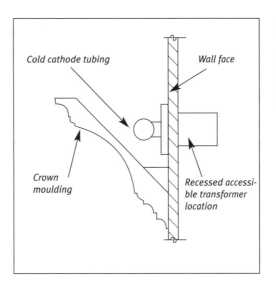

Figure 7.7
Cold cathode can be mounted behind crown moulding to provide uplight (local codes need to be checked before installation.)

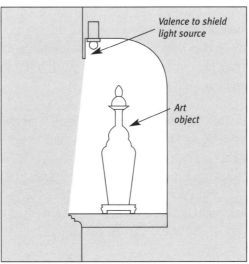

Figure 7.8
Cold cathode can be used to light the inside of a niche (local codes need to be checked before installation.)

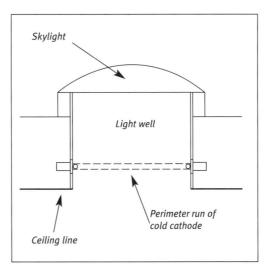

Figure 7.9
Cold cathode can be installed on the light well of a skylight (local codes need to be checked before installation.)

To keep the light level constant throughout the length of the run, you should keep the length of a fiber optic run to 100 feet or less and loop the run back to the illuminator. Optionally, place an illuminator at both ends.

light output or allows for a gradual shift from one color to the next. Remember the 1950s when everyone had a silver metal Christmas tree and a motorized light that passed colored lenses in front of a spotlight on a weighted base? Well, this is just a more refined version of the same principle.

Designers often mistakenly assume that edge-lit fiber optics are as bright as neon and are a viable substitute for neon or cold cathode on a project. This is not the case. While fiber optics and neon can come close to the brightness of neon or cold cathode in certain environments, the true advantages of fiber optics are what they can do better than neon. Flexibility, ease of installation, and low maintenance have made fiber optics better suited for many functions usually reserved for other light sources.

Edge-lit Fiber Optics
Edge-lit fiber optics can do a good job of approximating the look of a neon sign or sculpture. One of its main advantages over neon or cold cathode is the ability to change the color at will (see Plates 2.46, 2.47, 2.48 and 2.49). Red neon will always be red neon. Only replacement of the tube will give you a different color, while a simple change of lens is all that is required in fiber optics. The environment needs to be relatively dark for the fiber optics to "read" as neon. If there is too much other lighting in the spaces then the illumination from the fiber-optic run is washed out.

Another advantage to fiber optics is that since there is no electricity actually going through the tube, a fiber-optic run can be integrated into water environments. How about your client's signature or the outline of a giant fish in the bottom of the pool? You can also inset a fiber-optic run into the edge of the clients' pool or hot tub for a dramatic effect (see Figure 7.11). You could also backlight glass tile set in a bathroom floor for a very different type of night-light. If these glass tiles are a frosted whites then inserting a color filter in front of the light source could change the color.

Figure 7.10
A sandblasted acrylic handrail glows from within through the use of a fiber optic bundle running in a channel along the underside.

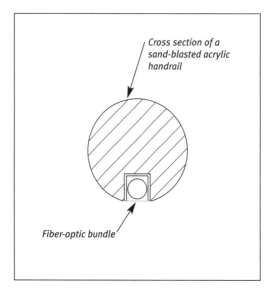

Cross section of a sand-blasted acrylic handrail

Fiber-optic bundle

Fiber-optic runs can also be snaked through walls of glass block to add another dimension to that architectural detail at night. The light source is remotely located in the illuminator, so the homeowner never has to go into the wall to replace the lamp (see Figure 7.12).

You can consider illuminating a sandblasted acrylic handrail from within by inserting an edge-lighted fiber-optic bundle through the center if it's a hollow straight run. Or you can fit it into a rout on the underside if it's a curved solid rail (see Figure 7.10). You could edge-light a table, a piano, or the steps

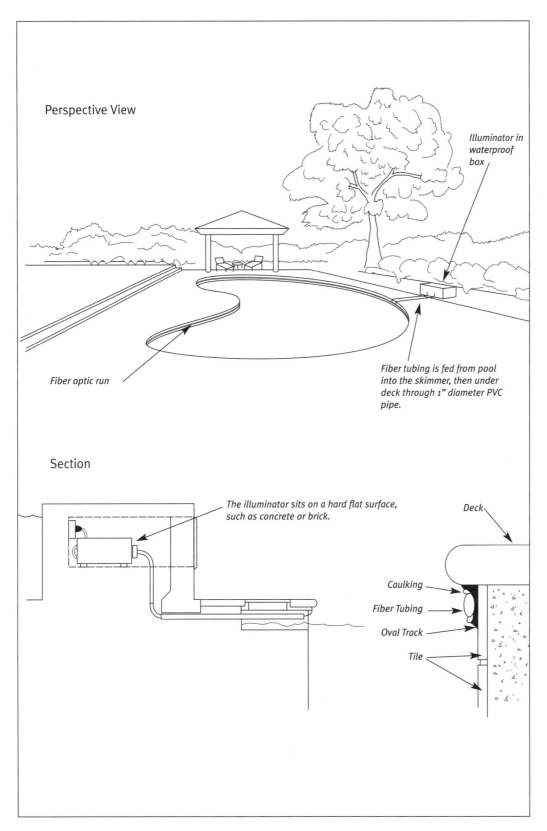

Figure 7.11
Fiber optics can be used to edge light a pool.

Design concept by Fiberstars.

Perspective View

Illuminator in waterproof box

Fiber optic run

Fiber tubing is fed from pool into the skimmer, then under deck through 1" diameter PVC pipe.

Section

The illuminator sits on a hard flat surface, such as concrete or brick.

Deck

Caulking

Fiber Tubing

Oval Track

Tile

Figure 7.12
Edge lighting of glass block
with fiber optics blends art
with architecture.

Design concept by Fiberstars.

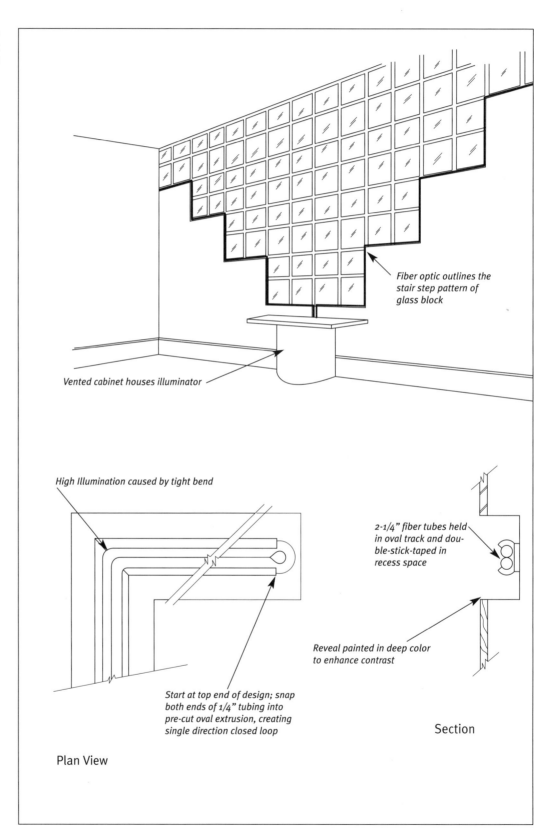

Fiber optic outlines the
stair step pattern of
glass block

Vented cabinet houses illuminator

High Illumination caused by tight bend

2-1/4" fiber tubes held
in oval track and dou-
ble-stick-taped in
recess space

Reveal painted in deep color
to enhance contrast

Start at top end of design; snap
both ends of 1/4" tubing into
pre-cut oval extrusion, creating
single direction closed loop

Section

Plan View

leading to your clients' front door, outline an architectural detail, or create an art piece.

Fiber optics are dimmable, but since the output of illumination can be subtle, dimming is often not necessary. To keep the light level constant throughout length of the run, you should keep the length of a fiber-optic run to 100 feet or less and loop the run back to the illuminator. Optionally, place an illuminator at both ends.

End-lit Fiber Optics

End-lit fiber optics can perform a variety of interesting functions. For example, single strands of fiber optics can be pulled through a ceiling to create a starry-night effect. The color wheel can do its trick of gradually changing the hue and intensity of those man-made constellations. You can also consider creating the effect of fireflies to a garden on the West Coast, where fireflies don't exist, by hiding fiber-optics at different heights in a stand of bamboo.

End-lit fiber optics (offered by Fiberstars, Lucifer Lighting, and other manufacturers) are also being integrated into display lighting and downlights, where removing the light source is advantageous for maintenance purposes. Also, because fiber optics do not emit ultraviolet (UV) rays, they are an excellent source of illumination when conservation of what is being illuminated is an issue.

Fiber optics can be a very good way of adding a little sparkle or flexible accent light to a project. These examples are just a taste of what is possible.

LEDs (Light-Emitting Diodes)

LEDs are very new on the market as a source of illumination for residential and commercial projects. Until recently LEDs were primarily used to light up instrument panels, clock faces, and dashboards in cars. The next generation of LEDs became the source of illumination for traffic lights. Look closely at a newer traffic light—you'll notice a series of smaller points of light instead of one large source of illumination. Since LEDs have an extremely long life (up to 400,000 hours) and intense colors, they were a perfect solution for this use.

Now the commercial market is using LEDs to backlight plastic lettering on signage. Here too, the intense light and the long life of the source make it a better way of backlighting than fluorescent or neon. Neon is fragile and costly, while fluorescent sources have a more limited lamp life than LEDs, have little flexibility, and don't work well in cold temperatures.

The residential market is just opening up for LEDs. The first items to hit the market were backlit house numbers and doorbell indicator lights. These products allowed for the use of the intense colors generally available in LEDs. A viable white LED light source has not yet been successfully developed—as of this writing, LED manufacturers have developed a white light source that is only one-third as bright as the other colors. But give them time. If there is a market out there that demands a high lumen white LED, be assured that the manufacturers will come up with a solution.

The other application of LEDs in a residence is their use in cove lighting, indirect illumination that runs around the perimeter of a room. The light source is normally hidden in some kind of architectural detail. An LED system with a color changer can create a glow of light on the ceiling that goes from red to blue to green to purple. While this may not be suitable for a dining room application, it would work magnificently for a home theater. The white-to-yellow color range would be better for living rooms, dining rooms, and bedrooms.

The Bottom Line

Remember, a little goes a long way. Let your project wear one or two pieces of great architectural jewelry—don't empty the whole jewel box.

Section Two

Using Light

Reprinted by permission of
The New Yorker.

"'Incandescent' is how he thinks, but 'fluorescent' is what I want."

Chapter Eight

KITCHENS—THE NEW GATHERING PLACES

Kitchens have
become the new
centers for
entertaining.
The impact on
lighting is that the
kitchen should
now be as inviting
as the rest of
the house.

Kitchens have become the new centers for entertaining. One reason for this is the change in the way we entertain. It's now more casual than it was previously, with a relaxed and interactive feel. Today it's likely that guests will gather in the kitchen as the meal is being prepared, often lending a hand while sipping a glass of wine.

New homes are being laid out by architects and builders to accommodate this change. As a result, the trend is toward open plan houses, where the rooms flow together. The solid walls between the kitchen, dining room, and family room have disappeared. This newly defined space is often referred to as a "great room".

The impact on lighting design is that the kitchen should now be as inviting as the rest of the house. It too must have controllable lighting levels, so that guests look as good and feel as comfortable as they do in the other parts of the house (see Figure 8.1). This definitely changes some of the lighting methods that have been around for a long time (see Plate 2.22).

Sadly, we still see new kitchens, expensive kitchens, with a single source of illumination in the center of the room. Whether this is incandescent or fluorescent, it is essentially a "glare bomb" that provides little in the way of adequate task, ambient or accent lighting. As our eyes adjust to the glare, the rest of the kitchen seems even darker than it actually is. We see only the light source, and little of the surrounding room (see Figure 8.5).

As you have learned, there is no single luminaire that can perform all the required functions of lighting for a space. Here, as almost everywhere else in the house, it is the layering of various light sources that creates a comfortable and flexible lighting design (see Plate 2.23).

In the 1970s, builders seemed compelled to put a run of track in the center of the kitchen. Track lighting is best used as a source of accent lighting. If you try to use it to light the inside

Figure 8.1
A room filled with ambient light helps soften the shadows on faces. The additional layer of fill light is what helps humanize a given space.

Figure 8.2
A room filled with only recessed down lights casts harsh shadows onto people's faces, placing their features in deep shadow and making their features unattractive.

Figure 8.3
At first appearance this kitchen appears to be adequately illuminated, but in reality the series of recessed downlights create an inhospitable environment for the family members and their guests. The addition of wall sconces, mounted on the mullions in between the windows, would have provided much-needed ambient light. The addition of recessed lighting on the refrigerator is a total mystery.

Figure 8.4
The corner of this cleanly styled kitchen uses two sources of illumination to provide the appropriate task lighting. Recessed wall wash fixtures provide illumination for the open shelves, while low voltage linear light offers shadow free illumination along the counter.

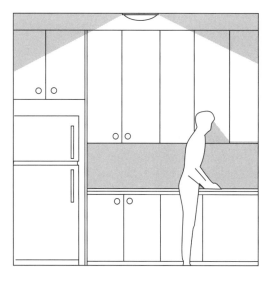

*Figure 8.5
The illumination from a surface-mounted luminaire in
the center of the room is
blocked by one's own body.*

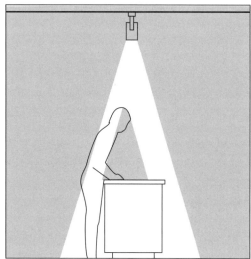

*Figure 8.6
Track lighting is a poor
source of task light. Clients
will be forced into working in
their own shadows.*

*Figure 8.7
Linear task lights
mounted towards the back of
the cabinet create a distracting glare when people sit at
the table.*

of cabinets or the countertops, your own head can get in the way, casting shadows onto the work surface (see Figure 8.6). The old surface-mounted luminaire in the middle of the ceiling can cause the same problems.

In the '80s there was a shift toward using a series of recessed downlights installed in a grid pattern in the ceiling. This was a little better, but by themselves they cast harsh, unflattering shadows on people's faces and your own head still eclipses the work surface (see Figures 8.2 and 8.3).

Under-Cabinet Lighting

The first step toward successful light layering in the kitchen is the introduction of lighting mounted below the wall cabinets. This type of lighting provides an even level of illumination along the countertops. Since it comes between the work surface and your head, the lighting is much more shadow-free (see Figure 8.4).

These linear task luminaires come in a great variety of styles and lamp sources. What we commonly see is a fluorescent strip luminaire mounted at the back of the cabinet. The drawback to this placement is that when people are sitting down in the breakfast area or the adjacent dining room, the light source can hit them right in the eye (see Figure 8.7). They also come as a mini recessed or surface mounted luminaire called a puck light.

What has been on the market for a while now are linear task lights in incandescent or fluorescent versions that mount toward the front of the cabinet. They project a portion of the illumination toward the back splash, which then bounces light without glare onto the work surfaces and out toward the center of the kitchen (see Figure 8.8). This works well when the countertop is a material with a non specular surface, such as a matte-finish plastic laminate, unpolished marble, or Corian.

Lighting designers are often faced with the challenge of lighting highly reflective counter-tops, such as polished black granite or glossy tile. These shiny surfaces act like mirrors, revealing the light source under the cabinets. In this situation, a solid reflector could be installed along the underside of the luminaire so that the light is directed only toward the backsplash.

In the worst case-scenario, both countertop and backsplash have a reflective finish. This is a true lighting nightmare. If the clients are not willing to choose a surface with a matte finish, then the only solution is to install miniature recessed adjustable luminaires with louvers covering the face of the lamps. Inside the cabinets, a false bottom would need to be created in order to hide the luminaire housings (see Figure 8.9).

Note: The incandescent linear task lights (including halogen and xenon) produce heat and can affect the food stored inside of the cabinet — items such as baker's chocolate can melt. It's a good idea to instruct your clients to store perishables on an upper shelf if heat is a factor.

General Illumination

Ambient lighting plays an important role in the overall lighting design for the kitchen, just as it does for the other main rooms in the house. It is this soft fill light that helps humanize the space. Note that the color temperature of the lamps in all the lighting used in the kitchen should match, or at least be similar to, the color temperature in other areas of the house.

There are a variety of ways to provide ambient lighting. One way, when dealing with 9-foot or higher ceilings, is to install a pendant-hung luminaire or a series of pendants along the centerline of the space. They can be made of an opaque material, such as plaster, or have

Note: The incandescent linear task lights (including halogen and xenon) produce heat and can affect the items being stored inside of the cabinet. Items such as baker's chocolate can melt. It's a good idea to store perishables on an upper shelf if heat is a factor.

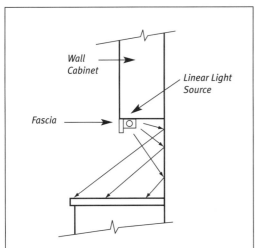

Wall Cabinet

Linear Light Source

Fascia

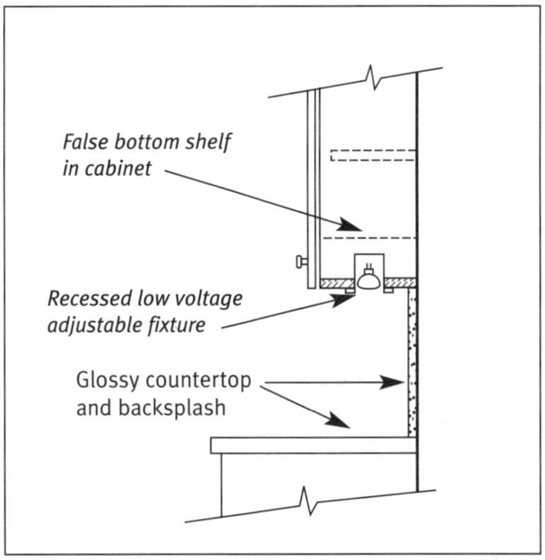

False bottom shelf in cabinet

Recessed low voltage adjustable fixture

Glossy countertop and backsplash

Figure 8.8 (left)
A linear task light mounted at the front of the cabinet bounces illumination off the backsplash and onto the countertop.

Figure 8.9 (right)
The only way to control glare when both the backsplash and the countertop are a gloss finish is to provide cross-illumination from recessed luminaire mounted inside the cabinets.

*Figure 8.10
A series of pendant
luminaires can provide a
wonderful, inviting
ambient light.*

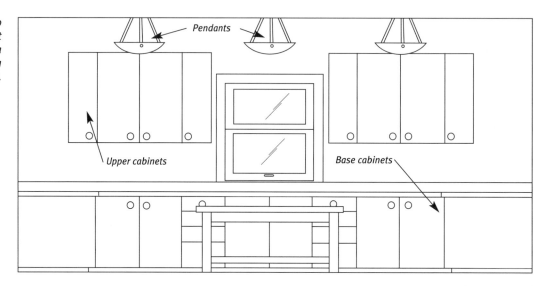

Pendants

Upper cabinets

Base cabinets

*Figure 8.11 (left)
California's Title 24 states
that either the center luminaire or the undercabinet
lights must be fluorescent.*

*Figure 8.12(right)
California's Title 24 states
that if there are two or more
light sources in the room, the
center luminaire must be fluorescent.*

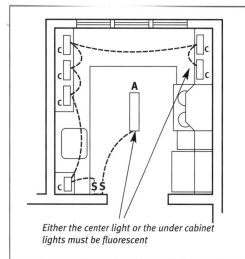

Either the center light or the under cabinet
lights must be fluorescent

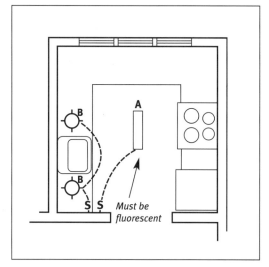

Must be
fluorescent

*Figure 8.13 (left)
California's Title 24 states
that if there is only one luminaire in the room, it must be
fluorescent.*

*Figure 8.14 (right)
California's Title 24 states
that if only undercabinet
lights are used, then they
must be fluorescent.*

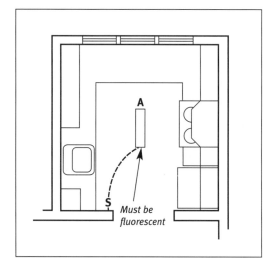

Must be
fluorescent

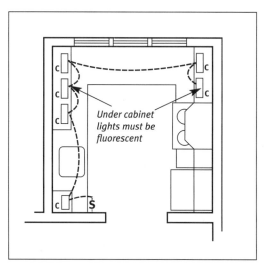

Under cabinet
lights must be
fluorescent

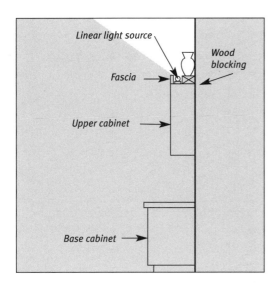

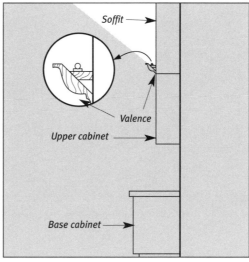

Figure 8.15 (left)
Side section
Indirect lighting mounted on top of the cabinets not only produces ambient illumination, but could also highlight a client's collection.

Figure 8.16 (right)
Side Section
If the wall is soffitted down to the tops of the cabinet, a valence of crown moulding could be installed to house a linear light source.

a more translucent quality such as alabaster. Not only will they produce a wonderful ambient illumination, but they will also add a more human scale to the kitchen (see Figure 8.10).

Another ambient lighting option is to mount linear luminaires above the cabinets, provided there is open space between them and the ceiling (see Figure 8.15). This can be a wonderfully subtle way of producing much-needed ambient light. If the cabinets don't have a deep enough reveal on top, a fascia (a wooden trim piece) can be added to hide the luminaires from view. You can add a shelf that is at the same height as the fascia behind the light to create a potential display area along the top of the cabinet. Without the shelf, the display items would be visually cut off at the bottom.

If the wall has already been bumped out or soffited above the cabinets, there is still an opportunity to build a cove or valence detail out of crown molding in which to house an indirect light source (see Figure 8.16).

The light source for this indirect lighting can be incandescent (including halogen and xenon) or fluorescent. Standard 3-foot, 4-foot, and compact fluorescent tubes are easily and quietly dimmed using solid-state (electronic) dimming ballasts. This can also fulfill Title 24 requirements in California (see Figures 8.11–8.14).

California requires that the first switch in a kitchen or a bathroom must operate a fluorescent luminaire and have an efficiency of at least 40 lumens per watt. Be sure to check local and state codes for building and energy regulations. California is not the only state to have codes that emphasize energy efficiency. The emerging trend is to incorporate energy conservation into building standards throughout the United States.

A less traditional approach to providing ambient illumination would be to install a series of wall sconces on the face of the soffit, instead of using a crown molding detail (see Figure 8.17). The illumination from these fixtures would not be especially even, but a pattern of

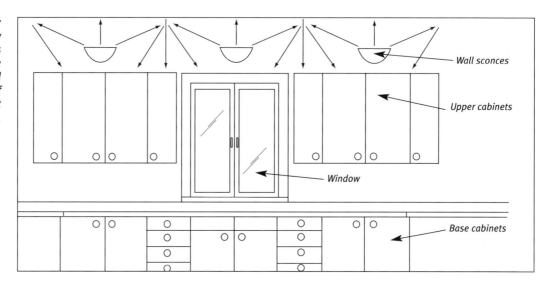

Figure 8.17
Front view
A series of wall sconces mounted on the soffit above the overhead cabinets will provide a modern source of ambient illumination.

light might add some visual interest to a ceiling with little architectural detail.

Skylights can be a great source of general illumination during the day. This is especially true if they are made of a white opal acrylic material or are fitted with a diffusing material (refer to Chapter 5). At night, light sources mounted within the light well can produce adequate fill light (see Figure 8.18), while at the same time keeping the skylight from becoming a "black hole" after dark. Don't let the fact that the kitchen you are designing is on the first floor of a three-story building stop you from installing a skylight. You can still install a faux skylight by opening up a recess in the ceiling (see Figure 8.19) or using a ready-made faux skylight available from various manufacturers. This will create a feeling of increased height and openness.

Accent Lighting

Your client might have a few art pieces that can stand up to an occasional splash of marinara sauce. They deserve to be highlighted. This helps make the kitchen part of the overall open-home plan. One tasty effect is to dim the ambient and task lights in the kitchen down to a glow, once the party has moved to another area, letting the accented art catch the attention.

Many facets of your kitchen design will determine the way it is lighted. Not only do such variables as ceiling height, natural light, and work surfaces affect the placement or amount of light used, but there are other factors you should consider as well. Here is a checklist:

1. Color. Darker finished surfaces are more light absorptive. An all-white kitchen requires dramatically less light (40-50 percent) than a kitchen with dark wood cabinets and walls.

2. *Reflectance.* A highly polished countertop has a high degree of reflectance and acts just like a mirror. Any under-cabinet lighting will show its reflection.

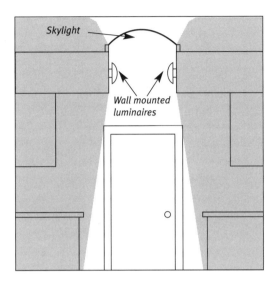

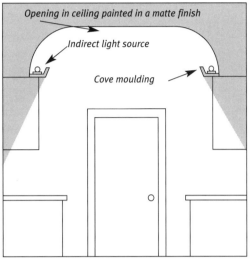

*Figure 8.18 (left)
Side Section. Light luminaires mounted on the inside of the light well can help provide ambient illumination for the kitchen at night.*

*Figure 8.19 (right)
A faux skylight can be created to provide "daylight" even if the kitchen is on the first floor of a three story building.*

3. *Texture.* If your end design includes brickwork or stucco, you might choose to show off the textural quality of those surfaces. This is accomplished by directing light at an acute angle onto the textured surface. Luminaires located too far away from the wall will smooth it out (which might be a good idea for bad drywall jobs).

4. *Mood.* Floor plans are more open now. Guests will flow from the living room to the kitchen to the dining room. The kitchen should be just as inviting as the rest of the house. Make sure that there is enough ambient light in the kitchen. This softens the lines on people's faces and creates a warm, inviting glow.

5. *Tone.* The warm end of the color spectrum works well with incandescent light, but cooler colors are adversely affected by the amber quality of incandescent light. Whites turn yellow and reds can turn orange. Make a color temperature choice that works well with skin tones and room colors.

6. *Code.* In California, designers must conform to Title 24 (the State Energy Commission's requirements for new construction and remodel work that affects more than 50 percent of the existing space). General lighting must be fluorescent (or have an efficacy of at least 40 lumens per watt) in kitchens and baths, and must be the first switch as you enter the room. Today many decorative luminaires are made to take compact fluorescent lamps, which are now dimmable. (California is not the only state with such regulations. In the near future, most states will be affected (refer to Figures 8.12 - 8.15).

7. *Windows.* Windows that let wonderful light stream in during the day, showing off landscaping, will become black, reflective mirrors at night unless thought is given to exterior lighting. Outside lighting will visually expand the interior space out into the exterior (see Chapter 15).

8. *Sloped ceilings.* Even if there is enough space above a sloped ceiling to install recessed luminaires, special care must be taken to select units that don't glare. Some luminaires are

made specifically for sloped ceilings, while others have a 90-degree aiming angle to accommodate the slope.

9. *Pot racks.* A pot rack may look just perfect over that center island on the plan, but it's extremely difficult to light a work surface through cookware. If a pot rack is demanded, consider installing recessed adjustable luminaires to cross-illuminate the counter surface of the island or position them above the center of the rack. Still, the shadows cannot be eliminated, so having the option of increasing the ambient light is a way of combating the glare.

10. *Door swings.* Make sure that switches are on the unhinged side of a door. Otherwise, your client will have to reach around the back of the door to turn on the lights. Make sure that any swing changes that occur during the installation process are forwarded to you and all the design team members so that you can make sure that the design works in the end.

Of course, many aspects of this checklist apply to other rooms in the house, so feel free to refer to the list as you go from area to area.

Getting a Lighting Professional on the Team

Just as interior designers and architects are pulling in kitchen specialists on their projects, those specialists are now turning to lighting experts to make the projects glow. Since the lighting consultant specializes only in lighting, he or she has a vast library of catalogs and information relating solely to light and lighting products. The consultant can turn out a quality design in a short amount of time, saving the kitchen designer's time and ultimately reducing the client's cost.

The Bottom Line

A successful kitchen design is a foot-in-the-door, maybe an introduction to do the interior design work for the rest of the client's house (and their neighbor's house).

Chapter Nine

ENTRANCES—SETTING THE TONE

Too often,
a foyer in a home
is restricted in
space, but with
lighting and
related design
techniques, the
space can be sub-
tly transformed
into a vastly more
welcoming place.

Just as you judge people by your first impression upon meeting them, you judge a home by what you see and how you feel as you come into the entry. This makes it doubly important to set just the right mood and tone. The correct lighting is crucial to how people will respond, as well as where their attention will be drawn (see Plates 1.18, 1.19, 1.20, 1.21 and 1.22).

Outside, as evening guests approach a house, the lighting should provide an eye-catching, welcoming feel, as well as security. You will also need to give specific cues showing which way to approach and enter. Be sure to light the house number (see Figure 9.1). Chapter 15 discusses illumination for the outside in more detail.

Inside the home, ambient illumination should surround the entry with welcoming light. Fill light is especially important in this area. People need a gentle glow of illumination to help them feel at ease in a new surrounding. This complimentary light also allows the home-owners to look their best when greeting people. Good ambient light in the entry will help transform what is often an awkward moment into a more comfortable and enjoyable encounter. Entry lighting can also energize a person's impression of a home. Highlighting a dramatic painting, sculpture, or architectural detail can help guests feel at once welcomed and impressed (see Figure 9.2).

People respond to what they sense, not always to what is real. A room can be made to look large, airy, and open when the reality may actually be quite the opposite. Too often, an entrance in a home is restricted in space, but with lighting and related design techniques, the space can be subtly transformed into a vastly more welcoming place.

Illusion

Not all lighting solutions directly involve the use of luminaires. Mirrors, for instance, can be used to create the illusion of greater space or more light. Mirroring one wall can make a room appear to expand in size. Mirrors will keep wall areas located farthest from the windows from falling into darkness or seeming less important.

Entries come in all shapes and sizes. Lighting can help you redefine the envelope of the space. Do you want the entry to look larger or more intimate? Do you want a look that dazzles or a look of homey comfort? How about a combination of both? It is possible (see Plates 1.2, 1.3 and 1.4). For example, in a cramped entry area, you can often use illusion and lighting to "steal" part of another room. In addition to using mirrors, you might consider installing glass block or directing an accent light onto a sculpture, flower arrangement, or painting in an adjacent area to visually make it a part of the small entry.

Stairways in an entry area can provide additional opportunities for expansiveness. Illuminated, they make the room seem larger and provide another focus for the guest's attention upon entering the home. Lighting a painting mounted on the wall along the stairway or illuminating plants or a sculpture on a stair landing can also help a small entry assume the appearance of a grander entrance hall.

Switching and dimming systems can take the same entry that was made to look huge and dramatic for a big party or event and instantly transform it into a cozy and intimate greeting area for small, friendly gatherings. Lighting can and should be that flexible.

With an integrated dimming system, your clients can create whatever kind of setting they would like. There's nothing wrong with making the house seem foreboding when uninvited guests stop by, or having the lights go to full brightness when it's time for guests to depart. Review the section on pre-set dimming systems in Chapter 6 to get a better handle on the idea of creating lighting "scenes".

Lighting directed toward the ceiling helps open up a space and makes it feel larger, and at the same time friendly and inviting. Illumination pointed down onto the floor makes an entry seem smaller because the darkened ceiling feels lower. Adding accent light to a darkened space creates highly dramatic settings. Accent light layered with ambient light provides a friendly environment with a bit of visual punch. Positioning the accent lights for the particular art piece is critical (see Figures 9.2, 9.3, 9.4, and 9.5).

Too often entries end up looking unintentionally dark and uninviting, even if elegantly decorated. Usually it's because the addition of ambient light has not even been considered. Either it was omitted entirely or the walls and ceiling may be too dark for indirect light to be reflected and diffused effectively throughout the space (see Plate 1.20). If the ceiling is not adequately lit, the space seems small, and beams, coffers, moldings, ceiling frescoes, and other design components lose their potential to be marvelous welcoming details. Lighting architectural details well gives people something to engage their interest as they enter, and helps enlarge the feel of the room by expanding the space visually upward. For parties, entrances can serve as auxiliary gathering spots when they are properly lit for people's comfort.

Planning

It's essential that you take lighting needs into consideration at the beginning of the design stage, because additions later will cost much more than adding appropriate lighting touches at the front end of a project. A common approach to lighting an entry is to put a decorative luminaire, such as a chandelier, in the center of a ceiling as the only source of illumination (see Figure 9.1). If this is your design choice, then the bottom of an entry or hall pendant should be a minimum of 6 feet 8 inches off the floor.

As a result, this one luminaire draws all the attention. Art, moldings, ceiling details, and flower arrangements fall into secondary importance. Your clients, as they greet guests, will end up in silhouette, which does not give them a flattering appearance.

Daylight also should be integrated into the design of an entry, if possible. Use available windows or add windows or skylights to provide some or all of the ambient light during daylight hours. (Look back at Chapter 5 for some application ideas.) This is when light layering comes into play. For example, think about installing a source of ambient light so that an existing chandelier can be dimmed to a subtle sparkle (see Figure 9.2).

Ambient Lighting

One option for **ambient lighting** would be to install a pair of wall sconces flanking an art piece to provide the necessary glow of illumination. Translucent versions may draw too much attention to themselves; opaque-bottom sconces (made of metal, bisque, or plaster) will cast light upward, softening the shadows on faces and filling the entry with a pleasing glow of illumination (see Figure 9.8).

Rule of Thumb — Mount opaque-bottom wall sconces above eye level; normally 6 to 6-1/2 feet above the finished floor. This applies to 8- or 9-foot ceilings. When working with a higher ceiling, the luminaire can be mounted higher.

Figure 9.1 (left)
Using only a chandelier in the center of the ceiling draws too much attention to itself and the rest of the room and the people are not illuminated properly.

Figure 9.2 (right)
Wall sconces provide the ambient light for the room, and allow the chandelier to be dimmed, so that it gives the illusion of providing the illumination, without attracting too much attention to itself.

Figure 9.3
The uplighting on the façade of this house reaches only to the underside of the second story windows. Passersby are given little clue as to the rest of the architecture. Mounting the fixtures further back would have allowed the light to travel up the full height of the house. Care needs to be taken so that these accent lights do not hit people in the eye as they exit the building.

Figure 9.4
A small wooden dog sculpture is bathed in its own pool of light, in this living room space. In the background a square column blends with the philodendron to create an impressive silhouette.

*Figure 9.5 (left)
The direct overhead lighting
for this seated Buddha causes its facial features to fall
into shadow. If the fixture
would have been located
more in front instead of
directly over the piece, much
better illumination could
have been provided for the
sculpture.*

*Figure 9.6 (right)
This wooden sculpture is
successfully illuminated from
above because the recessed
light fixture is located slightly
in front of the art instead of
directly on top of it.*

Figure 9.7
This collection of art objects uses a series of shallow recessed fixtures called Puk *lights, manufactured by Lucifer Lighting. Note how the pieces are staggered to allow the light to reach to the lower shelves.*

Figure 9.8
This more classically-styled opaque wall sconce, by Boyd Lighting, produces a good amount of fill light from a 150-watt halogen source.

Figure 9.9
Torchères can also be a good,
easy way of adding ambient
light. They provide the illumi-
nation that people will think
comes from the chandelier,
which can be dimmed to an
appropriate level.

Figure 9.10
Cove lighting inside the
moulding detail provides
ambient light without glare.
Again, the chandelier gives
the illusion of providing illu-
mination, but is dimmed so it
will not produce too much
distracting brightness.

Figure 9.11
A pendant-hung indirect
luminaire can be substituted
for the chandelier, to provide
the necessary ambient light.
Candlestick wall sconces
could be added for sparkle.

Rule of Thumb: Mount opaque-bottom wall sconces above eye level, normally 6 to 6-1/2 feet above the finished floor. This applies to 8 or 9-foot ceilings. When working with a higher ceiling, the luminaire can be mounted higher. Do not mount the luminaire closer than 2 feet from the ceiling; otherwise there'll be a hot spot above the sconce.

A second possible source of ambient lighting is the torchère (see Figure 9.9). If electrical outlets are already available, then an electrician is not needed. Torchères are the quickest and easiest way of adding ambient light to a room. Remember to choose a luminaire with a solid reflector-type shade that provides uplight only. Otherwise attention will be drawn away from the other more interesting aspects of the entry. A half-switched receptacle would allow your clients to turn on the torchère using a wall switch instead of turning it on at the luminaire itself (refer back to Figure 6.1 in Chapter 6).

A more architecturally integrated solution to the question of ambient light would be to install cove lighting (see Figure 9.10). A linear light source can be hidden behind molding details to uplight the ceiling along the perimeter of the entry. In new construction, this is an inexpensive addition to overall building cost. In a remodel situation, this could be the costliest and most labor-intensive of the ambient lighting solutions. Adding a series of opaque wall sconces would create an interesting pattern of light in an entry hall (see Plate 2.1).

Lastly, you could substitute an opaque-housing, pendant-hung, indirect luminaire in place of a chandelier to create the necessary fill light (see Figure 9.11). This would eliminate the source of sparkle, so you could install translucent or candlestick-type wall sconces on either side of the art as the sparkle of light for the entry. Decorative wall sconces are normally mounted at 5-1/2 feet on center (centerline of the junction box) above the finished floor.

Accent Lighting

Now that you have addressed the decorative and ambient light questions, you can tackle the accent lighting. While the common choice for accent lighting is apt to be track lighting, it is generally not the best solution. For some rooms it may be the only feasible choice because of the architecture, construction complications, or cost. But track lighting visually intrudes into a room and makes people feel as though they're onstage or on display.

When possible, recessed adjustable luminaires mounted in the ceiling are the better solution. These can be directed to particular spots that need highlighting, and are much more low-profile. Even in an existing home, recessed luminaires made especially for remodel can often be installed within a reasonable budget and with a minimum of mess. Always hire a professional electrician to get the job done properly. A well-installed job makes the interior designer or lighting designer look good too.

Can Halogen Lamps Be Used as Downlights?

The big question here is: What is the best use of downlights? The worst place to use downlights is over seating areas. They cause hard, unflattering shadows on people's faces, making them look tired and older than their true age. Who wants that? Fixed downlights should be installed only over stationary objects, such as sculptures, niches, or planters built into the architecture.

The trend we are seeing in the industry is the use of recessed adjustable luminaires that allow people to easily redirect the lighting as art and furniture are moved around. Interiors are no longer as static as they were in the 1950s and 1960s. Both MR16's and MR11's are halogen sources and can be great sources of accent light.

So can halogen lamps be used for downlights? The answer is yes. However, whether you choose to use downlighting in a project becomes the more pertinent question. In magazines, we constantly see rooms filled with a series of recessed downlights casting light in circles on the floor. Their intended purpose is to provide ambient illumination. Downlights, no matter what lamp is used, are a poor source of fill light because of the shadows they cast and the absence of light to reflect back toward the ceiling. Use other sources, such as wall sconces or cove lighting, for the ambient lighting. Use adjustable downlights for accent lighting. In extremely rare situations it might be necessary to use downlights where no other solution is possible (this does not mean a limited-budget situation).

Avoid specifying straight downlights. They don't give the flexibility needed to highlight different sizes, shapes, and mounting heights. As was mentioned before, interiors are not static anymore. With today's modern transient lifestyle, flexibility is necessary. in order to accommodate new furnishings or new homeowners. A straight downlight offers very few

Try not to place downlights over seating areas. They cast hard shadows onto people's faces, making them look older.

Figure 9.12 (left) Weighted bases are available that can hold track heads, so they can be used as portable accent lights.

Figure 9.13 (right) Stake lights in planters can cast intriguing shadows on the walls and ceilings.

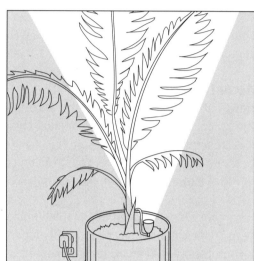

options and limits your client's choices. On the other hand, don't go crazy with recessed adjustable luminaires and fill the entire ceiling with holes, often referred to as the *planetarium effect* or **Swiss cheese effect**. Don't feel you have to light everything in a room.

Accent light does not have to be permanently installed. There are a number of portable luminaires readily available that will work in temporary, lower-budget, or historically protected homes. In addition, most track lighting companies manufacture weighted bases to accommodate their track heads, converting them into portable accent lights (see Figure 9.12). There are also stake lights that fit into planter pots to uplight plants and cast intriguing shadow patterns on the ceiling (see Figure 9.13). This can add wonderful texture to a space. Refer to Chapter 4 for other portable options.

The Bottom Line

Be sure to hide light sources as much as possible. Let what is being highlighted come into focus, not the luminaires themselves. Use your design know-how and your client's assets, whatever they are, to turn straw into gold. Well-designed lighting can be powerful alchemy in the entry and throughout the rest of the house.

Chapter Ten

LIVING ROOMS—LAYERING COMFORT WITH DRAMA

Lighting in the living room should be as flexible as the rest of the home's components, and it needs to be controllable enough to satisfy a variety of needs.

The way we view living rooms today is very different from the way they were often experienced years ago. Then, living rooms seemed to be off-limits. No one would enter unless company came over. It was as if an invisible braided rope kept the family out. It's almost like the way people treat guest towels—as "too nice to use."

Not that it was a place anyone really wanted to go, anyway. The furniture was formal and uncomfortable. Sometimes it had plastic slipcovers that stuck to people's legs in the summertime. Even the lamp shades may have had plastic covers — the kind that looked like big shower caps. That "hands-off" feeling is finally softening a bit. The furniture is getting more comfortable and arrangements more relaxed (see Plates 1.23, 1.24 and 1.25).

Nowadays, families have reclaimed the living room. It's not just reserved for special occasions anymore. Furniture plans are less static (see Plates 2.16, 2.17, 2.18 and 2.19). It used to be that everything stayed in exactly the same place. Now, paintings, sculpture, and plants are rotated around the house to keep the look fresh. The living room is often rearranged at holidays to accommodate a Christmas tree or Hanukkah display, or to set up a buffet for a Fourth of July feast.

Lighting should be as flexible as the rest of the home's components, and it needs to be controllable enough to satisfy a variety of needs. Straight downlights are too inflexible for the way people live today. Putting recessed fixtures over a seating area puts people in a very bad light (refer back to Figure 8.2 in Chapter 8). Refer to Figure 10.1 to see how a living room looks with regular downlights installed over a sofa.

Although entertaining at home is very popular, it's still the owners of the house who spend the greatest amount of time there. The designer's first concern is to give them adequate illumination for their day-to-day activities. Then layer that with lighting options for entertaining.

Ask your clients what they plan to do in the living room. Will they read there? Will they watch television? If they have children, will they want to do puzzles on the floor or board games on the coffee table? Getting a picture of how the space will be used will help you decide how to light it.

Ambient Lighting

The first concern is to create adequate ambient light. There are many ways to provide ambient light. The typical 8-foot ceiling offers the least number of options. One solution would be the installation of two or four opaque wall sconces (see Figure 10.1), mounting them 2 feet down from the ceiling. These can be made of various materials. Sometimes they may look like one material but are actually something totally different (see Figures 10.5 and 10.6).

A possible alternative would be to place a pair of torchères flanking the fireplace or a major piece of furniture, although the illumination would be less even than with the four wall sconces (see Figure 10.2). If the room is large, consider using two torchères on a diagonal. Torchères provide excellent ambient light for a room. Their main job is to fill the volume of space with an overall illumination that softens the shadows on people's faces and shows off the architectural detailing.

If you have a white or light-colored ceiling, the torchère can provide suitable secondary task lighting for reading, though it should be used only for light reading such as newspapers and magazines. For serious reading, such books or balancing the checkbook, pharmacy-type lamps that position the light between your head and the work surface work best.

In a living room with 9-foot or higher ceilings, you have more open options. In a smaller living room, a single pendant fixture that provides both ambient and decorative illumination is a good possibility (see Figure 10.4). A pair of pendant luminaires with an overall length of two feet to thirty inches would work well for a nine to twelve-foot flat ceiling in a room 15 feet wide and 15 feet long (see Figure 10.7). A pitched ceiling would require luminaires adapted for the slope.

Figure 10.1 (left) Floor plan: A series of four wall sconces would be a viable solution to provide adequate ambient light for this living room.

Figure 10.2 (right) Two torchères can also provide the room's ambient light, but it will not be as evenly lighted as when four wall sconces are used.

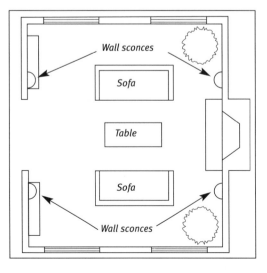

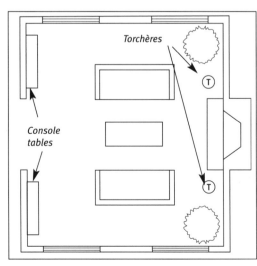

Figure 10.3
Note what happens when two recessed fixtures are mounted very close to the wall and over a seating area. The resulting coning pattern of light becomes the focal point of the space, which is very distracting.

Figure 10.4
This Arts and Crafts-inspired fixture, manufactured by the Mica Lamp Company, would be a good source of ambient and decorative lighting for period homes built during that era, or newly built homes reflecting that style.

Figure 10.5
Here we see an artisan working on what appears to be a plaster fixture, from the Sirmos Lighting line of fixtures. This piece is actually made of cast resin, which is much more durable than plaster.

Figure 10.6
Another artisan at Sirmos, working on what appears to be a highly polished metal wall sconce. This fixture is also actually made of cast resin.

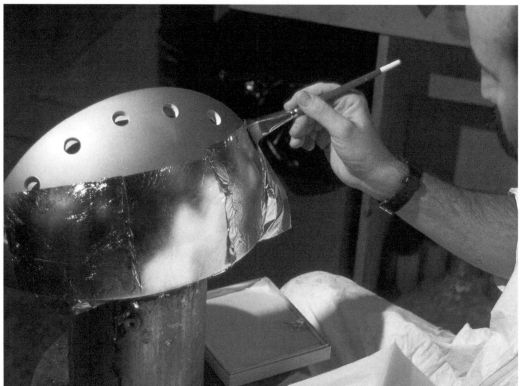

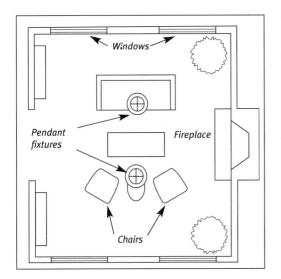

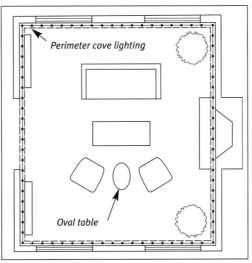

Figure 10.7 (left)
Two pendant luminaires would do a great job of providing ambient light, as long as the ceilings are nine-foot or taller.

Figure 10.8 (right)
Perimeter cove lighting is a very clean, architecturally integrated way of getting ambient light into the living room.

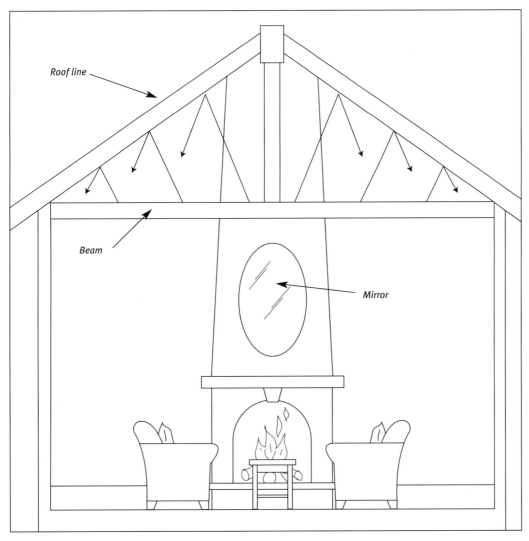

Figure 10.9
For living rooms with gabled ceilings and beams that are parallel to the floor, you have the option of locating indirect lighting on top of the beams.

A higher ceiling would also work well in conjunction with a cove lighting detail, where the light source is hidden behind a crown molding or valence, or a cantilevered detail (see Figure 10.8 and Plate 2.45). Living rooms with gabled ceilings and support beams that are parallel to the floor offer an additional option. In this situation, linear strip lighting can be mounted on top of the beams to provide ambient light from a totally hidden source (see Figure 10.9).

There are four different methods of installing this linear lighting:

1. Rout a channel in the top of the beam.

2. Place it in a surface channel on top of the beam.

3. Run a length of quarter-round molding along either side of the luminaire.

4. Wrap fascia boards around the beam to create a channel (see Figure 10.6).

Figure 10.10
Here are four methods of masking the linear lights mounted on top of vertical support beams.

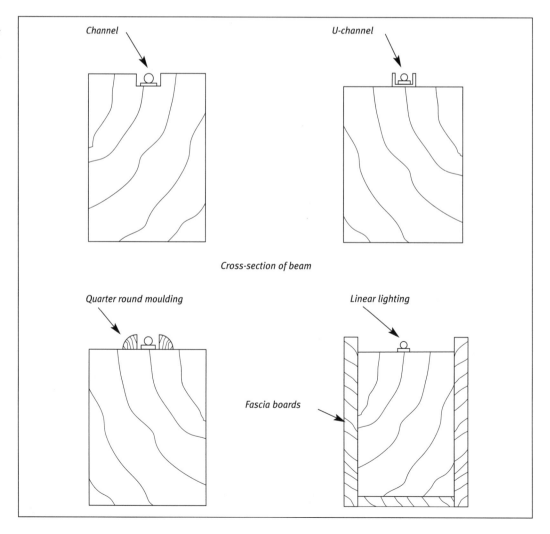

Channel

U-channel

Cross-section of beam

Quarter round moulding

Linear lighting

Fascia boards

Asymmetrically sloped ceilings are becoming more common architectural elements. This results in one very tall wall that often becomes a dead space, because it is too high to hang art. It is a perfect spot to mount a series of wall sconces that fill the room with an abundant amount of ambient illumination (see Figure 10.11).

Accent Lighting

Once you have decided what method you'll use to give the living room its fill light, the next step is to decide on accent lighting. The type of luminaire you choose for the source of accent lighting needs to be flexible. As your clients move furniture and art around, the lighting needs to accommodate each new arrangement (see Plate 2.44).

Remember, when straight downlights are used for accent lighting, they offer no flexibility at all. If the highlighted object is moved, the clients are left with a circle of light on the floor. If you specify recessed adjustable luminaires, you will provide clients with the adaptability they need. There are both line-voltage and low-voltage versions of these luminaires (refer to Chapter 4 for comparisons between these two options). One of the advantages of a low-voltage recessed adjustable luminaire is the ability to use a smaller-aperture trim in the ceiling, which draws less attention to the unit itself.

If you are working on an existing home that already has recessed luminaires, it is possible to leave the housings (the main part of a recessed luminaire installed inside the ceiling) and replace the trims (the visible part of a recessed unit, which is attached to the housing) with line- or low-voltage adjustable versions. In new construction and remodel projects, placement of these accent lights is dependent on what is to be highlighted. That's why it's so important to know the furniture plan before laying out the lighting.

Figure 10.12 shows a living room with furniture centered around a fireplace. Recessed adjustable accent lights are positioned to highlight various parts of the overall design. On the north wall, the sculpture on the table is illuminated with a single recessed adjustable luminaire.

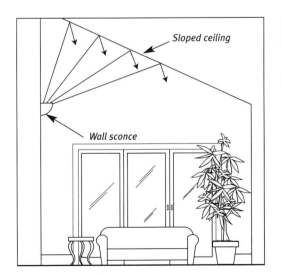

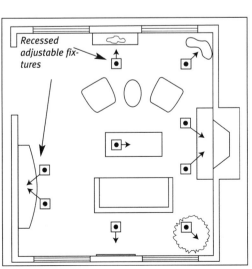

Figure 10.11 (left)
Make use of the tall wall by installing a series of wall sconces for the much-needed ambient illumination.

Figure 10.12 (right)
This is a partial lighting plan showing recessed adjustable luminaires used for accent lighting.

Angle of reflectance— The angle at which a light source hits a specular reflective surface equals the angle at which the resulting glare is reflected back.

On the east and west walls, two pairs of recessed adjustable luminaires cross-illuminate the art over the console and the fireplace. It's better to use two luminaires to light a painting that has a glass or Plexiglas® face, because a single accent light centered on the art could simply reflect back into people's eyes. By cross-illuminating, light is directed away from the normal viewing angle. The angle of reflectance plays a role whether one, two, or more luminaires are used.

The single recessed adjustable accent light on the south and east walls illuminate objects on a small table, a plant, and a corner sculpture. The luminaire in the center highlights the coffee table. The flexibility of recessed adjustable accent lights allows the coffee table to be illuminated even though the luminaire isn't centered over the table itself.

Track Lighting

Sometimes track lighting ends up being the design choice when other options aren't available (see Plates 1.26 and 1.27). For example, if there is inadequate ceiling depth in which to house recessed luminaires, a surface-mounted system must be used. If track lighting is your choice, a good arrangement in the living room would be to run it around the perimeter (see Figure 10.15). You can make the track seem more architecturally integrated by installing a run of molding on either side of the track (see Figure 10.15).

Halogen Bridge Systems

An alternative to recessed and track lighting is a relatively new product, generically called a halogen bridge system or cable system. This is a low-voltage set up of two wires strung parallel to each other across a ceiling space. Luminaires, normally using MR16 or MR11 lamps, can be clipped and locked into place along the wires to highlight various objects below (see Figure 10.17). This works especially well in homes where the ceilings are sloped; otherwise, changing the lamps in recessed or track luminaires would be difficult because of their inaccessibility. These systems also come in rail versions that are sturdier than the wire versions. They can be bent to follow curving hallways (see Figure 10.13) or simply curved to add visual interest.

Even though these luminaires are low in wattage, they are high in amperage, requiring a specific gauge of wire. Make sure the installing electrician knows this and uses the correct gauge. The high amperage also limits the number of luminaires per transformer. Normally the maximum load is 300 watts, or six 50-watt lamps. The lighting showroom that distributes the cable system or the manufacturer's representative will help you or the electrician to put the correct components together.

Task Lighting

The last consideration in the layout of the lighting design is task lighting. The main function of task lighting in the living room is for reading or related activities. Since the best position for a reading light is between one's head and where one's attention is focused, a pharmacy-type luminaire or a tabletop luminaire will work very well (see Figure 4.3 in Chapter 4).

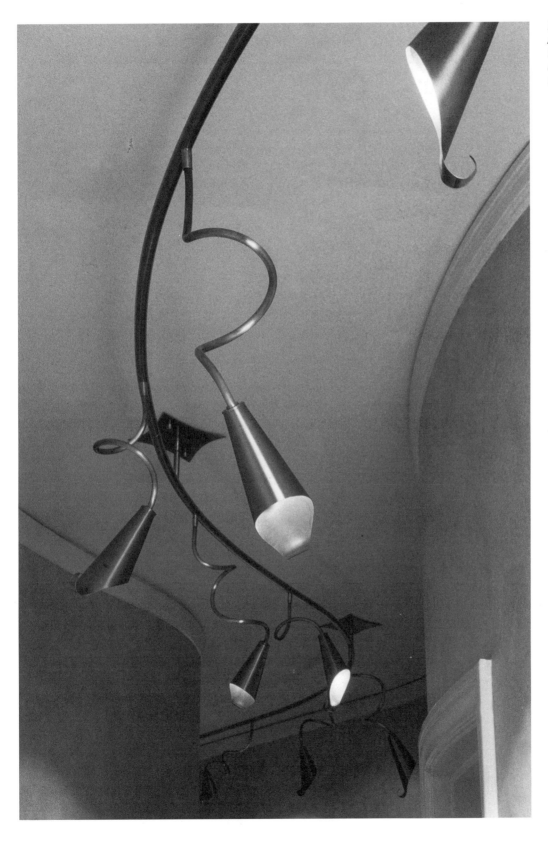

Figure 10.13
A sculptural track lighting system, designed by Terry Ohm, adds a fanciful flare to this undulating hallway.

Figure 10.14
If recessed luminaires aren't a possibility on a particular project, track lights set up in a perimeter pattern would do an acceptable job.

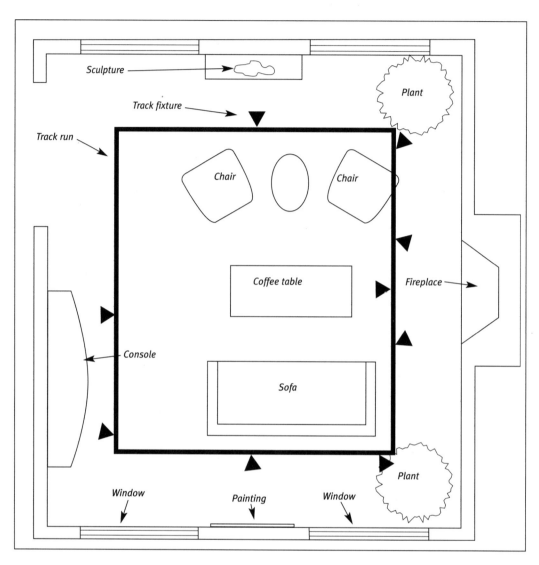

Figure 10.15 (left)
Side section
The addition of moldings on either side of the track run will help it blend in a little more architecturally.

Figure 10.16 (right)
Using a "halogen bridge" system lets the luminaires be reached more easily, to change bulbs or readjust the lights.

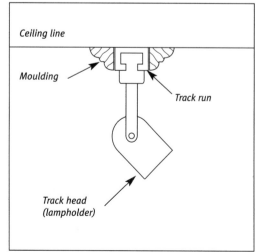

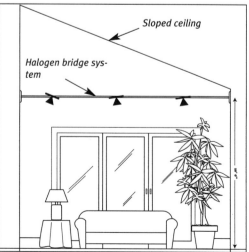

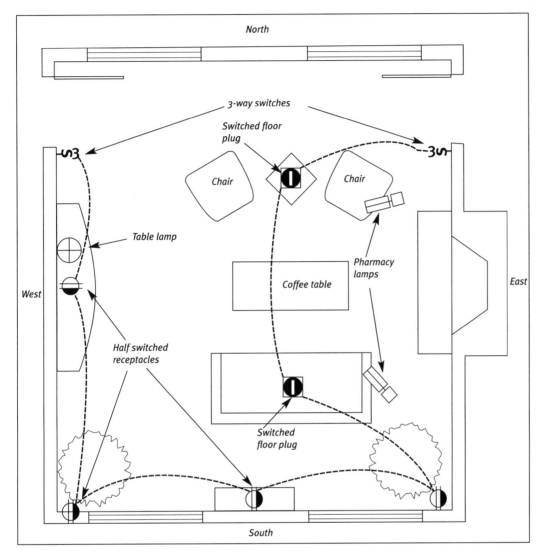

North

3-way switches

Switched floor
plug

S3

Chair

Chair

Table lamp

Pharmacy
lamps

West   Coffee table   East

Half switched
receptacles

Switched
floor plug

South

Figure 10.17
Switched floor plugs help
keep cords from being tripped
over.

If the floor plan has furniture in the middle of the room, it's a good idea to specify floor plugs so that cords don't cross the floor to a wall outlet. With these, crawl space or basement accessibility is a bonus for the electrician in a remodel project.

In Figure 10.17, the sofa and the occasional table both have a switched floor receptacle in which to plug the pharmacy luminaires. These luminaires can be placed on either side of each sofa. The west and south walls have half-switched receptacles (refer back to Figure 6.1 in Chapter 6), so that possible table luminaires and uplights for the plants can come on with the flip of a switch, instead of the homeowner having to go from luminaire to luminaire.

The Bottom Line
Remember, all the elements of lighting (task, ambient, decorative, and accent) must be considered to create a totally functional and adaptable lighting design. They are the "fantastic four," and they work best as a team.

Chapter Eleven

DINING ROOMS—THE MAIN EVENT

Dining rooms have been transformed in some homes into multi-use spaces. These changes set up a need for adjustable lighting and have forced homeowners and designers to rethink the use of a chandelier.

Dining rooms used to be the last holdout for a traditional static furniture arrangement. Now they too have been transformed in some homes into multiple-use spaces. Homeowners realized how little of their time was spent actually entertaining, and they wanted to reclaim this often under utilized room for additional purposes.

Previously, the dining room table itself was always too big for anything other than a meal for eight or ten people. Today, tables have become more flexible in size, folding down to more intimate seating for four, or able to be divided in two to make a pair of game tables. Even homeowners who have kept their large table want to be able to push it against a wall for buffet dining. All of these changes set up a need for adjustable lighting and forced homeowners and designers to rethink the use of a chandelier.

Rethinking Chandeliers

For eons, the dining room table has been centered under the chandelier. Many people spent countless hours of their lives making sure that this alignment was just perfect (see Plate 2.38). As dining room tables began to be moved around, the chandelier in the center of the space started getting in the way. For those clients who want a traditional feel but with the flexibility to create a more multifunctional room, there are a good number of choices:

1. Specify a decorative luminaire that hugs the ceiling so that it doesn't look odd when the table isn't in the center of the room (see Figure 11.1).

2. Select a pendant light on a pulley system that allows your client to raise or lower the luminaire (see Plate 2.34). There are a good number of European-designed pendants available, primarily contemporary styles (see Figure 11.2).

3. A traditional multiarmed chandelier of brass or crystal could be hung in a recessed dome or coffer so that it is visually linked to the ceiling configuration rather than the table location (see Figure 11.3). In a remodel project where it is too expensive or there is inadequate

Figure 11.1 (left)
A decorative luminaire
mounted tightly to the ceiling
will be less distracting when
the table is
moved aside.

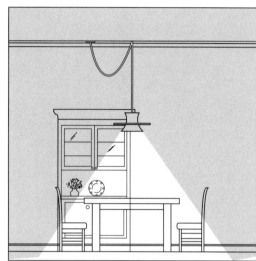

Figure 11.2 (right)
A pendant light on a pulley
system can be raised out of
the way when the table
is moved.

Figure 11.3 (left)
A dome detail in the ceiling
will allow for a more tradi-
tional hanging chandelier
without hitting people in the
head when the table
is relocated.

Figure 11.4 (right)
A table with no chandelier
makes use of three recessed
adjustable luminaires to
highlight the table setting, as
well as
the centerpiece.

attic space for a dome, a decorative ceiling medallion will create a similar illusion.

The decorative luminaire mounted over the table should be at least 12 inches narrower than the tabletop, and the bottom of the fixture should be 30 to 36 inches from the top of the table. If the ceiling is higher than 8 feet, add 3 inches per foot over the 8-foot height, but this can vary depending on the layout of the room and whether the ceiling slopes. These are just guidelines (see Plate 2.35). The chandeliers normally come with additional lengths of chain or cable to allow for an on-site adjustment. It really comes down to an aesthetic call.

Many clients in more modern-style homes are forgoing any decorative luminaire at all and are relying instead on recessed adjustable luminaires to provide illumination for the table, no matter where the table is placed (see Figure 11.7). In Figure 11.4, three recessed adjustable luminaires are used. The middle one highlights a flower arrangement in the center of the table. The two outside luminaires cross-illuminate the tabletop itself, adding sparkle to the dishes and silverware. Make sure the two outside luminaires are not pointed straight down. This would cast harsh shadows on the people at both ends of the table and could create glare from glass, lacquer, or highly polished wood table. Keep these two luminaires pointed at an angle from the vertical that is less than 45 degrees. At 45 degrees or more, the light may glare into people's eyes (see Plate 2.37). If luminaires are aimed at an angle less than 45 degrees, light will hit the tabletop first, giving a soft, complimentary underlighting of people's faces. Figure 11.5 shows how these same luminaires can be redirected toward the wall when the table is being used for a buffet.

For those clients happy with a traditional setting in their dining room, the addition of two recessed adjustable lights on either side of a chandelier will help add drama to the table. This allows the chandelier to be dimmed to a pleasing glow, while giving the impression of providing the table's illumination (see Figure 11.6).

A large chandelier may require additional support at the junction box. Most standard junction boxes will support up to 50 pounds. Check with the manufacturer to find out what the weight is so that the electrical contractor can accommodate the weight. Large or ornate chandeliers installed in rooms with a high ceiling, may require a pulley mechanism that is mounted above the ceiling to lower the chandelier for ease of relamping and cleaning.

Decorative sconces can act as "jewelry" for a dining room (see Figures 11.8 and 11.9). Think of the chandelier as the crown and the sconces as the earrings.

Ambient Lighting

Whatever solution you choose for table illumination, this alone will not complete the lighting scenario. Ambient light and additional accent lighting should still be considered. While it's true that the decorative luminaires will provide some illumination for the dining room, they can easily overpower the rest of the elements in the space if turned up too brightly (see Figure 11.10). This is the same problem that occurs in entrances (see Figure 9.1 in Chapter 9).

Figure 11.5 (left)
Recessed adjustable luminaires over the dining room table can be redirected to light the table when it is against the wall serving as a buffet.

Figure 11.6 (right)
Two recessed adjustable luminaires in combination with a chandelier give highlighting to the table and let the decorative luminaires take all the credit.

Figure 11.7 (left)
In this dining room, the built-in display case uses a series of recessed low-voltage downlights to highlight the collection of crystal and art objects. In the foreground, two recessed adjustable low-voltage fixtures cross-illuminate the dining room table.

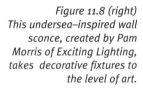

Figure 11.8 (right)
This undersea-inspired wall sconce, created by Pam Morris of Exciting Lighting, takes decorative fixtures to the level of art.

Figure 11.9 (left)
This vintage Art Deco light fixture, rescued from a 1920s movie palace, found its way to a new home in a high-end home theater.

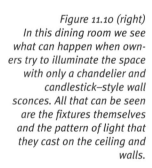

Figure 11.10 (right)
In this dining room we see what can happen when owners try to illuminate the space with only a chandelier and candlestick-style wall sconces. All that can be seen are the fixtures themselves and the pattern of light that they cast on the ceiling and walls.

Adding ambient lighting is relatively straightforward. Many of the options mentioned in previous chapters work here as well: torchères, wall sconces, and cove lighting. If the dining room you are working on has a dome detail, the perimeter can be illuminated with low-profile cove lighting so that fill light is bounced off the dome's interior. If it is a beamed ceiling, channels can be used, as discussed in Chapter 10 (see Figures 10.9 and 10.10).

Accent Lighting

The two or three recessed adjustable luminaires located over the dining room table already address accent light for the table itself and the centerpiece (see Plate 2.36). Single downlights integrated into some specially modified chandeliers may be used to provide accent light for centerpieces as well (see Plate 2.34). The next spaces to look at for possible areas in need of accent light are the walls, the side table or buffet, and plants.

For art on the wall, don't feel that every piece has to be illuminated. It's all right to let some pieces fall into secondary importance. It lets them be "discovered" as guests take a second look around the room. Add one or two recessed adjustable luminaires to accent the side table, buffet, or console. A silver tea service will sparkle and a buffet dinner will look even more scrumptious when highlighted.

Plants can be uplighted, downlighted, or both. Broadleaf plants such as fiddle-leaf figs are better illuminated from above or backlighted. More airy-leafed plants, such as a ficus tree, can be illuminated from the front, casting leaf patterns on the walls and floor. They can also be uplighted, which creates a shadow pattern on the walls and ceiling. Palms are best shown off when they are lighted both from the top and from below. The sculptural quality of a cactus calls for lighting from the front at a 45-degree angle, preferably off to one side, in order to add dimension. Lighting plants outside can also visually expand the dining room and make the outside feel a part of the inside (see Plate 2.55).

Candles Do Count

Candles should be used correctly as well. No light source gets overlooked in this book (see Plates 2.35 and 2.55). Typically, at the dinner table you artfully place candlesticks flanking the centerpiece. When you and your guests sit down at the table, that candle flame is right at eye level. When you look at the flame for a while and then cast your gaze toward the guests, you'll notice that there is a black hole where their heads used to be. This is much like the effect you experience after someone has taken a flash picture of you. To solve this problem, use candles that are either lower or higher than eye level. That way you'll get that soft golden glow, but the candle will not distract from looking at the person across the table. Reviewing Figures 11.15, 11.16, and 11.17 should give you an idea of what can happen.

Figures 11.11 and 11.12 illustrate one way a traditional dining room layout can be lighted. This particular design used a traditional chandelier flanked by two recessed adjustable luminaires (as shown in Figure 11.6). In addition, four wall sconces are being used to provide the fill light, while five more recessed adjustable luminaires have been installed to highlight the art and tabletops.

*Figure 11.11
This is a possible lighting
layout for a more traditional
dining room furniture plan.*

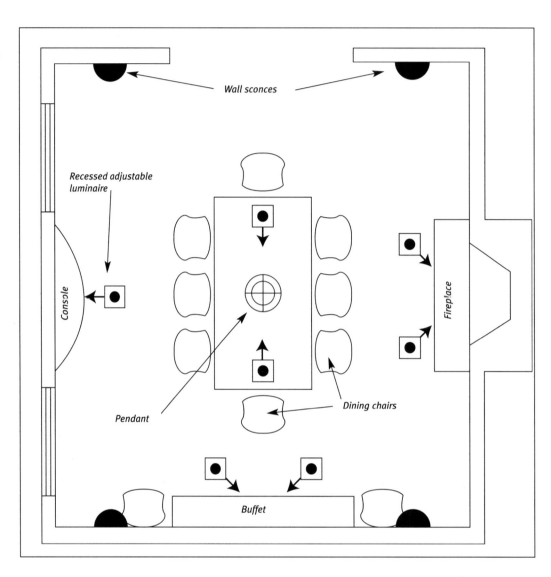

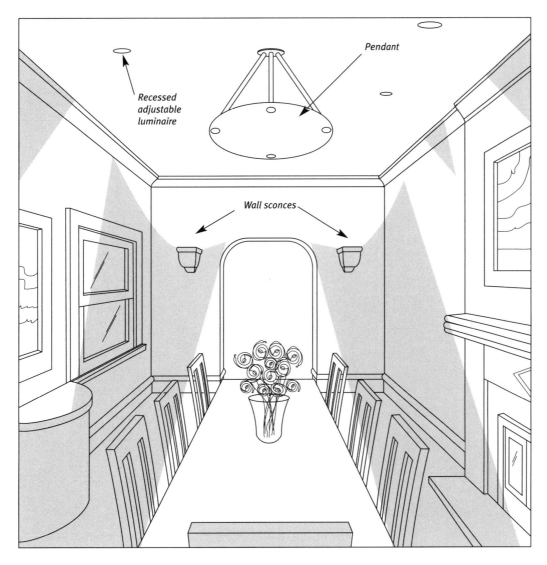

Pendant

Recessed
adjustable
luminaire

Wall sconces

Figure 11.12
This perspective drawing
shows what the room looks
like when translated from the
lighting plan shown
in Figure 11.11.

Figure 11.13
This is a more non-traditional furniture plan. Note that the table can be separated to make smaller tables.

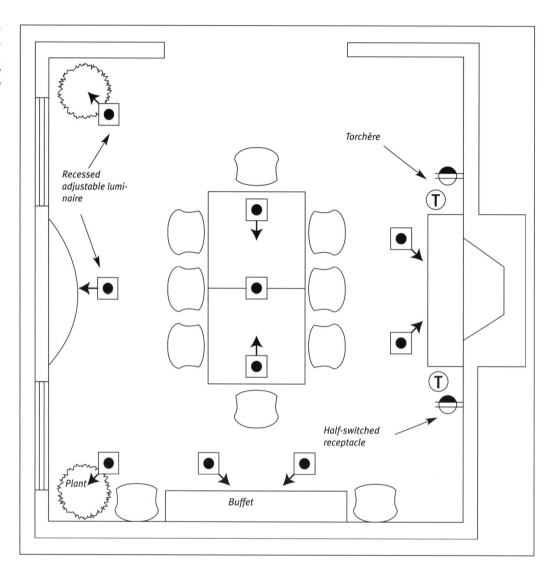

Recessed
adjustable lumi-
naire

Torchère

Half-switched
receptacle

Plant

Buffet

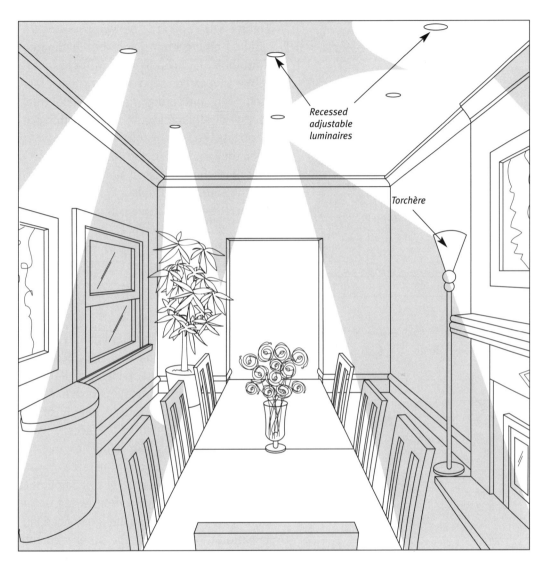

Recessed
adjustable
luminaires

Torchère

Figure 11.14
This perspective drawing
shows what the dining room
looks like with the lighting
and furniture in place (the
floor plan with the lighting
layout is shown on
Figure 11.13.)

Figure 11.15
Standard-height candles
obstruct your view of the per-
son across the table.

Figures 11.13 and 11.14 show how a less traditional dining room might be illuminated.
The table is actually two 4-foot square
tables that can be separated for smaller family dinners and card games. The use of three
recessed adjustable luminaires in this scenario lets the lighting follow the tables wher-
ever they end up in the room. This time a
pair of torchères located along the east wall
are the sources of ambient light. Seven additional recessed adjustable luminaires accent
the art above the fireplace, the sculpture on
the west wall, and the two plants in the
northwest and southwest corners of the
room.

The Bottom Line

As in the rest of the house, light layering in
the dining room is the key. The addition of
dimmers can offer many levels of illumination. Dimming the chandelier down to a glow
will help bring out the true beauty of the
luminaire, while dimming the accent lights
and walls sconces will allow for the full
brightness needed to clear the table or work
on a puzzle or a lower level to compliment
the other lighting in the room when entertaining. The goal is to create a balanced illumination that enhances the other elements
of your design.

Figure 11.16
A low votive candle provides a
soft, complimentary uplight-
ing.

Figure 11.17
A tall candle adds the
romance without the glare.

Chapter Twelve

BEDROOMS—PRIVATE SANCTUARIES

This is the one room where ambient light is first and foremost. People are the main event in a bedroom setting. Help erase dark circles and soften age lines. Your clients will love you for it.

Often it's the bedrooms that are thought of as unimportant areas when a lighting plan is being put together. They are usually left with a fixture in the center of the ceiling and a couple of half-switched receptacles (refer back to Figure 6.1 in Chapter 6). Think about how much time we spend in our bedrooms. Statistics show that we spend one–third of our lives sleeping. Many individuals spend that time sleeping with a significant other. People would like to look their best in such an intimate setting (see Plates 2.20 and 2.21).

Ambient Lighting

This is the one room where ambient light is first and foremost. People are the main event in a bedroom setting. Help erase dark circles and soften age lines. Your clients will love you for it. If there is an existing luminaire in the center of the ceiling, an easy upgrade would be to replace it with a pendant–hung indirect fixture (refer back to Figure 4.15 in Chapter 4). This will provide illumination that bounces off the ceiling and walls to create a flattering, shadowless light (see Figure 12.1).

Quite often now, we see many homes built with sloped ceilings. The tall wall area above the door line is often considered a dead space. Mounting a series of two or three wall sconces up there will create great fill light without wasting any of the art wall space at the normal viewing heights.

Another architectural style change is the tray ceiling (see Figure 12.2). This aspect lends itself to a perimeter cove lighting detail. The light helps emphasize the architect's ceiling concept, while filling the bedroom with ambient light. Sometimes clients

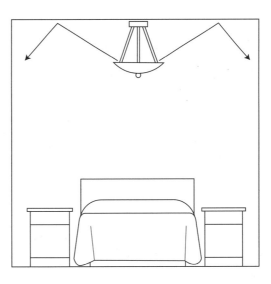

Figure 12.1
Replace the existing ceiling luminaire with a pendant-hung indirect version for a good source of fill light.

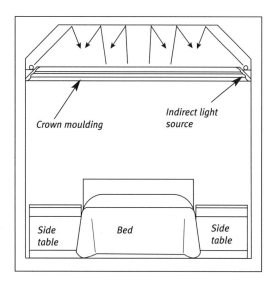

Figure 12.2
A "tray-style" ceiling lends itself perfectly to a cove lighting detail.

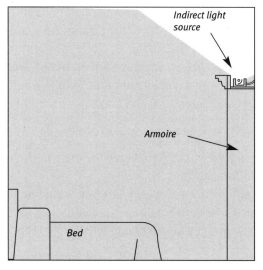

Figure 12.3
A tall piece of furniture such as this armoire is a great spot to hide a source of ambient light.

Figure 12.4
If you choose traditional bedside lamps for reading, specify shades with opaque liners, so that the other person in bed can get some sleep.

are reticent about putting a lot of time and money into architecturally integrated lighting design solutions. For these more cost-conscious customers, a pair of torchères should do the trick (see Figure 4.4 in Chapter 4).

Also, you could place a halogen indirect light source on top of a tall piece of furniture, such as an armoire (see Figure 12.3). Often there is a recess on the top of these furniture pieces that provides a great hiding spot for an indirect source of illumination. In some homes there is a canopy bed with a solid top. This too can be a great location for a hidden indirect light (see Figure 4.12 in Chapter 4).

Task Lighting

In addition to the ambient light, another function of light should be considered. This is reading illumination, which comes under the category of task lighting. Typically a pair of portable luminaires (table lamps) are placed on the bedside tables. If you choose this approach, there are a few things to consider:

1. Select reading lights that have opaque shades. This will help direct the light down and across the person's work surface. Additionally, the opaque shade helps shield the light from the person's bedmate (see Figure 12.4).

2. Install wall-mounted swing-arm lamps (see Figure 12.5). They are a flexible source of illumination that doesn't take up space on the bedside tables. Mounting them at the correct height is critical, however. If they are too high, they will be a source of glare. If they are too low, the client may have to slump into an uncomfortable position in order to read. They should be mounted just

above shoulder height when sitting in bed.

The best way to find the correct mounting height is to have your clients get into bed and hunker down against the pillows in their normal reading position. Then measure from the floor to just above their shoulder height. Why? Because the optimum spot to position task lighting is between the person's head and the work surface. Clients sharing a bed may nest in at different heights. Some compromise should be made on both sides so that the reading lights can be mounted at matching heights.

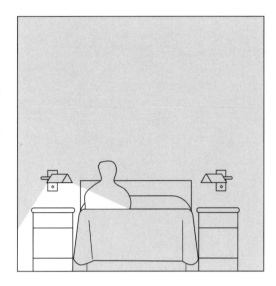

Figure 12.5
Swing-arm lamps provide good task light, without taking up space on the bedside table. Mount them at just above your clients' shoulder height. Yes, put them in bed and measure.

3. A third option for reading lights is to install a pair of recessed adjustable low-voltage luminaires in the ceiling above the bed (see Figure 12.6). This is the airline approach to providing light for reading. You may have noticed that the reading lights in the airplane are not directly over your seat, but actually over the seat of the person sitting next to you. That's because the passenger's head would block the light if it was installed directly overhead.

The same principle applies in the bedroom. The person on the right controls the recessed adjustable luminaire over the partner's side of the bed, and vice versa. By using a lamp with a tight beam spread, such as the MR16 ESX (20-watt spot), the light is confined to a circle of illumination about the size of a magazine. If all the clients read are paperbacks, then you can use an MR16 EZX, which projects a very narrow spot.

Using a recessed luminaire like this that has a small aperture, helps reduce the possibility of glare. Some recessed adjustable low-voltage lights come with apertures as small as 1–1/2 inches. It also helps if the luminaire specified has a black-painted interior. Otherwise, the dichroic reflectors of the MR16 and MR11 create a visible pink glow of light inside the recessed housing. Remember to place the dimmers for the reading lights on either side of the bed just above the night tables. Your clients should not have to get out of bed to control the lights.

Special Effects

Some designers like to have underlighting (see Figure 12.7) along the edge of a bed. This is a more modern effect that creates the illusion of the bed levitating slightly off the floor. It can also be a great night-light for those clients who make frequent trips to the bathroom or occasional trips to the fridge.

Don't use undimmed cooler-colored fluorescent as your source of underlighting; it gives skin unattractive tones. If you decide to use fluorescent, then a dimmable fluorescent source in a warm color temperature would be a more comfortable choice. Another option is

Figure 12.6
Cross-illumination
above the bed provides
"quiet" reading light that
doesn't disturb the other bed
occupant.

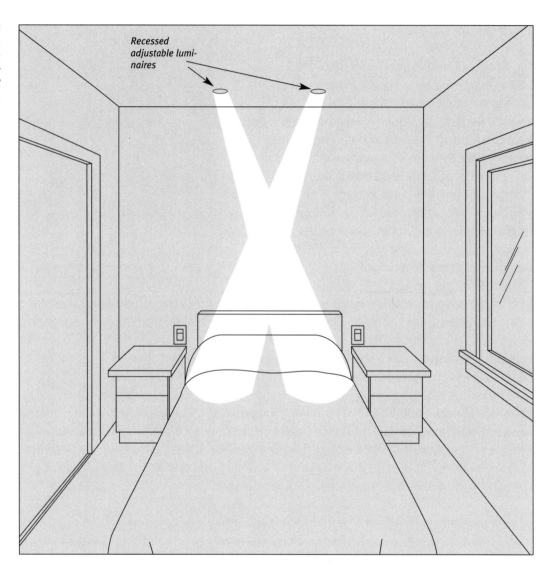

low-voltage tube lighting using half-watt lamps on 1-inch centers. The tubing is flexible and goes around corners easily. The end effect will be just a gentle glow of light.

At least once in your design career someone is going to ask for a mirror above the bed (see Figure 12.8). Believe it or not, we often look our best when lying down. Gravity works to our advantage, smoothing away lines and excess folds of skin. An old Hollywood trick is for stars to have their close-ups taken while lying on their backs. So how do you light people in bed? Cross–illumination, of course. Three recessed adjustable lights flanking the two long sides of the mirror will give a fabulous even illumination. Use MR16's (50-watt FNV) to provide a soft overall glow. You can slip in a peach–colored filter to add a flattering hue to their skin tone.

A Television Technique

One last item to consider doesn't have as much to do with lighting as it does with visibility. Today, new master bedrooms are often quite enormous. The bed will be near one wall and fifteen or twenty feet away on the opposite wall will be an armoire with a television inside. That's simply too far away for people to watch without using binoculars. A more practical solution would be to place a console at the end of the bed that houses a pop-up TV (see Figure 12.9). The television disappears into the console when not in use. There are manufacturers who make this device for flat-screen televisions too. Your clients will very likely be impressed with this great idea.

The Bottom Line

Make the bedroom into the ultimate refuge of the house. It is the one place to find a little escape from the world, and it is that last holdout for romance. Light your clients well in this room and you will have clients for life.

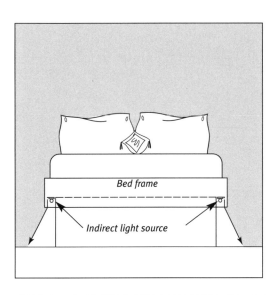

Figure 12.7
Underlighting the bed gives a sense of hovering, like the bed is about to take off.

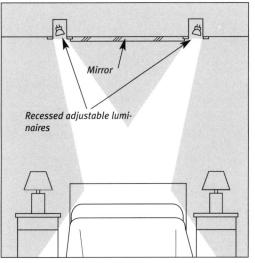

Figure 12.8
If you have clients who want a mirror above the bed, then cross-illuminate them with three recessed adjustable lights on each of the long sides of the bed, using lamps with complementary wide beam spreads.

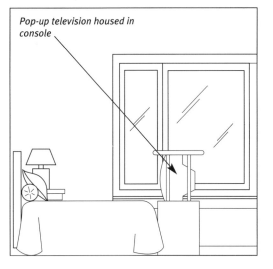

Figure 12.9
Do your clients a favor and locate the television at the foot of the bed instead of way across the room. There are consoles available that allow the television to pop up when being watched, and disappear inside when not in use.

Using Light

COLOR SECTION TWO

How lighting is incorporated into a space can affect the architecture, interior design and the mood of the people in that space. Great lighting happens when all the functions of light are seamlessly blended together. This applies to both interior and exterior spaces.

Plate 2.1- This rather plain entry takes on a dramatic architectural flare when day turns to dusk. The barrel-vaulted ceiling is uplighted with a series of opaque wall sconces that create an intriguing pattern of illumination. Two runs of standard cove lighting would have turned the space into a train tunnel. Instead, this more cost-effective solution creates a much more inviting first impression.

Plate 2.2 - This dramatic entryway uses recessed adjustable fixtures to project pools of illumination onto the objects in the space. Since this is a pass-through area there is not a specific need for ambient light. Recessed fixtures and wall sconces are all that are needed to show off the owner's collection and to give visual cues as to where guests should go next.

Plate 2.3- The opposite side of the entry shows a wall sconce with Japanesque styling. The bronze metal plays off the chocolate brown walls. The doorway leading to the powder room is sand-blasted so that the natural light can flow inside during the day and the artificial light can flow out at night. A normal solid door would prevent the possibility of these two desirable effects. Sometimes it is not lighting alone that makes a space work but it is the lighting in combination with the interior design and the architecture that makes a cohesive feel of the space.

Plate 2.4 - The row of wall sconces leads visitors from the entry to the living room. People are always drawn to the brightest source of illumination, so use this technique to direct people to where you want them to go next. Recessed adjustable low-voltage fixtures also provide illumination for the art pieces.

Plate 2.5 - Sometimes it is not just interior lighting design alone that will make a space work. In this case an architect was also brought in to be part of the design team. In this kitchen remodel, the main visual problem was the strong diagonal line at the ceiling created by the staircase leading to the upper level. The architect resolved the problem by creating two barrel vaults to conceal the stairway profile. Here you can begin to see the framework installed to form the vaults.

Plate 2.6 - This "after" shot shows a striking difference. The strong diagonal line of the staircase is totally concealed by a lower barrel vault. A line of pendant fixtures help add a human scale to the narrow galley kitchen. At the entry a translucent paper sculpture and tall candles mark the entry to the kitchen, helping to integrate it into the rest of the space.

Plate 2.7 - The lower part of the staircase that leads to the upstairs is open to the galley kitchen. From this location you can see the upper glass-faced cabinets are gently illuminated from within. The countertops are illuminated with shallow 20-watt puck lights, while the orchid in the foreground is highlighted from a recessed light above.

Plate 2.8 - The view from the galley kitchen towards the dining area. Notice that the pendant fixture is not located over the table but centered in the room. Its proximity to the ceiling allows the table a greater variety of positions not predicated by a standard decorative fixture hung closer to the tabletop. On the right hand side a pair of square sconces casts an impressive pattern of light onto the wall. The counter top in the foreground is illuminated with a row of recessed fixtures that act as both task lights and accent lights for the objects placed there.

Plates 2.9, 2.10, 2.11 - These three images show what this media room looked like prior to the remodel. This space was actually used as a store-front for many years, including a grocery, a model train store, a TV repair shop, and a beauty salon.

Plate 2.13 - A close up of the tall wooden sculpture shows how a single light source coming from the side enhances the shadowing of the piece.

Plate 2.14 - In one corner a recessed adjustable low-voltage fixture highlights the orchid and Indian chest. The glass block, although it appears to be illuminated, is actually not. What you are seeing is the wall behind the glass block washed with light. This creates the illusion that the glass block is illuminated.

Plate 2.15 - In the opposite corner, a single recessed adjustable low-voltage fixture, fitted with a daylight blue filter, shows off the abstract painting and tablescape. The paper lantern gives the feeling that it is providing all the light in this area, when in fact it contains only a 15-watt lamp.

Plate 2.12 - This old storefront has been greatly transformed. Here light layering plays a major role in the success of the space. A pair of yellow glass Murano pendants provide both a decorative and an ambient source of illumination. An opening at the top of each of the fixtures allows the 100-watt halogen lamp to offer a flattering indirect light for the space. A vintage Noguchi lantern adds another decorative lighting element to the room. Recessed adjustable low-voltage fixtures illuminate the tabletop, the artwork and the tall wooden sculpture. Beyond the window an illuminated magnolia tree helps visually expand the space at night.

Plate 2.16 - This shot shows the living room side of a wide great room. In the center a tall woven wood floor lamp helps add texture to the space. Recessed adjustable low-voltage fixtures provide focus to the framed photographs and the natural fiber weavings on the wall.

Plate 2.17 - A close-up of the niche located next to the fireplace, displaying an art glass vase. This piece is illuminated with a single 10-watt puck light.

Plate 2.18 - A shot of the opposite side of the great room shows a center fireplace that is open on both spaces. Beyond the fireplace is the dining area. Recessed adjustable low-voltage fixtures project light onto the art and tabletops.

Plate 2.19 - In a corner of the dining area three lighting elements are at play. In the upper left corner, a wall sconce features slumped and sand blasted glass painted on the inside to add an additional layer of texture. A single recessed adjustable low-voltage fixture, with a 20-watt spot (ESX), highlights the ceramic vessel. Another recessed adjustable low-voltage fixture creates an interesting shadow pattern on the shoji doors of the buffet.

Plate 2.20 - What we are seeing in this image is the entryway to a master bedroom. The floating staircase takes on a strong sculptural feel when set against the illuminated foliage. A pair of lanterns from Bali helps lead you into the master bedroom. Three recessed adjustable low-voltage fixtures help add depth and dimension by highlighting the shoji panels, the tansu, and the woven reed cushion.

Plate 2.21 - As you enter the main part of the master bedroom the first thing that you see is a tall French table lamp, covered in a translucent fabric. This is the decorative element for the space. Two recessed adjustable low-voltage fixtures, located above the bed, offer individual reading lights. Additional recessed adjustable low-voltage fixtures show off the painting above the headboard and the objects on the bedside tables. The city view beyond the well-illuminated foreground plantings becomes part of the overall scene, because the black mirror effect has been circumvented.

Plate 2.22- This kitchen uses many functions of light, while maintaining its 1940s feel. A chrome and glass center fixture offers good ambient light without glare. Two recessed compact fluorescent fixtures provide cross illumination at the sink. Additional task light on the counter tops comes from linear low-voltage halogen sources, mounted on the underside of the overhead cabinets. More of the same types of linear fixtures illuminate the two display shelves above the cook top.

Plate 2.23- You may be surprised to learn that all the lighting in this kitchen uses fluorescent sources. The two alabaster pendant fixtures use dimmable compact fluorescent lamps with a color temperature of 2700-degrees Kelvin. The recessed fixtures and the linear task lighting also use fluorescent lamps with 2700-degree color temperature. Using a buttery yellow color on the walls enhances the warmth of the room. The result is a very inviting kitchen that is also very energy efficient.

Plate 2.24 - This is probably one of the largest residential kitchens that you will ever see. The space opens up into an equally generous family room. The L-shaped island divides the two spaces. A row of cast glass and metal pendants offers a sense of separation between the two areas. Recessed adjustable low-voltage fixtures project additional light onto the butcher-block table and countertops.

Plate 2.25 - A detail of the pendant fixtures, designed by Christina Spann, showing their hand-forged quality.

Plate 2.26 - Interior designers these days are creating bathrooms where design elements continue in from neighboring spaces. Here glass block walls allow natural light to flow into the bathroom. Now that art is becoming a standard element in bathroom spaces, recessed adjustable low-voltage fixtures specifically made to be installed in wet locations can be used to accent objects in tub and shower areas.

Plate 2.27 - A close up of the sink area reveals a pair of Frank Lloyd Wright inspired wall sconces, providing excellent cross illumination at the mirror. For master baths each vanity light should have at least 100-watts of illumination because this is where major work needs to be done.

Plate 2.28 - This sumptuous master bath uses two pairs of vanity lights to illuminate the sinks. Each of these fixtures holds three 50-watt G lamps. One recessed adjustable low-voltage fixture draws attention to the raku vessel that is located between the sinks. Another recessed adjustable low-voltage fixture, rated for wet locations, is installed over the walk–in shower area. Outside, an impressive shadow pattern shows up on the frosted glass as light passes through the overhanging branches.

Plate 2.29 - Powder rooms can afford to be more daring than master baths. Here guests need only need to wash their hands or check to see if there is spinach in their teeth, so the light level does not have to be as intense. In this particular powder room, wall sconces are mounted on the return walls instead of either side of the mirror, to help make this small space appear a bit larger. Three recessed adjustable low-voltage fixtures show off the stone sink, the Macintosh inspired chair and the Japanese silk screen (as seen reflected in the mirror).

Plate 2.30 - During the day no one is aware of the lighting element nestled in among the plantings.

Plate 2.31 - As the sun begins to set, this glass sculpture, illuminated from within, begins to make its presence known.

Plate 2.32 - After night falls, this piece, designed by Pam Morris, becomes a visual icon that helps lead guests to the front door.

Plate 2.33 - In this study many lighting elements are at play. On the wall above the sofa
two mica and metal sconces offer the decorative layer of illumination. On the opposite wall
(just out of camera range) a pair of torchères
provide the much-needed fill light for this
space. A directional uplight, sitting on the
floor, enhances the form of the wooden sculpture. Recessed adjustable low-voltage fixtures
bring attention to the coffee table, the painting, and the low teak console. The images of
objects located on the other side of the shoji
panel appear as intriguing silhouettes.

Plate 2.34 - A pass-through between the kitchen and the dining room of this home offers a glimpse of a formal dining room (a shot of the dining room itself is on the cover of this book). Two recessed adjustable low-voltage fixtures highlight the small African sculpture and arrangement of grasses in the foreground. The sculptural "Flotation" lantern, designed by Ingo Maurer, draws people up to the dining room table.

Plate 2.35- In this very traditional dining room only one recessed adjustable low-voltage fixture is used to add a layer of light beyond the candles, chandelier, and wall sconces. The 50-watt MR16 spot (EXT) illuminates the urn and casts an impressive shadow pattern from the peach blossoms onto the window covering.

Plate 2.36 - The very large painting is cross-illuminated using two recessed adjustable low-voltage fixtures with 50-watt MR16 narrow floods (EXN). On either side of the painting are cast glass and bronze sconces using 75-watt A19 IF lamps. The dining room table uses a single recessed adjustable low-voltage fixture to bring attention to the flower arrangement and table setting.

Plate 2.37 - For this dining room the interior designer opted not to hang any decorative fixtures over the table. Instead recessed fixtures are used to provide the necessary illumination. The two outside fixtures cross illuminate the tabletop, while a center recessed fixture on its own dimmer shows off the flowers. Two sconces flank the French doors to help provide ambient light for the space. Lighting from outside creates a serendipitous art piece on the opposite wall.

Plate 2.38 - A 1960s-era pendant fixture becomes an illuminated sculpture over the table. A pair of recessed fixtures, cross illuminate the tabletop, while one additional recessed adjustable low-voltage fixture illuminates the monochromatic painting on the back wall.

Plate 2.39 - During the day the bronze 'X'-shaped art piece draws little attention to itself.

Plate 2.40 - At night the red neon, integrated onto the backside of the piece, creates a stunning field of vibrant crimson.

Plate 2.42 - What you are looking at here is a striking pink metal and blue neon sculpture as seen from the front. A single low-voltage track head projects light onto the face of the piece to pick up the pink color of the metal form and to keep the neon from overpowering the piece.

Plate 2.43 - A side view of the same neon piece shows how people see the shape of the sculpture as they enter the front door. The illumination on the solid orange color field painting draws people into the living room where they are then confronted with the red neon 'X' that is hidden behind the wing wall.

Plate 2.41 - A close up of the sculpture shows an 'X shaped channel cut into the face of the piece, which allows the color of the neon to bleed through the front. Two low-voltage track heads cross illuminate the bronze casing to keep the metal from falling completely into silhouette against the strong neon light source.

Plate 2.44 - This magnificent mid-century modern home comes to life at night. Recessed adjustable low voltage fixtures are used to create pools of illumination to help add depth and dimension to this very large living room. A pair of opaque wall sconces, flanking the Kormandel screen, look like modern interpretations of torches. Ambient light comes from linear xenon lighting, mounted on top of a cantilever that runs around three-quarters of the room.

Plate 2.45 - Another view of this massive living room feels more intimate through the use of well-placed lighting. Recessed adjustable low-voltage fixtures cross-illuminate the large black and white art piece above the sofa and the red art glass collection on the tansu. A modern Italian table light draws people to the seating area. In the upper right hand corner a glimpse of the perimeter ambient light can be seen.

Plate 2.46 - Side-lit fiber optics are used to create an illuminated handrail. The illuminator, located in a closet off to the left, houses the light source and a color filter. Presently the handrail is lavender but by simply changing the filter in the illuminator, the handrail can become any color of the rainbow.

Plate 2.47 - End-lit fiber optics changes the color of the cascading water feature to a radiant burnt sienna hue.

Plate 2.48 - The same water feature now becomes pale blue when the filter is changed. In this instance a revolving color wheel allows an ever-changing lighting effect.

Plate 2.49 - During daylight hours this compact dining area gets very little natural light from the north facing windows.

Plate 2.50 - After dark, a gently radiant neon sculpture becomes a focal point on the deck, located beyond the bank of floor to ceiling glass doors. A pair of shielded exterior fixtures, mounted in the corners above the door line, cross-illuminate the plantings and pottery. In the upper right corner a hanging lantern uses a single candle to add a touch of romance.

Plate 2.51 - The red metal sculpture and gentle water feature are fore-lighted from a pair of shielded directional exterior fixtures, mounted on the eave of the house. The stand of three palm trees is illuminated with a pair of additional directional fixtures, mounted behind the low stone wall. The single palm tree in the distance is allowed to fall into silhouette against the evening sky to help enhance the feeling of depth.

Plate 2.52 - This spectacular dining room uses a variety of lighting techniques to produce an aura of suffused radiance. The giant chandelier creates a floating crown of luminosity above the table. A pair of recessed adjustable low-voltage fixtures (located one foot out from each side of the chandelier) gently cross illuminate the Han dynasty figure in the center of the table. The two ornate columns, which flank the French doors leading out onto the deck, are up-lit from below to bring out the impressive detail. Beyond the French doors, a riot of brightly illuminated greenery creates a magnificent background for an unforgettable dining experience.

Chapter Thirteen

BATHROOMS—FUNCTIONAL LUXURY

The most important thing to remember in lighting the bathroom is that good illumination for tasks is primary, because looking good is *hard work*.

Well-designed lighting is of the utmost importance in the bathroom. Yet more often than not, people use inadequate lighting techniques for much-needed task illumination. How many times have we seen a dramatic photograph of a vanity with the recessed downlight directly over the sink? It makes for a great shot, but imagine yourself standing at the mirror with that harsh light hitting the top of your head. Remember when, as a child, you would hold a flashlight under your chin to create a scary face? With downlights, the same thing happens, only in reverse. Long dark shadows appear under your eyes, nose, and chin. This is extremely bad lighting for applying makeup or shaving (refer back to Figure 8.2 in Chapter 8).

Another typical arrangement is the use of one luminaire that is surface-mounted above the mirror. This is only slightly better than the recessed luminaire. At best, it illuminates the top half of the face, letting the bottom half fall into shadow. This is an especially hard light by which to shave. There are only so many ways you can tilt your head to catch the light (see Figure 13.6).

Task Lighting at the Sink

For the best task lighting, use two luminaires flanking the mirror area above the sink to provide the necessary cross illumination (see Figure 13.1 and Plates 2.27 and 2.28). The principle of cross illumination on the vertical axis originated in the theater, where actors applied make up in front of mirrors surrounded by bare lamps in porcelain sockets. These provided even, complimentary illumination on peoples faces, like their own halo of ambient illumination (refer back to Figure 8.1 in Chapter 8).

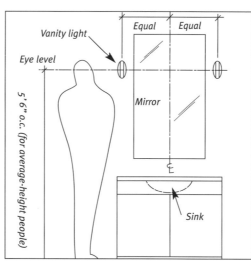

Figure 13.1
Vanity lights are optimally mounted at eye level, flanking the mirror.

In imitation of this technique, about twenty years ago luminaire manufacturers started to put vanity light bars on the market. Soon homes everywhere were sporting the now ubiquitous three-lamp brass or chrome bars above the mirror. Remember, these bars work best when mounted on each side of the mirror. A third luminaire could be mounted above the mirror, but it is not necessary for good task lighting. A luminaire mounted above the mirror by itself is not an adequate source of work light.

A more recent trend in providing cross-illumination is to wall-mount translucent luminaires at eye level on either side of sinks (see Figure 13.2 and 13.3). These task lights can flank a hanging mirror or be mounted on a full-wall mirror (see Figure 13.2). For inset sink areas, the mirror lights can be mounted on the return walls (see Figure 13.4). Many new, well-designed American and European luminaires are perfect for this application. To protect the homeowner from electric shock, luminaires located this close to water should be installed with an instantaneous circuit shutoff, called a ground fault interrupter (**GFI**) (see Figure 13.5).

Figure 13.2 (left)
Two sinks mounted too far apart need a pair of light luminaires per sink.

Figure 13.3 (right)
Two sinks mounted closer together can share three light luminaires.

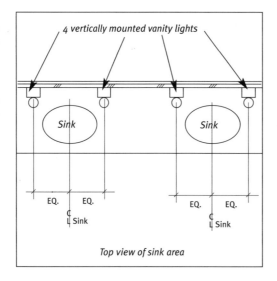

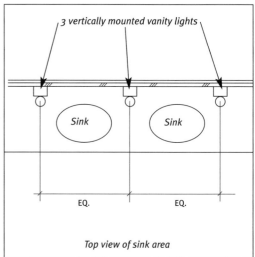

Figure 13.4 (left)
In small vanity areas, task lights can be mounted on the return walls.

Figure 13.5 (right)
A GFI (ground fault interrupter) prevents people from being shocked if they touch water and an electrical appliance at the same time.

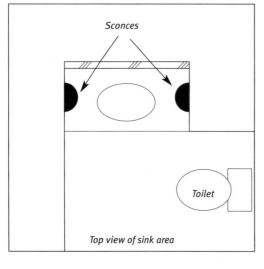

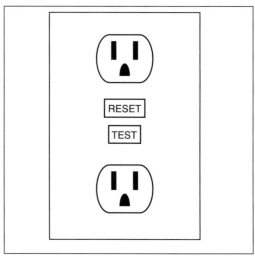

Figure 13.6
This is typically what we see in a bathroom, one light fixture mounted over the mirror. This provides a perfect light if you are shaving or applying makeup only to your forehead. Two light fixtures flanking the mirror, mounted at eye level, is the proper way to provide shadowless task light at the sink.

Figure 13.7
This tall linear wall sconce
from Boyd Lighting would be
a good choice for task illumi-
nation, installed on either
side of the mirror in a bath or
powder room.

Many builders and architects have a propensity for installing fluorescent or incandescent light in soffits, fitted with either acrylic diffusers or egg-crate louvers, located over the vanity areas. They too mostly illuminate the top half of a person's face. A white or glossy counter can help reflect some light from below by bouncing illumination up onto the lower part of the face. You are cross-lighting from top to bottom in this instance. This is not the optimal solution, but a passable substitute. Consider this only if vertical cross illumination is impossible to install. Remember, the more stuff that ends up on the counter, such as towels and containers, the less reflective surface there will be.

Lighting for Tubs and Showers

While the task area at the vanity is the most critical to illuminate correctly, other areas of the bath bear consideration. Tubs and showers need a good general light. For this purpose, recessed luminaires with white opal diffusers are commonly used and relatively effective. One drawback is that many of the units on the marketplace project approximately 2 inches below the ceiling line and may not be visually comfortable. They also tend to collect dead bugs. Also, these luminaires are usually limited to 60 watts of light, which is not very much. They call out for a normal household bulb (**A lamp**) which throws as much light back into the fixture as it projects out. This is not very effective.

We're all a little sensitive to bright light t first thing in the morning. Fully recessed luminaires with lenses flush or slightly recessed into the ceiling will render the upper third of the shower or tub area a little dimmer (see Figure 13.8). These luminaires do a better job at reducing glare and allow the use of higher-wattage bulbs.

A recent development makes lighting wet locations a little more exciting. Some luminaire manufacturers now offer recessed adjustable low-voltage fixtures that rated for wet environments. As designers are specifying interesting tile, plumbing fixtures, and even niches for art, they can install directional fixtures to highlight these exciting elements (see Plate 2.26).

Make sure that all luminaires, whether recessed or surface mounted, that are to be used in the shower, in the steam room, and over the tub are listed for wet locations by UL, **ETL**, or another approved testing laboratory. If Underwriters Laboratories tests them, they will have a blue UL label that indicates they are rated for a wet location. Also check to see if these luminaires should be circuited with GFIs for extra safety. Additionally, code requirements should be checked when specifying a surface-mounted fixture over a spa or bathtub. The national electric code now requires that the bottom of the luminaire be 8 feet above the high-water level.

Make sure that all luminaires in the shower are listed for wet locations by UL, ETL or other approved testing laboratory. If they are tested by Underwriters Laboratories, they will have a *blue* UL label. Also check to see if these luminaires should be circuited with GFIs for extra safety.

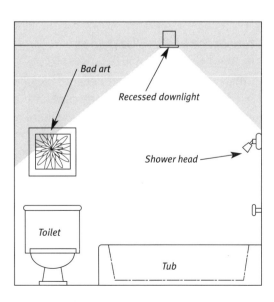

Figure 13.8
Recessed downlights may help reduce glare, but the downside is that they aren' t adequate sources of fill light.

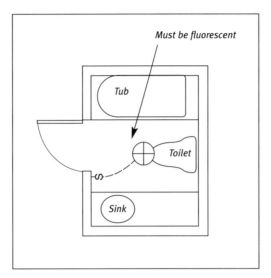

Figure 13.9 (left) California's Title 24 states that if there is only a single light source, then it must be fluorescent.

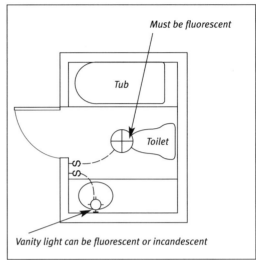

Figure 13.10 (right) California's Title 24 states that, in this design, the general illumination must be fluorescent, but the vanity lights can be incandescent or fluorescent.

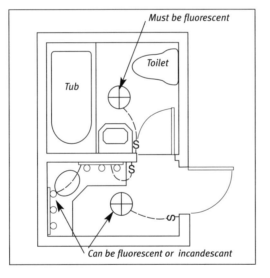

Figure 13.11 (left) California's Title 24 states that here the part of the bath with the toilet must be fluorescent, while either the general illumination or the vanity lights can be fluorescent. or incandescent.

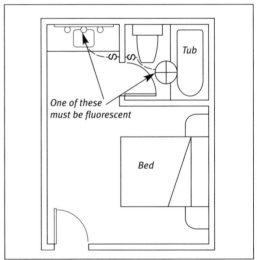

Figure 13.12 (right) California's Title 24 states that here, either the vanity lights or the general illumination in the toilet area must be fluorescent.

Fluorescent in the Bathroom

The fluorescent option is important today. Several states demand fluorescent light sources in the construction or remodeling of residential bathrooms. The reasoning behind this is forced energy efficiency. Fluorescents are at least three times more energy-efficient than incandescent lamps. For those designers and architects doing work in California, a state code called Title 24 requires that the general illumination in bathrooms (and kitchens, as mentioned in Chapter 8) that are for new construction or remodel projects that affect more than 50 percent of the existing space must be from fluorescent luminaires (see Figures 13.9–13.12). It also must be the first switch as you enter the bathroom. Recently the code changed to allow incandescent light in bathrooms if storage areas and garages use fluorescent fixtures or if outdoor decorative lanterns are hardwired for fluorescent.

Note that this code specifically states that it is the bathroom with the toilet in it. So if the toilet is in a separate space, such as a water closet that has a door between it and the rest of the bathroom, then this is the only area that requires fluorescent. Do not put a recessed fluorescent or any recessed fixture of any kind over the toilet. It is a common mistake that creates the most unflattering shadows imaginable (see Figure 13.14).

Getting past your client's fear of fluorescent lighting will be the hardest part of the project. Fortunately, the color temperatures of many of today's fluorescent lamps are very flattering to skin tones. In response to color rendition criticism, most manufacturers have introduced recessed and surface-mounted luminaires that use lamps with color-correcting phosphors, including the newer compact fluorescents (CFLs). Refer to Figure 13.15 to see a bathroom with a series of wall sconces using a compact fluorescent source.

Not only do these lamps greatly improve color rendering, but the 13-watt version produces an amount of illumination close to that of a 60-watt incandescent bulb. Many luminaires today even use two 13-watt tubes or a 26-watt quad tube that puts out as much light as a 120-watt incandescent source for 26 watts of power. Because one of the color temperatures available in the compact fluorescent lamp is close to that of incandescent (2,700°K), both light sources can be used in one's bath without creating disconcerting color variations.

Two drawbacks to some of the compact fluorescent lamps, as mentioned in Chapter 3, are an inherent hum and the lack of a rapid-start ballast. The latter deficiency causes the lamp to flicker two or three times before stabilizing. It's a good idea to let clients know the downsides as well as the advantages of this lamp if you specify it. Quad versions are much quieter because they use an electronic (solid-state) ballast and have a relatively rapid start-up. Dimming of compact fluorescents is now a reality. These advances, along with the improved colors, long life, and quiet operation, make fluorescent lighting worth a second look. (Chapter 3 covers your fluorescent options, including the newer lamps that can be dimmed with an incandescent dimmer instead of the more expensive fluorescent dimmer.)

Exhaust Fans

Windowless interior bathrooms may require an exhaust fan. Bathrooms with operable windows are not required by code to have an exhaust fan, although many homeowners like to have fans to help remove steam and odors. Units are now available with compact fluorescent sources that meet energy conservation requirements. Specifying a combination fan and light is a quick fix, but not an attractive choice. Make sure to specify separate switching for the fan and light, if allowed by code, so that the fan doesn't automatically go on when someone runs into the bathroom to grab a tissue or wash their hands.

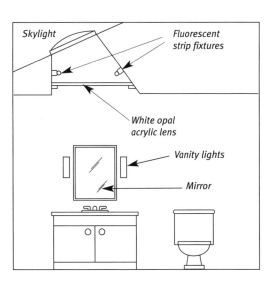

Figure 13.13
Lighting can be located within the light well to provide additional illumination at night, instead of becoming a "black hole" at night.

Figure 13.14 (left)
The effect of placing one recessed downlight over the toilet can be very dishearten-ing. Note the long shadows under the rolls of toilet paper and towel and imagine your appendages under this same quality of light. A little ambi-ent light in the form of one or two wall sconces would go a long way towards creating a much more pleasant environment.

Figure 13.15 (right)
In this rather long bathroom, a series of plaster wall sconces manufactured by the Phoenix Day Company pro-vide a very pleasant light which eliminates shadows on people's faces. Surprisingly, this light source is fluorescent

Figure 13.16
The wall sconces flanking the sink in this guest bath are grossly overscaled. The main danger is that the guests may use the wall sconces as sup-port while testing the temper-ature of the water, resulting in a possible shocking surprise for them.

Ambient Lighting

Indirect lighting in a bathroom adds a warm overall glow to the space. Wall sconces or cove lighting that directs light upward can provide gentle ambient illumination. Both of these can use miniature incandescent lamps, warm-colored compact fluorescents, or the standard-length color-corrected fluorescent lamps. The fluorescent choices not only comply with tighter energy restrictions, but also provide comfortable, low-maintenance light for the entire room. For bathrooms with higher ceilings, pendant-hung units can also be considered as a source of fill light.

Skylights

Often skylights are installed to supplement or replace electric lighting during the daytime hours. Clear glass or acrylic skylights project a hard beam of light, shaped like the skylight opening, onto the floor of the bath (as mentioned in Chapter 5). Bronze-colored skylights cast a dimmer version of the same shape, while a white opal acrylic skylight diffuses and softens the natural light, producing a more gentle light that fills the bath more completely. Existing clear or bronze skylights can be fitted with a white acrylic panel at or above the ceiling line to soften the light they cast (see Figure 13.13).

All specified skylights should have ultraviolet filters to slow the deterioration or fading of materials, caused by the sun's ultraviolet rays. If **UV filters** are not available from the skylight manufacturer, they often can be obtained from companies that manufacture fluorescent outdoor signs. The original fabricator of these filtering sheets of plastic is Rohm and Haas of Philadelphia. Their product is called a UF3 ultraviolet-filtering acrylic sheet.

If the light well is deep enough, low-maintenance fluorescent strip lights or luminaires with long-life incandescent lamps can be mounted between the acrylic panel and the skylight (see Figure 13.13). These inexpensive lights can be used to keep the skylight from appearing as a dark recess in the ceiling at night.

If fluorescent luminaires are used, dimming ballasts can be specified to allow control over the amount of light being emitted. Although such ballasts are not inexpensive, one of the advantages of dimming fluorescents is that they don't change color temperature significantly when dimmed. In this regard, they are unlike incandescents, which become more amber as they are dimmed. A new breed of screw-in fluorescent, such as the Earthlight by Phillips, can be dimmed with a standard incandescent dimmer. This offers a low-cost, energy-efficient dimmable option for the lighting within the skylight.

Another good reason for adding some type of ambient illumination in bathrooms is that they are becoming multifunctional areas. Homeowners now have exercise areas, dressing rooms, lounging areas, and whirlpools. Some bathrooms have become intimate entertaining areas that deserve all the design care that you give to the other main areas in the house.

Figure 13.17
This wall sconce with a perfo-rated paper shade projects a romantic pattern of light onto the wall.

Accent Lighting

Along with this newfound need for ambient illumination comes an opportunity for accent lighting. Plants and art pieces can be highlighted (see Plate 2.26).

When clients are entertaining, the room most frequently visited by their guests will likely be the powder room. This space can be treated differently than the other bathrooms. No serious tasks are going to be performed by guests (see Plate 2.29). This is a place where people will wash their hands or check their hair and make up before rejoining the soirée. Choosing the correct size of these fixtures is important. Take a look at Figure 13.16 for an example of sconces that are way too big. Here lights should be just a flattering glow. Sometimes a pair of translucent luminaires on either side of the mirror (see Figure 13.17,) or a single wall sconce with a fixture in the middle of the ceiling will do the trick.

Some powder rooms do double duty as guest baths for overnight houseguests. If this is the case, light the bath as you would a master bath, also making sure to put the various lights on dimmers to allow for flexible control over the illumination levels.

The Bottom Line

Bathrooms, along with kitchens, are the two areas in which people are most willing to invest their money, because a well-done remodel in these two rooms adds immediate value to the home. Clients can normally recoup the money they have invested when the home goes on the market.

The most important thing to remember in lighting the bathroom is that good illumination for tasks is primary, because looking good is hard work.

Chapter Fourteen

HOME OFFICES—WORK SPACES THAT REALLY WORK

Designers seek a more residential feel for work environments. They gravitate toward color, texture, round edges, plush carpeting, plants, and warm comfortable illumination. This design trend has made its mark as America's work force is moving back home.

With the advent of personal computers, e-mail, the Internet, and cell phones, an amazing number of people have moved their offices into their homes. Gone is the aggravation of the commute, along with the overhead costs of a separate work space. Some designers and related professionals find that they spend most of their time with clients at job sites or showrooms, making a separate office unnecessary.

For many more individuals, the home office serves as an important supplement to the main office space. Information can be obtained through the home personal computer or laptop, faxes can be received and sent, and a few very productive hours of work can be put in without leaving the house. The question is, how do you make this office space usable and comfortable for yourself or for your client?

Often the office area is visible from the rest of the house. How do you make it truly work-oriented without creating a commercial-looking office environment? The trend to humanize office environments has been going on for the last seven or eight years. The early to mid-eighties were the culmination of years of hard-edged commercial design. Lighting design seemed to follow the same route. The trend was to fill rooms with flat, shadowless, almost hospital like illumination. Depth and dimension were lost. Softness and texture were eliminated.

Finally, people grew tired of it and longed for a more welcoming place to work. Now designers create a more residential feel for work environments. They gravitate toward color, texture, round edges, plush carpeting, plants, and warm, comfortable illumination. This design trend has made its mark as America's workforce is moving back home.

Ambient Lighting

With business now so computer-oriented, a designer's major focus shifts to how lighting affects people working at a computer's VDT (visual display terminal) or monitor. Since much of our work these days is done on the computer, we have genuine concerns about eyestrain,

A common misconception is that the more light there is, the better people can see.

fatigue and headaches. These can often be caused by contrast and reflection. Glare is an uncomfortable light level or location, caused by contrast and reflection. Surprisingly, even what you wear will affect the reflection. A white shirt or blouse will show up on the screen and keep you from seeing areas of the data display (see Figure 14.1).

Here are some considerations when putting together a design:

1. A common misconception is that the more light there is, the better people can see. In the case of monitors, if there is too much light in the room, the monitor becomes difficult to read because of the amount of light hitting the surface of the screen (see Figure 14.2).

2. Another factor is the difference between the surface brightness of the document from which the computer operator is taking information and the brightness of the screen itself. Going back and forth from a brightly illuminated document to a more dimly lit screen will cause eye fatigue. Try to balance the amount of illumination on the documents with the illumination level of the monitor.

3. The third problem concerns disconcerting bright spots on the screen. A ceiling filled with recessed luminaires or track lights can cause little glare spots on the mirror like surface of the screen (see Figure 14.3).

What steps can you take to minimize these problems? A lot of the answer relates to the interior design and space planning:

1. Step one would be to keep the color contrast between the walls and ceiling to a minimum. Stay away from using glossy finishes that could reflect distractingly onto the screen.

2. Another planning consideration is to avoid positioning people with their backs to a window. The image of a bright window will overpower data on the monitor.

3. There are antiglare screens available, but you can't rely on them totally. They must be used in conjunction with proper lighting.

4. If recessed or track lighting is being considered, then specify units that have louvers or baffles that create a virtual cutoff at the face of the unit. Louvers have also been used as a way of reducing glare for monitors when situated at certain angles to the luminaires. A light source aimed directly at the monitor will create glare even if it is fitted with a baffle or louver. Instead of using recessed luminaires or track lighting, consider using a source of ambient illumination instead. Torchères would be a serviceable solution in a home office setting (see Figure 4.4 in Chapter 4). They can produce a soft, relatively even illumination across the ceiling and screen without the typical hot spots created by recessed or track lighting.

5. If the monitor is in a corner, an uplight positioned behind the screen will help soften the contrast between the screen and the corner walls (see Figure 14.4).

Figure 14.1 (left)
Even a light-colored shirt or blouse or clown makeup can cause a reflection on the monitor, obscuring some of the data displayed.

Figure 14.2 (right)
Positioning the screen away from the windows or other highly reflective surfaces will help reduce glare on the monitor.

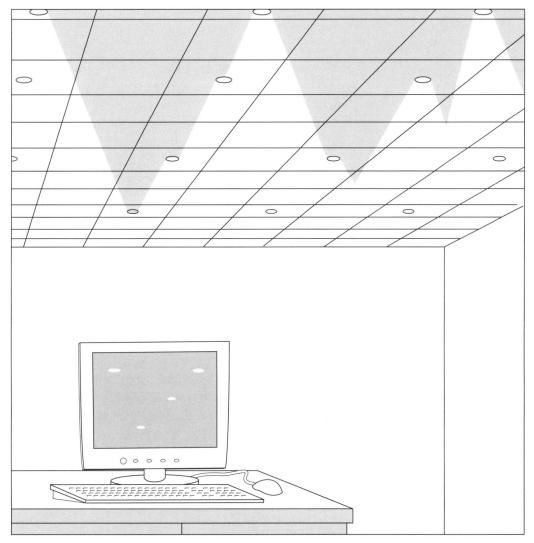

Figure 14.3
A series of recessed luminaires will cause hot spots of glare to appear on the monitor.

Figure 14.4
Placing an uplight behind the computer can help lessen the contrast between the screen and the wall color.

Figure 14.5
Using a flexible tabletop task light provides lighting for the work surface without putting any reflection onto the surface itself.

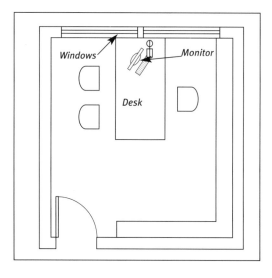

Figure 14.6
Make good use of the natural light coming in through the windows. Use some type of shade to control the light level when using the computer.

6. Make sure that light coming through the windows is controllable, using some sort of shade or blind (see Figure 14.6).

Task Lighting

Layered with this general illumination should be some flexible, task-oriented lighting. A tabletop or wall-mounted luminaire with a swingarm and some variability in light levels would be a good way of lighting documents and the keyboard without spilling light onto the screen itself. Select a luminaire with an opaque shade, so that the image of the luminaire itself won't reflect onto the monitor screen (see Figure 14.5). Remember that optimal task light is located between your head and the work surface.

Accent Lighting

In the home office accent lighting is not as important for the day-to-day tasks of running a business. Where it comes into play is at night when the home office is closed and your clients are entertaining friends. Turning off task lights, dimming down ambient light, and turning on accent lights helps integrate the home office into the rest of the house.

Daylight

Remember, natural light can be a very usable source of illumination and should be utilized to the best advantage. Daylight is totally free and should be utilized as a viable source of illumination. As was mentioned earlier, try to position the monitor with its back to the window in order to avoid reflection on the screen. Nothing can compete with the intensity of daylight (see Figure 14.6).

The Bottom Line

The main objective is to integrate the office into the rest of the home environment without sacrificing the needs of a well-appointed workspace.

Chapter Fifteen

EXTERIOR ROOMS—EXPANDING INTERIOR SPACES VISUALLY

In reality, the illumination of exterior spaces can be directly related to how the interior areas are perceived. One of the great benefits of exterior lighting is that it can visually expand the interior rooms of a residence.

As a designer of interior spaces, you may not feel a need to incorporate exterior lighting as a part of the overall design. In reality, the illumination of exterior spaces can be directly related to how the interior areas are perceived. One of the great benefits of exterior lighting is that it can visually expand the interior rooms of a residence. When there is no illumination outside, windows become highly reflective at night. This is known as the black mirror effect (see Plates 1.28 and 1.29). The windows end up reflecting the lights in the room, so that all the clients can see at night is their own reflection instead of the view beyond (see Figure 15.1). Unfortunately, window treatments only tend to accentuate the problem by framing the black mirror. Closing the draperies only confirms the dimensions of a smaller-size room.

People often feel boxed in at night when they are surrounded by these black mirrors. The room can seem smaller than it actually is. The rule of thumb is to try to balance the amount of light inside and outside the house. This allows the windows to become more transparent, as they are during the day (see Plate 1.31).

Psychologically, people also feel safer when they can see the yard area around them. They feel more vulnerable inside the house when there is no lighting outside (see Plates 1.38 and 1.39). You don't have to light up the exterior like the White House. That type of illumination would come under the heading of security lighting.

Security Lighting

Security lighting and landscape lighting are two different things. Yet often you will see people trying to use the same lights to per-

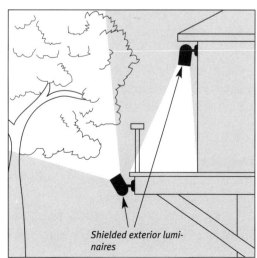

Shielded exterior luminaires

Figure 15.1
Fore lighting the deck from under the eaves and uplighting the trees from under the deck will help make the outside feel like part of the interior spaces.

Some areas have "light pollution" regulations requiring fixtures to be shielded or aimed to prevent illumination that may disturb the neighbors.

form both functions. Security lighting is often simply a source of lighting that immediately floods the yard with a good punch of illumination. This is what clients turn on when they hear a noise outside. Security lighting does not have to be confrontational. The main objective is to provide enough light so that homeowners can see what is causing the disturbance outside.

Security lights should be mounted as high as possible under the eaves. Specifying "double bullets" (see Figure 15.2) aimed in different directions and angled out and down will provide good yard illumination. Some residential neighborhoods have light pollution regulations, requiring fixtures to be shielded or aimed downward to prevent illumination that may disturb the neighbors or the evening sky (see Figure 15.3).

Security lighting is optimally controlled by a **panic switch** located next to the bed in the master bedroom and in the bedroom of another responsible person in the household, such

Figure 15.2 (left)
Security lighting is normally mounted at the roof-line along the perimeter of the house.

Figure 15.3 (right)
Reasonably priced bullet shaped luminaires are a good source of security lighting.

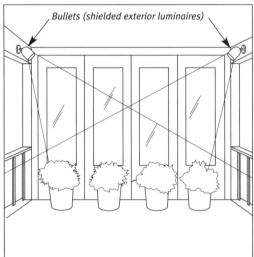

Bullets (shielded exterior luminaires)

as a grandparent, au pair, or oldest child. A motion sensor (see Chapter 6) can also control these security lights.

Security lights do not come on as part of the landscape lighting. There is nothing worse than driving up to someone's home, only to be assaulted by glaring security lights mounted on the corner of the house. As a guest, you may feel like you've been caught in the middle of a prison break.

Landscape Lighting Defined

What do you do when you have clients who've installed this confrontational kind of system, thinking they've got landscape lighting? One approach would be to say, "Oh, how wonderful! I see that you've put in an effective security lighting system. Now, let's talk about the landscape lighting." This way the clients don't lose face and are possibly more open to ideas on additional lighting concepts.

Landscape lighting needs to be subtle. Attention should be drawn to the plantings, sculpture, and outbuildings, not the luminaires themselves. Decorative exterior luminaires, such as lanterns, can't do the job by themselves. They can easily overpower the facade of the house and the yard area if they are the only source of illumination. Typically you will see two lanterns flanking the front door and maybe a post light at the end of the driveway. These just become disturbing hot spots that leave everything else in silhouette (see Figure 15.4).

Still, they play an important role in the overall lighting design. Their job is to create the illusion that they are providing all of the exterior lighting, when in reality they should provide no more than 25 watts of illumination each. They serve the same purpose as interior decorative luminaires. Think of them as architectural jewelry. Visually, they should be more along the lines of a subtle pair of pearl earrings than a diamond-encrusted tiara.

Another aspect to consider when selecting an exterior lantern is the type of glass. Too often they are chosen with a clear or beveled glass. The result is that at night people only see the lamps inside, instead of the luminaire itself. If you choose a luminaire that has frosted glass, iridescent stained glass (see Figure 15.6), or sandblasted "seedy" glass (glass filled with tiny bubbles that resemble seeds), then you see the volume of the lantern instead of just the lightbulb (see Figure 15.5).

It is possible to have the glass in the existing lanterns sandblasted. Often, mirror companies will do sandblasting as a sideline. Remember to have only the inside sandblasted—if you do the outside, fingerprints will show because of the oil in our skin.

Correct sizing of exterior fixtures can be tricky. Lanterns displayed in lighting showrooms appear about 25 percent larger than they do when installed on a home. The eye tends to make a visual room out of the surrounding fixtures in the showroom, so the lantern is viewed in a very small space. The result is that people tend to select fixtures that are too diminutive in size. One low-tech way of determining the correct scale for a particular house

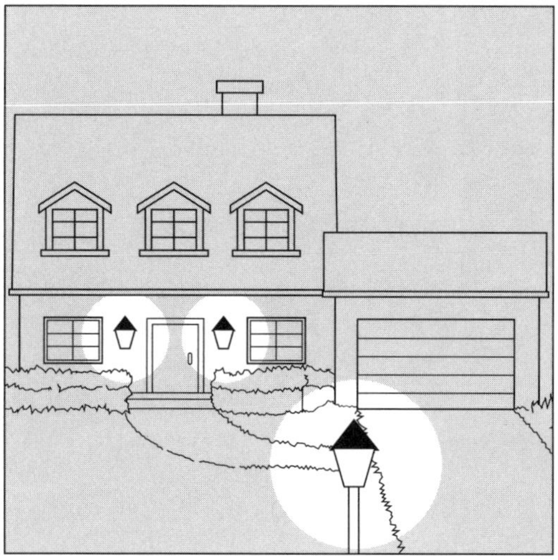

If the lanterns are existing, it is possible to have the glass in them sandblasted. This helps obscure the view of the light bulb within.

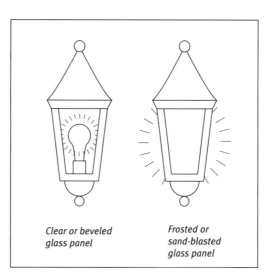

Figure 15.4 (left)
Decorative luminaires alone become too predominant, leaving the rest of the yard and house in relative darkness.

Figure 15.5 (right)
Selecting a luminaire that has clear or beveled glass shows off only the light bulb at night. Specifying sandblasted or frosted panels allows the luminaire itself to be the focal point.

Clear or beveled
glass panel

Frosted or
sand-blasted
glass panel

Figure 15.6
This Arts and Crafts style
lantern, made by Hinkley
Lighting, uses an iridescent
opal glass to obscure the
light bulb.

Figure 15.7
Determining the correct scale
and mounting height of exte-
rior lanterns is extremely
important. In this picture you
can see how these oversize
lanterns mounted 30 inches
off the ground make for a
rather comical entryway.

is to cut out a piece of cardboard the size of the prospective lantern. Hang it on the house and then back away to view it from the street or driveway. Choosing the correct mounting height is just as important. Take a look at Figure 15.7 to see a strange installation using very expensive luminaires.

Landscape Lighting Techniques

In designing the landscape lighting, a decision must be made as to which voltage system will be used. The choices are line voltage (120 volts, also known as house current) or low voltage (normally 12-volt or 24-volt systems, although other voltages are sometimes used).

One of the determining factors is what is already existing on the property. If some exterior lighting has already been done and there is 120-volt current out in the yard, then you are home free. Using one or more transformers, you can branch off from the line voltage and install low-voltage luminaires. Adding additional 120-volt luminaires to the lighting installation of an existing 120-volt system will be expensive and disruptive to the plants due to the trenching that will be required. The electrical code for 120-volt systems requires the wiring to be buried in conduit or directly buried 18 inches below the surface of the lawn.

Check local codes for permit requirements. Twelve-volt lighting systems are less restrictive, and installation is relatively easy. Low-voltage 12-gauge cable does not have to be buried, but hiding it under a layer of bark or a shallow layer of dirt is more visually appealing.

Low-voltage systems can use much less power and may not require any additional circuits. Their flexibility makes altering the original lighting design feasible and easy without costly rewiring. Luminaires for 120-volt systems are often larger than those using 12-volt lamps and may visually overpower the yard during the day.

When laying out a 12-volt system, remember to include the location of the transformer as part of the design. Voltage drop must be taken into consideration if it is necessary to have a run of over 75 feet from one of the transformers.

Often the best landscape lighting comes from a combination of both low-voltage and line-voltage fixtures. The line-voltage luminaires can highlight tall trees and provide an appropriate level of fill light for the yard area. This fill light is especially important when people are looking at the outside landscape through the window of an illuminated interior room (see Plate 1.43). Remember that balancing interior and exterior light levels helps keep the windows from becoming "black mirrors".

There are many techniques for landscape lighting from which you can choose. When working with new construction, it is important to specify a number of outside duplex GFI receptacles for future landscaping or portable luminaires for parties. Planning ahead for switching and transformer locations will save your clients money when the landscaping is started. Save time and construction costs by having power lines or conduit installed under the driveway or patio before paving or bricking. Small plants and trees continue to grow, some

Voltage drop— a loss of electrical current due to overload or long length runs (usually over 100 feet), causing lamps at the end of the run to produce a dimmer light than those at the beginning of the run.

*Figure 15.8
When the lighted object
can be viewed from one direction only, above-grade accent
lights are the logical choice.
To prevent direct glare, fixtures are aimed away from
observers. Place the accent
lights behind shrubbery to
keep a natural looking landscape.*

*Used by permission of
Kim Lighting.*

*Figure 15.9
If the lighted object may be
viewed from any direction,
well lights are the ideal solution. These below-grade luminaires are louvered to further
reduce the potential for glare.
Use the optional directional
louver to gain efficiency when
the lamp must be tilted within
the well.*

*Used by permission of
Kim Lighting.*

*Figure 15.10
Trees and shrubs with interesting branch structure are
dramatic when silhouetted
against a wall or building
facade. This combination
of landscape and facade lighting provides additional security near the building.*

*Used by permission of
Kim Lighting.*

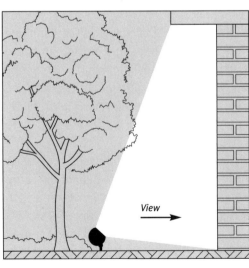

slowly and some more rapidly. Plan for maximum growth and install smaller-wattage
lamps that can be replaced with higher
wattages as the foliage matures. Using a
variety of lighting techniques will keep the
design interesting. Using only one technique may create a design that looks too
commercial. The following are some options
to consider.

Uplighting

This can be a very dramatic way of lighting
trees that have a sculptural quality to them
(see Figures 15.8 and 15.9). The luminaires
can be ground-mounted (see Figure 15.11) or
actually installed below-grade. These buried
luminaires are known as "well lights" (see
Figure 15.12). Well lights have little or no
adjustability, so they work best for mature
trees.

Above ground directional luminaires have a
much greater flexibility and therefore do a
better job of lighting younger trees as they
mature. Use shrubbery or rocks to conceal
the light source from view (see Figure 15.13).
A below-grade junction box for a line-voltage fixture will allow the luminaire to be situated closer to ground level. Low-voltage
fixtures have stakes to help affix them to the
ground. These are easily movable as the
garden matures. Have the electrician leave
an extra loop of wiring per fixture to allow
for some adjustment later on in the life of
the garden.

Silhouetting or Backlighting

Silhouetting or backlighting , done by lighting the wall behind the feature to be highlighted, can be a very effective landscape
lighting technique. Solid objects can be
more dramatic when illuminated from
behind or used to project a strong shadow
pattern (see Figure 15.14 and Plates 1.40

Figure 15.11
This ground mounted exterior fixture, manufactured by Kim Lighting, sticks out like a sore thumb in the center of this flat grassy area. Landscaping lighting is meant to be subtle and fixtures should be integrated into the plantings.

Figure 15.12
Here we see an example of a well light, an exterior fixture mounted below grade and fitted with a louvered face that keeps leaves and other debris out of the fixture. Diligence must be used in trimming back vegetation that could cover the face of the fixture, otherwise the effect of the lighting will be lost.

Figure 15.13
This directional uplight, by Kim Lighting, is nestled among low-level plantings to help it visually disappear. Its weathered copper (or verdigris) finish also helps the fixture blend into the foliage

Figure 15.14
Sometimes the shadow of a piece of art can be as intriguing as the object itself. Here an illuminated fish sculpture creates an expressive dual image.

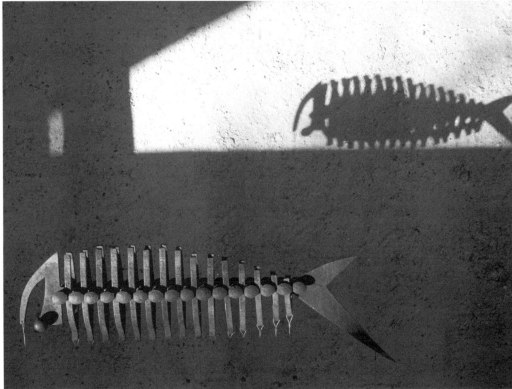

Figure 15.15
Two adjustable low-voltage fixtures with a transformer located inside the mounting canopy, by Lumiere Lighting, are specified with a white finish to match the color of the house. Using the lighter color instead of a more traditional bronze or verdigris finish makes them less apparent in daylight.

Figure 15.16
An exterior directional fixture, manufactured by BK Lighting, is affixed to a tree branch using a nylon strap. The strap can be adjusted as the diameter of the branch increases so that the tree is not harmed.

*Figure 15.17
Downlighting—For outdoor
activity areas, luminaires
placed above eye level provide efficient lighting for
recreation, safety and security. Overlapping light patterns
will soften shadows and create a more uniform lighting
effect. Mount to trellises,
gazebos, facades, eaves, or
trees.*

*Used by permission of
Kim Lighting.*

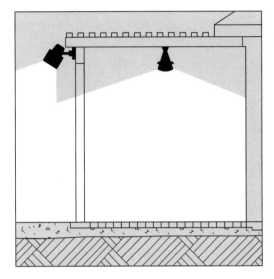

*Figure 15.18
Spotlighting—Special objects
such as statues, sculpture, or
specimen shrubs should be
lighted with luminaires that
provide good shielding of the
lamp. Mounting lights overhead on eaves or trellises
helps reduce glare. If ground-
mounted luminaires are used,
conceal them
with shrubbery.*

*Used by permission of
Kim Lighting.*

*Figure 15.19
Fully shielded mushroom-
type lights highlight pathways and ground cover without drawing attention to
themselves.*

*Used by permission of
Kim Lighting.*

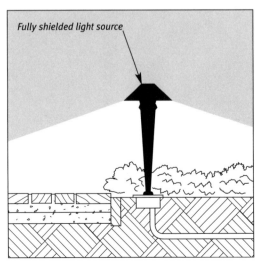

Fully shielded light source

and 1.41). This can work inside as well (see Plate 2.33). There are now fluorescent luminaires that do a good job of wall washing, consuming a small amount of power and with a long lamp life (see Figure 15.10). Remember to specify a ballast designed for low temperatures if your project is located in a cold part of the country.

Downlighting

This type of lighting is to be used for outdoor activity areas. It's best to overlap the spreads of illumination to help reduce shadowing. The luminaires can be mounted on trellises, under eaves (see Figure 15.15), or gazebos, and within the branches of mature trees (see Figures 15.16 and 15.17).

Spotlighting

Use spotlighting sparingly. Statues, sculpture, or specimen plants do deserve to be highlighted (see Figure 15.23). They will tend to dominate the view as people look outside (see Figure 15.18). Spotlights should be shielded to avoid glare if they are in direct view. They should be mounted on tall stakes if the surrounding plantings might cover them (see Figure 15.24). Layer this type of lighting with some of the other techniques to keep the landscaping from looking too spotty (see Plates 1.44, 1.45 and 2.54).

Path Lighting

This is one lighting technique that needs to be done judiciously. Too often we see walkways or driveways flanked with rows of pagoda lights, used as the only source of exterior illumination. This tends to look like an airport runway (see Plate 1.32). When a pathway light is needed, consider using an opaque mushroom light that projects light down without figure attention to it (see Figures 15.19 and 15.20).

These luminaires should not exceed 14 inches in height. This, in combination with additional lighting sources, will help create a comfortable exterior environment. Spacing of path lights will depend on the style of the luminaire and lamp options. Many lighting showrooms now have landscape displays to help you make an informed choice.

Step or Stair Lighting

Steplighting fixtures can be recessed in the sidewalls or the steps themselves to illuminate the risers. This will provide safety as well as background fill illumination for the landscape design (see Figure 15.21). Path lighting is most important at stairs so that a stroller is warned of changes in elevation.

Moon Lighting

This is the most naturalistic way of lighting an exterior space. The effect is as if the area were being illuminated by a full moon (see Plates 1.32, 1.33. 1.34, 1.35,1.36 and 1.37). A dappled pattern of light and shadow is created along pathways on water features, statuary and across low-level plantings (see Figure 15.25). This is accomplished by mounting luminaires in mature trees, some pointed down to create the patterned effect and some pointed up to highlight the canopy of foliage (see Figure 15.22).

Controls

It's best not to dim exterior lighting. Many outdoor luminaires use incandescent sources. When incandescent lamps are dimmed, the light becomes more amber, and the yellow cast makes the plantings look sickly. The whiter the light, the healthier the plants look. You can, though, divide the lights into different switching groups. A typical arrangement would be to have the decorative exterior lights on one switching group, possibly on a timer that would come

Partially shielded light source

Figure 15.20
Partially-shielded path lights create a glare when placed within taller shrubs. The surrounding shrubbery may filter light onto the pathway, reducing glare. A fully shielded fixture is a better choice.

Used by permission of Kim Lighting.

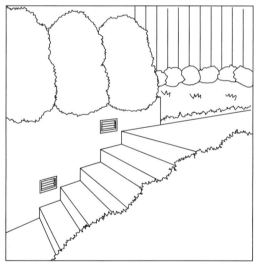

Figure 15.21`
Step lights can be mounted in the side walls of the stairway to provide safe illumination.

Figure 15.22
Moon lighting—The effect of moonlight filtering through trees is another pleasing and functional outdoor lighting technique. Both up and down lighting is used to create this effect. With luminaires properly placed in trees, both the trees and ground are beautifully illuminated. Ground lighting provides security, and is accented by shadows from leaves and branches.

Used by permission of Kim Lighting.

Please note that GFIs (ground-fault interrupters) are required on all outdoor circuits in some areas. Local codes should be checked prior to installing the system.

on and go off even if your clients aren't home. The second group could be the accent lighting throughout the yard, and the third would be the security lighting.

Note that GFIs (groundfault interrupters) are required on all outdoor circuits in some areas. Local codes should be checked prior to installing the system. If your client wants to dim the outside lighting, it is possible for the GFIs to be tripped erroneously if the lights are dimmed with phase-controlled dimmers.

Filters

It's best to stay away from most colored filters. They tend to change the look of plants to an unrealistic color. When designing with incandescent sources, one filter you can consider is what's called a daylight blue filter. It filters out the amber hue of incandescent light to produce a blue-white light that is very complementary to plants, making them look lush and green. Many manufacturers offer daylight-blue filters (sometimes called "ice-blue" or "color correction" filters) as an accessory. This small addition can make a huge difference in the overall look of the landscape lighting. For more information, refer back to Chapter 2's section on color temperature and plants and Chapter 4's section on color filters. Blue light is also better for pools and fountains, as yellow water is not very inviting (see Plate 1.42).

Light color is also a factor when considering the insect population of your clients' gardens or exterior spaces. Insects are attracted to blue light, which is why bug zappers have blue lights. Bug lights, which repel insects, are yellow. Put a bug zapper in the far corner of the yard, or make a gift of blue light to a neighbor.

HID and Fluorescent Sources for Landscape Lighting

There are many more exterior luminaires now available, using fluorescent and HID sources that are suitable for residential installations. Some mercury vapor and metal halide lamps, as well as the cooler-colored fluorescent sources, can do a wonderful job of providing a crisp blue-white light. These work best for illumination of very tall trees and building facades. They have a long lamp life and are very energy-efficient.

The Bottom Line

Don't limit your design work to interior spaces. There is a ton of money to be made creating outdoor rooms. Think about the possibilities of alfresco dining, pool areas, gazebos, and statuary. This is the last frontier for design, and you'd better jump on the bandwagon or you will be left behind in the dust.

Figure 15.23
This fascinating sculpture of a horse by artist Deborah Butterfield appears to be made of driftwood. It is actually cast in bronze from the original wood model. This piece is lit both from above and below to help it stand out against the dense foliage in the background.

Figure 15.24
A detail of one of the fixtures, manufactured by Lumiere, used to uplight the horse sculpture. Note that it is mounted on a tall stake to keep it from being covered by the plantings.

*Figure 15.25
Low-voltage lighting mounted in the overhead branches
of a tree creates an intriguing
shadow pattern on this lion
head fountain.*

Chapter Sixteen

APPLYING LIGHTING TECHNIQUES

This section allows you to hone your lighting design skills. It is a chance to combine what you may already know with the information and ideas put forth in this book.

Part A shows guidelines for drawing a reflected ceiling plan.

Part B provides guidelines for writing lighting specifications clearly and completely.

Part C is a questionnaire form that you can give to clients to get them thinking about lighting and the various functions it serves. The more they understand the importance of well-integrated lighting, the more they may be willing to invest.

Part D is a sample lighting project on which you will provide the lighting layout for a condominium project. A sample layout is provided in Appendix Two.

Part E is a review exam covering much of the information covered in Chapters 1 through 15. Sample answers are provided in Appendix Two.

Part A—Guidelines for Drawing a Reflected Ceiling Plan (Lighting Plan)

Everyone has different styles of presentation. The important thing is to get information across clearly and concisely. Remember, your lighting plan must be read and understood by people who aren't familiar with your design: architects, interior designers, Kitchen & Bath designers, sound system engineers, contractors, landscape designers, and of course... the clients.

1. Create an Architectural Background:
Start with the plan of the building (or room), with all walls and door swings as background (in a gray-tone or half-tone). This enables everyone to see the architecture without it competing with the lighting layout. Add to it (in dashed lines) all ceiling features, overhangs, skylights, columns, and beams that have a bearing on your lighting design (see Figure 16.1)

2. Place the Furniture in Each Room:
Layout the furniture next. This is very important. You cannot do a viable lighting design without knowing where the furniture is placed. For example, a seating arrangement that 'floats' in the center of a room will need floor plugs for table lamps and reading lights(refer back to figure 4.24 in Chapter 4). Without knowing where the major furniture pieces are being positioned it is impossible to locate the correct placement for the floor plugs. Another example relates to the placement dining room table. If you install a chandelier in the center of the ceiling and the table ends up being off center because a buffet has been place along one wall, then the chandelier is not over the center of the table.

You don't have to pick the style or fabric for the furniture, just size and placement. All the finish details come later. Selecting which walls will be used for hanging art is also important.

Figure 16.1
Make your lighting plan as clear as possible. The more information you provide, the less time you will spend on the phone or at the site explaining what you want done.

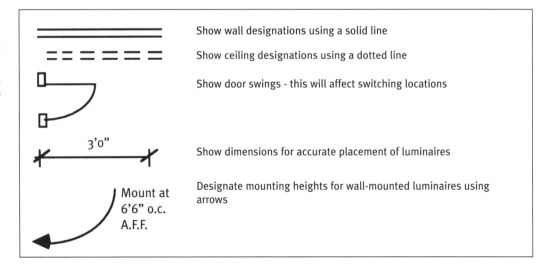

3. Create a Library of Symbols:

Draw your luminaires using clear and consistent lighting symbols along with clear symbols for components such as switches, dimmers, floor plugs, etc. Be sure to include a symbol list (legend) on the drawing. If you have any unusual luminaires, try to use a simple symbol which suggest that luminaire. This simplicity saves drawing time and is less confusing or distracting to the reader of the drawings (see Figure 16.2).

Decorative luminaires are usually selected by committee. The project interior designer, the architect, and the homeowners will all have their respective opinions. In order to keep the project moving forward, you can refrain from specifying the decorative luminaires on the legend, and use the note "to be specified by interior designer or homeowners" (see Figure 16.2, under Decorative). This gives the design team time to select luminaires at a later date, while allowing you to complete the lighting legend for the lighting design package.

4. Don't be Stingy with the Information:

On your plans, be sure to provide dimensions, distances, and spacings of your luminaires with respect to the architectural elements, because the location of the luminaire is critical to your design. In most cases, lighting symbols are larger than the actual luminaires you specify, and the drawing may not be accurately drafted for a number of reasons.

As a result, it may not be safe to allow the installers to take measurements off the plan for luminaire locations. Show dimensions to be sure! (See Figure 16.1). The electrician will kill you if he has to use an architectural scale to measure every fixture location. On CAD drawings use a fine/light pen weight to give the dimensions. This allows the lighting symbols to be the boldest line weight on the plans so they stand out. The background of architectural details and furniture should be the lightest of the three line weights.

The Bottom Line

The more information you provide, the less questions will arise during the bidding and installation phases. The fewer times you have to answer the phone on a particular project allows you to work on something else that makes you money.

Part B—Guidelines for Writing Lighting Specifications

A specification (or "spec") is a detailed description of the lighting equipment and components you have chosen for your project. This is a document that will be used by contractors, distributors, and manufacturers who want to bid on the project. Don't be generic. A specification that just say 'recessed adjustable low voltage downlight' is open to a lot of interpretation. Take special care to indicate exactly what you want or risk getting something you didn't want. Without clear and concise specifications you may end up with inferior luminaires installed on the job. The finishes may be different than you wanted and won't blend with the room and may look awkward.

Just because a luminaire, made by another manufacturer, may look like the one you want, it may not distribute the light in the way you intended. Giving full and complete specifications helps keep contractors from substituting inferior or inappropriate luminaires. Put a note on the plans that states that "any substitutions need to be approved of by the designer (you)."

Cover the following factors in your legend or on your plans:
1. Description of the luminaire (such as: opaque sconce)

2. Orientation of the luminaire (recessed, surface, wall-mounted, etc.)

3. Finish of the luminaire (white, chrome, gloss, matte, etc.)

4. Luminaire mounting height or suspension length (such as: 6'6" O.C., AFF.)

5. Type of lens, louver, or baffle, if appropriate (such as: daylight–blue filter)

6. Luminaire light distribution characteristics (e.g., asymmetric forward throw), if there is an option on the luminaire

7. Number of lamps (bulbs) per luminaire, lamp types, and color temperature (degrees Kelvin, for fluorescent or HID sources only), beam spreads and voltages (such as: 2- 100 Watt A 19 IF 120 Volt)

8. Ballast characteristics, such as dimming capabilities and voltage (such as: with Lutron Hi-lume dimming ballast 120 Volt)

Set-up in order of appearance, on the legend:
1. Generic description of luminaire or component (such as : opaque wall sconce)

2. Manufacturer's name and catalogue number (such as: Justice Design Group "Large Ambis" 1950)

3. Finish (such as : Bisque)

Recessed

 Arrow on recessed adjustable fixtures indicates which way they are directed. no arrow indicates down light position.

 IC Recessed adjustable low voltage integral transformer fixture rated for insulated ceilings (throughout). Lucifer DHI-M-120 DL2RX-W W/I50W MR16 EXN 12 Volts.

 IC Recessed adjustable low voltage integral transformer fixture rated for
WP insulated ceilings and wet locations (showers). Lucifer DHI-M-120 DL2RX-W w/I50W MR16 EXN 12 Volts.

 Recessed adjustable low voltage integral transformer fixture rated for non-insulated ceilings (exterior). Lucifer DHX-M-120 DL2RX-W w/I50W MR16 EXN 12 Volts.

 Recessed dimmable fluorescent fixture (kitchen). IRIS 5/32T SR/H w/Lutron dimming ballast w/1-32W 4-PIN CFL 35K 120 volts.

Decorative

Decorative fixtures are specified by the project interior designer or homeowners.

 Ceiling mounted light (throughout) to be specified by interior designer or homeowners.

 Wall sconce (throughout) to be specified by interior designer or homeowners.

 Table lamps (throughout) to be specified by interior designer or homeowners.

 Vanity light (bathrooms, new walk-in) to be specified by interior designer or homeowners.

 Mini pendant fixtures (kitchen) to be supplied by homeowners. Mount 30" above counter height, Confirm with owners prior to installation.

 Pharmacy lamps (throughout) to be specified by interior designer or homeowners.

Figure 16.2
This sample legend shows the symbol, generic description, and catalogue number for each luminaire. Keeping this information on computer will speed up the generation of future legends.

Fluorescent (excluding recessed)

Fluorescent wall mount fixture (existing bath). Progress 'eclipse' P7168-13ebw/1-26W 4-PIN CFL 27K 120V or equal.

Fluorescent ceiling mount fixture (bathrooms) to fulfill Title 24 requirements. Progress P3562-10EB w/2-13W QUAD 4-PIN CFL or equal. 15-1/4" diameter, 120 VOLTS.

Fluorescent under cabinet task light (laundry room). Progress P7007-30EB w/1-F17T8 35K lamp.available in 24", 36", and 48" lengths, 120 volts.

Fluorescent wall mount fixture (closets) on motion sensor. Progress P7094-30EB w/2-F17T8 35k lamps.available in 25-5/8", 37-5/8", and 49-5/8" lengths, 120 volts. The number 2, 3, or 4 designates approximate length.

Exterior

Exterior wall mount decorative fixture to be specified by interior designer or homeowners.

Exterior wall mounted directional fixture, FX luminaire copper spot LR-50-GS-HB W/BEM (brass eave mount) W/ PX-600-TCP-BZ transformer, 12 volts. For more information call mfg. Rep. Mark Thomas 916-419-4440.

Miscellaneous

Low voltage linear strip light (master bedrm., living rm., family rm., entry foyer, bedroom hallway). Starfire Xenflex XF-L-3-5-AOL-24 volts. Call Lumineering sales/ Sonia Danielson for quote pkg. (415) 469-8308.

Fan (bathrooms) to be specified by contractor. No integral light.

Range hood light supplied by range hood manufacturer. Hood light switch may be on hood, see manufacturer.

Power Outlets

Note: we recommend that switch plate receptacle covers all match throughout the house in style and color. Color and finish should be approved of by owners prior to ordering.

 Duplex receptacle outlet, to match Lutron Claro series

 Quadraplex receptacle outlet, to match Lutron Claro series

 1/2 hot switched outlet, to match Lutron Claro series

GFI Ground fault interrupter receptacle

WP Weather proof duplex receptacle outlet

WP Switched weather proof duplex outlet for holiday lights

220V 220 volt outlet

 Switched floor receptacle, to be specified by contractor

 Junction box (stub-out for future landscape lighting)

Switching/Dimming

Note: the color/finish of the following Lutron switches, dimmers, and controls need to be selected by the owners/design team before ordering.

PRESET 4   4 scene preset dimming system Lutron Grafik Eye GRX 3104-color/finish 4 zones. Verify component package with mfg's rep Greg Stewart (510)638-3800 ext. 133, or David Garibay ext. 139.

PRESET 6   4 scene preset dimming system Lutron Grafik Eye GRX 3104-color/finish 6 zones. Verify component package with mfg's rep Greg Stewart (510)638-3800 ext. 133, or David Garibay ext. 139.

M   Auxiliary master control, Lutron NTGX-4S-color/finish

Single pole switch, to match Lutron Diva Series Claro CA-1PSH-color/finish

3   3-way switch, to match Lutron Diva Series Claro CA-1PSH-color/finish

WP   Weatherproof switch

Incandescent dimmer - Lutron Diva Series DV600P-color/finish

3   Incandescent 3 way dimmer - Lutron Diva Series DV603P-color/finish

Switching/Dimming (continued)

⬤⊣ Low voltage dimmer - Lutron Diva Series DV600P-color/finish

⬤⊣ Low voltage 3 way dimmer - Lutron Diva Series DV603P-color/finish
₃

⬡25 Switching group - denotes which fixtures are controlled together

[MS]⊣ Motion sensor (closets) such as Wattstopper WA-100 or equal

[FS]⊣ Control switch for ceiling fan

Other Symbols

(SD) Smoke detector

✖ Ceiling fan

[C] Television cable inlet

[D]○ Doorbell

Other Symbols (continued)

(SL)   Tubular skylight, 10" 'Solatube' or equal

FAU   Forced air unit

(WH)   Water heater

GAS   Gas inlet

HB   Hose bib

▪▪▪▪▪▪   Dryer exhaust duct

◨   HVAC register

        Floor register at toe space

▣   Push button switch

        External operated disconnect switch

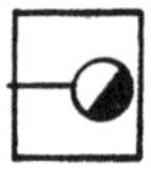

Ordering Guide

Use the table below to select the appropriate model number for Diva:

1. Determine the type of light.
2. Determine type of control.
3. Select the appropriate capacity.
4. Add your choice of color.

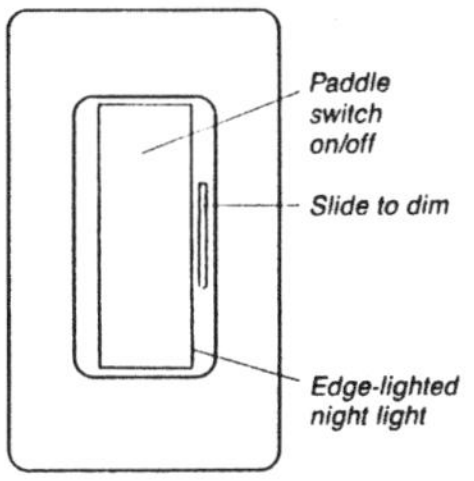
Paddle switch on/off
Slide to dim
Edge-lighted night light

DIVA

Type of Light	Type of Control	Model Code	Capacity 600W*	Capacity 1000W**	Color	
Incandescent	Single-pole	DV-	600P-	10P-	WH	White
	3-way	DV-	603P-	103P-	IV	Ivory
			600VA**	1000VA**	AL	Almond
					GR	Gray
Low-Voltage	Single-pole	DVLV-	600P-	10P-	BR	Brown
	3-way	DVLV-	603P-	103P-	BL	Black

Example: The model number for a low-voltage, 3-way, 600VA Diva dimmer in white is: DVLV-603P-WH.

*Available 4/30/92
**Available 5/29/92

Wallplate Options

Use Diva with Lutron SkyLine™ screwless wallplates or with any standard designer-style wallplate.
Both styles are available through your local electrical distributor in colors to match Symphony Series controls.
Wallplates are not included with Symphony Series controls.

Worldwide Technical and Sales Assistance

For help with applications, systems layout, or installation, call the toll-free ***Lutron Hotline:***
(800) 523-9466 (U.S.A.)
Outside the U.S.A., call (215) 282-3800
FAX: (215) 282-3090

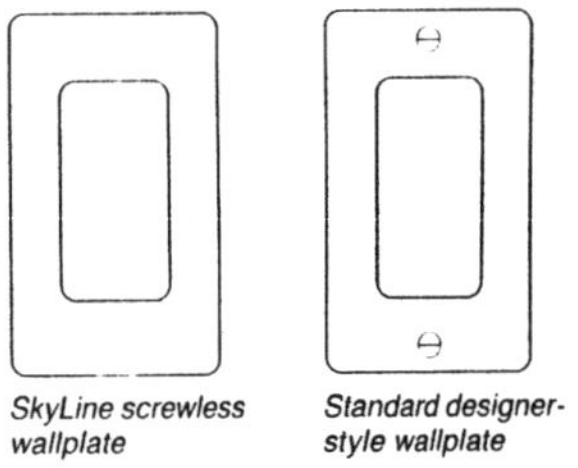
SkyLine screwless wallplate
Standard designer-style wallplate

Figure 16.3
This sample catalogue sheet marks which is the specified luminaire, along with the corresponding symbol.

Used by permission of Lutron.

Figure 16.4
This is an additional sample catalogue page with the specified luminaire highlighted and the corresponding symbol added to the page.

Used by permission of Justice Design Group.

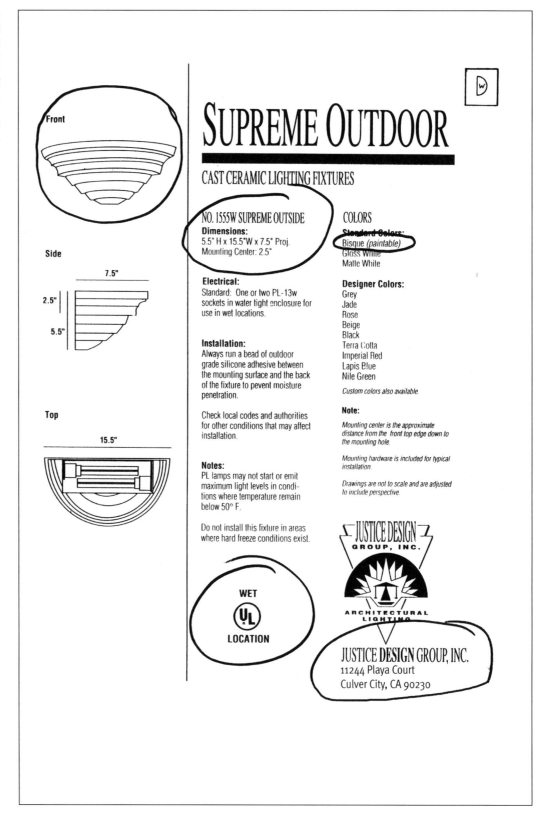

Front

Side

7.5"

2.5"

5.5"

Top

15.5"

SUPREME OUTDOOR

CAST CERAMIC LIGHTING FIXTURES

NO. 1555W SUPREME OUTSIDE

Dimensions:
5.5" H x 15.5"W x 7.5" Proj.
Mounting Center: 2.5"

Electrical:
Standard: One or two PL-13w sockets in water tight enclosure for use in wet locations.

Installation:
Always run a bead of outdoor grade silicone adhesive between the mounting surface and the back of the fixture to pevent moisture penetration.

Check local codes and authorities for other conditions that may affect installation.

Notes:
PL lamps may not start or emit maximum light levels in conditions where temperature remain below 50° F.

Do not install this fixture in areas where hard freeze conditions exist.

COLORS

Standard Colors:
Bisque *(paintable)*
Gloss White
Matte White

Designer Colors:
Grey
Jade
Rose
Beige
Black
Terra Cotta
Imperial Red
Lapis Blue
Nile Green

Custom colors also available.

Note:

Mounting center is the approximate distance from the front top edge down to the mounting hole.

Mounting hardware is included for typical installation.

Drawings are not to scale and are adjusted to include perspective.

WET
(UL)
LOCATION

JUSTICE DESIGN
GROUP, INC.

ARCHITECTURAL
LIGHTING

JUSTICE DESIGN GROUP, INC.
11244 Playa Court
Culver City, CA 90230

4. Lamping, plus louver or other attachments, if needed (such as 1- 13 Watt CFL quad, 2700 degrees Kelvin, and a glass diffuser)

5. Voltage (120 Volt , 12 Volt, etc.)

6. Special notes (such as: For additional information on this product please contact the manufacturer's rep: Mike Schultz, Pride Lighting 415-387-4856)

Examples of Complete Specifications

Wall sconce, Halo H2571 white, with Q150T3CL, 120V

Exterior wall-mounted directional luminaire, Hubbell 309-14, black with 75PAR30 flood with #1338 louver, 120V

Recessed adjustable low-voltage integral transformer luminaire, Lightolier 1102 P1 1152 white, with 50-watt MR16 EXN, 12V

Line voltage dimmer, Lutron Diva DV600P, white (For other colors and finishes contact the manufacturer's rep: Gregor Stewart, Associated Lighting Reps 510-638-2907 Ext: 133)

Dealing with Multiples of Fixture Types

You will notice in the sample legend (Figure 16.2) that a half-circle symbol always represents a wall sconce. If you have more than one style, designate each type with a letter: For example, if a symbol represents a wall sconce, and you have more than one style, designate each type with a letter, such as Ⓐ, Ⓑ, etc.

Recessed luminaires in the sample legend are represented by circles within squares. For example, a ⊡ represents a recessed, adjustable, low-voltage luminaire, while ⊙ represents a line-voltage downlight. Adding an "S" in the circle indicates that this downlight is wet-location rated for a shower or tub area.

Store Your Symbol Library on your Computer

These symbols, along with the names of the manufacturers you use most often can be entered into your computer to generate clear, explicit legends for each of the projects that include lighting. Building a database will save time on future jobs. The legend can be printed on a transparent, matte, sticky-back sheet, which can be affixed directly to the drawing if your office is not yet using a CAD system (computer-assisted drafting). If you are using CAD, place the legend on the last page of the plan set.

Specification/Submittal Books

Assemble a specification book that has photocopies of all the fixtures and related components, such as the dimmers, that you recommend. This will further clarify to the clients and contractors what you intend to have installed. A clear picture will answer a lot of questions in advance. It's also a good idea to draw the corresponding symbols at the top right-hand corner of each specification sheet to match the legend to the actual luminaire being specified. See samples 16.3 - 16.4.

Make a copy for the submittal booklet for the architect, interior designer, contractor, electrician, lighting designer, and the owners. It's a good idea to make one or two spare booklets and keep them in the client file. One of the players is always losing their copy and it will save you hours of recopying all the sheets again.

Cut Sheets

Circle or highlight the manufacturer's name on the catalogue cut sheet or spec sheet, along with the catalogue number and any other pertinent information. The upper right-hand corner shows the corresponding symbol.

Many manufacturers have their entire catalogues on the internet which can usually be entered through their website. This is great because they have printable digital files that you can print through your computer. It's great to just click "8 copies", instead of trying to make eight useable cut sheets from photocopies of pages in various catalogues. Also, many manufacturers have their catalogues in hard discs or compact discs to keep in your office and slip into your computer. Usually these can be obtained from the manufacturer's rep or directly from the manufacturer.

Put all the cut sheets in a binder or booklet for each of the players. Place a copy of the legend, resized to fit one or more 8 -1/2" x 11" sheets, and place this in the front of the booklet. Add a cover with the following title:

Lighting Submittals (this tells us what is in the binder)

Jones Project (this tells us what project it is for)

Saratoga, California (this identifies the project location)

Contractor's Copy (this identifies which particular team member the binder belongs to)

Part C—Lighting Questionnaire

The following questionnaire is a good starting point when meeting with your clients to discuss lighting. Getting these questions answered will help you create a design that suits the project. Note that this is a one-room project. If your project encompasses an entire house, then the same questions will apply to each room.

To Our Clients

There are many factors that affect the way a room is lighted. By answering the following questions, we will be able to give you the lighting design advice that best suits your needs.

1. Room Description (a scale drawing and a furniture layout are very important here).

_____

_____

2. Dimensions: _____
(If you have a scaled drawing, make sure that the scale is indicated, such as 1/4"= 1' 0").

3. New construction or remodel? (circle one)

If it is a remodel project, where are existing lights located? (Mark them on the plan).

4. Ceiling height _____   Sloped or flat (circle one)

5. Is there enough ceiling depth to consider recessed fixtures as an option? __Yes __No __ Don't Know

6. Are there Skylights? __Yes __No __ To be added
If so, how many and where are they located? (Mark them on the plan).

7. If you have, or want, skylights, are they clear, bronze, or white? (circle one)

8. Do you have a budget in mind? __Yes __No
If yes, how much? _____

9. What colors are the walls and ceiling to be painted? (Provide samples if possible).

_____

10. Where are the windows and doors located?(Show them on the plan).

_____

11. What do the windows look out onto? _____

_____

_____

Part D— Condominium Project

Your Assignment: You have been asked to design the lighting concepts for a new condo. The clients want you to tell them where to put lights and what type of luminaires you recommend (see Figure 16.5).

You are to use the sample list of symbols provided (see Figure 16.2) to designate the type of luminaires to be installed. If a symbol is not listed for a luminaire you would like to use, create one and identify it on the legend.

The reason to start using distinct symbols is to make the lighting plans easy to read. The norm in the industry for way too many years was to use the same symbol to represent almost everything: ceiling-mounted luminaires, wall-mounted luminaires, recessed luminaires, even table lamps. This is confusing to read and can lead to mistakes during the counting of each fixture needed , as well as, installation.

What you know about the clients:

1. They are a married couple, 30 years old, without children. The walls and ceilings are white and the floors are light oak.

2. You have already worked out the furniture plan and location of art with these clients. That furniture layout is shown on the plan.

3. They have enough money from their dual incomes and a home improvement loan to do whatever you recommend. You are not limited by budget.

4. There will be nine-foot ceilings throughout, except for the living room, which has a pitched ceiling that is 12' high at the apex (center) beam.

5. There is adequate space available for recessed luminaires.

6. The condo complex is located in Baton Rouge, Louisiana, and their unit is on the first floor.

What to Include in your lighting design:

Throughout the project, make sure you provide adequate lighting for task, ambient, and accent illumination. Don't forget to consider exterior lighting, as well.

Solution: A sample lighting layout is found in Appendix Two. This is not the only solution. There are as many possible solutions as there are different designers. It is a good look at what a finished lighting plan looks like. See if you can "read" it, understanding what the lighting designer intended.

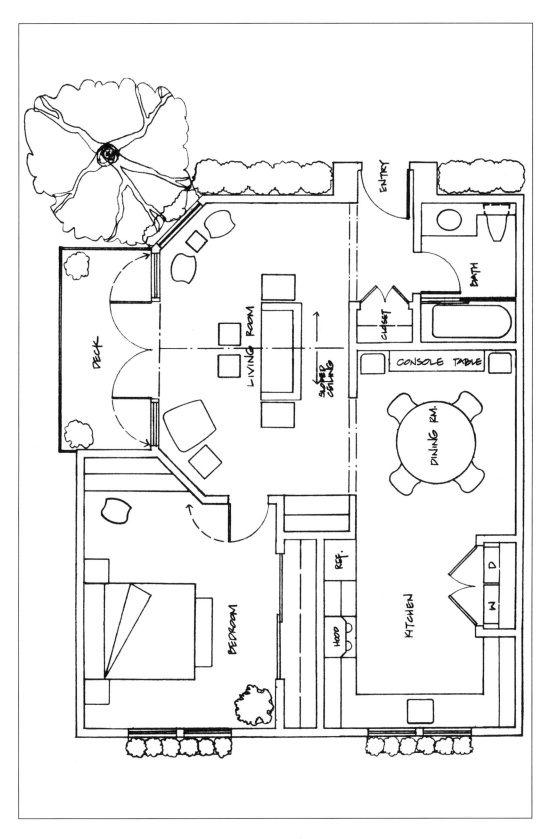

Figure 16.5
Condo Project.
Photocopy this page and try
your hand at developing a
lighting plan based on the
given client information.

Part E: Review Examination - Residential/Landscape Lighting

1. What is meant by layering light? Explain and give examples.

_____
_____

2. What 3 things are lit in a space? Which is the most important? Why?

_____
_____
_____
_____

3. What are color temperature and CRI? How would you use them to choose a lamp?

_____
_____
_____
_____
_____
_____

4. How do finishes and light sources interact in a space? Explain by giving examples.

_____
_____
_____
_____

5. What are some of the things to consider in specifying a fluorescent luminaire? How do they affect your decision?

_____
_____
_____
_____

6. If you were setting the scenes for a 4-scene preset dimmer system, what scenes might you use? Why? Describe.

_____
_____
_____
_____

7. How does Title 24 affect kitchen and bath lighting in California?

_____
_____
_____
_____

8. What are some of the considerations (other than Title 24) used when designing lighting for kitchens? Explain. _____

_____

_____

_____

_____

_____

9. When lighting landscapes, safety, security and beauty are to be considered. Choose one of these and describe some of the techniques used to accomplish this?

_____

_____

_____

_____

10. Why is it important to know which plant materials are being used when doing landscape lighting?

_____

_____

_____

11. What are some of the architectural constraints one must deal with in doing lighting design? Give an example._____

_____

_____

_____

_____

12. Describe the steps you would take in doing a lighting design from start to finish.

_____

_____

_____

_____

_____

13. Color temperature is measured in degrees of _____

14. Do green plants look better under a cooler or a warmer color temperature?_____

15. Name two benefits of ambient light.

1._____

_____

2._____

_____

16. Give two examples of task lighting in:

An Office: 1._____

               2._____

A Kitchen: 1._____

               2._____

17. How would you improve on the lighting in a dining room that is lighted only by a chandelier?_____

_____

_____

_____

18. What does the "MR" stand for in an MR16 lamp? _____

_____

(Hint: the answer is not "mister")

19. What is the diameter of an MR16 lamp?_____

20. To dim a quartz (tungsten halogen) lamp without significantly shortening its life, what percentage of time must it be burning at full capacity?_____

_____

21. Why are clients afraid of fluorescent and what can you do to "enlighten" them?

_____

_____

_____

_____

22. For task lighting at a vanity, where is the best place to locate the luminaires?

_____

_____

_____

_____

23. HID stands for _____

24. Mercury vapor lamps produce what color light?_____

_____

25. High-pressure sodium lamps produce what color light? _____

26. People tend to look rather unattractive under High Pressure Sodium light. What might look good under this light? _____

_____

27. Is "daylight" a warm color or a cool color temperature?_____

28. What does the "R" stand for in a 75R30 lamp? _____

29. Name two disadvantages of the compact fluorescent.
1._____
2._____

30. The four lamp categories are incandescent, fluorescent, LED and H.I.D. Which category does a quartz lamp fit into?_____

31. What are two advantages of fluorescent over incandescent?
1._____
_____
2._____
_____

32. Describe the "black mirror" effect._____
_____
_____

33. Describe the "moon lighting" effect._____
_____
_____
_____

34. Why is it necessary to light the clients as well as the art and architecture in a home?
_____
_____
_____
_____

35. If you were glowing from within, what color light would you emit to attract bugs?
_____

36. Give three advantages of low-voltage lighting.
1._____
2._____
3._____

37. Give three disadvantages of low-voltage lighting.
1._____
2._____
3._____

38. True or False? All "pagoda lights" should be sent to Wichita, Kansas to be used as landing lights._____

39. Describe the term "veiling reflection."_____
_____
_____
_____

40. What does not change significantly when you dim fluorescent?
_____
_____

41. What is the best way to light a piece of art with a reflective face (such as glass or Plexiglas™)?_____
_____
_____

42. When a client says, "How much light do I need for this room?," list at least three questions you need to ask them about the space.
1._____
2._____
3._____
4._____
5._____

43. What is a panic switch and where is it best located?
_____
_____

44. What is the most important element to any design project?
_____
_____

Glossary

Here is a quick reference guide for terms that are commonly used in lighting design. They have been put in layperson's terms so that you can effectively explain them to your clients.

A lamp—Refers to the shape of a standard household bulb. The A stands for arbitrary.

Absorption—Refers to a measure of the amount of light absorbed by an object, instead of being reflected. Dark-colored and matte surfaces are least likely to reflect light.

Accent lighting—Lighting directed at a particular object in order to focus attention upon it.

Alabaster—A stone with translucent qualities, used on decorative fixtures.

Ambient lighting—The soft, indirect light that fills the volume of a room with illumination. It softens shadows on people's faces and creates an inviting glow in the room.

Amperage—The amount of electrical current through a conductive source. Low voltage has more amperage than line voltage.

Angle of reflectance—The angle at which a light source hits a specular reflective surface equals the angle at which the resulting glare is reflected back.

ANSI—Five-digit numbering system in national use for designating lamp types.

Ballast—Device that transforms electrical energy. It is used by fluorescent, mercury vapor, high- and low-pressure sodium, or metal halide lamps so that the proper amount of power is provided to the lamp.

Beam spread—The diameter of the pattern of light produced by a lamp, or lamp and luminaire together.

Below grade—Recessed below ground level.

Black mirror—Refers to a glass door or window in a room that reflects the viewer's image and the light in the room around that person at night instead of seeing the objects or view beyond.

Bouillotte lamp—A portable luminaire with an opaque shade used for reading.

Bridge system—Two-wire low-voltage cable system.

Catalog Sheet—A page out of a catalogue that describes a lighting device or component. Also known as a cut sheet.

CFL—Compact fluorescent lamp.

Chandelier—A hanging decorative luminaire.

Cloudy Day Effect—Where the lighting in a space is so even that there is no depth or dimension.

Code—Electrical guidelines that must be followed in order to ensure a safe electrical installation. These can be national, state, or city-regulated.

Cold cathode—A neon like electric-discharge light source primarily used for illumination. Cold cathode can sometimes be used where fluorescent tubes would be too large or too hard to relamp.

Color Rendering Index (CRI)—A scale used to measure how well a lamp illuminates an object's color tones as compared with the color of daylight.

Color-corrected—The addition of phosphors in a lamp to create better color rendering.

Daylight—The mix of skylight and sunlight.

Daylight-blue filter—A light blue lens that reduces the amber hue of incandescent light.

Decorative luminaire—A light fixture that is designed to please the eye and provide focal illumination.

De-rating—The reduction of the amount of wattage used to prevent overheating. Related to ganging of dimmers. The more dimmers that are located in the same box, the less wattage they can control.

Diffusion filters—Glass lenses used to widen and soften light output.

Dimmer—A control that regulates light levels.

Dimming ballast—A device used with fluorescent lamps to control the light level. May also apply to HID sources.

Downlight—A luminaire that is used to project light toward the ground.

Downlighting—A technique that uses a luminaire to project light downward.

Efficacy—A measurement of the efficiency of a light source.

ETL—An independent testing facility, similar to UL.

Fade rate—The rate at which light levels decrease.

Fiber optics—An illuminating system composed of a lamp source, fiber, and output optics used to remotely light an area or object.

Filters—a glass or metal accessory used to alter beam patterns.

Fish tape—A device used to pull wires through tight spaces or conduit.

Floor plug—An electrical outlet recessed into the flooring of a room

Fluorescent lamp—A very energy-efficient type of lamp that produces light through the activation of the phosphor coating on the inside surface of a glass envelope. These lamps come in many shapes, wattages, and colors.

Framing projector—A luminaire that can be adjusted to precisely frame an object with light.

Ganging—The grouping of two or more controls in one enclosure.

GFI (ground fault interrupter) —An instantaneous disconnect device that turns off an electrical appliance or circuit when it comes in contact with water, in order to prevent electric shock.

Glare Bomb—A source of uncomfortably bright light that becomes the focus of attention rather than what it was meant to illuminate.

Glass block/glass brick—A transparent or translucent building material.

Halogen—An incandescent lamp containing halogen gas that recycles the tungsten. It is whiter in color than standard incandescent lamps but becomes more yellow when dimmed.

Hardwire—A method of luminaire installation using a junction box.

High-intensity discharge (HID) lamp—A category of lamp that emits light through electricity activating pressurized gas in a bulb. Mercury vapor, metal halide, and high- and low-pressure sodium lamps are all HID sources. They are bright and energy-efficient light sources, used mainly in exterior environments.

High-pressure sodium—An HID lamp that uses sodium vapor as the light-producing element. It produces a yellow-orange light.

Hole saw—A drill bit used to cut very clean holes in doors, walls, floors, and ceilings.

Housing—An enclosure for recessed sockets and trim installed above the ceiling line.

Incandescent lamp—The traditional type of lightbulb that produces light through electricity, causing a filament to glow. It is a very inefficient source of illumination.

Junction box—An enclosure for joining wires behind walls or ceilings.

Kelvin—In lighting design, a measure of color temperature.

Lamp—What the lighting industry calls a lightbulb; a glass envelope with gas, coating, or filament that glows when electricity is applied. Also a common word for a portable light fixture, but not used in the professional lighting community in this sense.

LED—Light-emitting diode.

Legend—A list of symbols that relate to lighting and electrical components used on a lighting plan.

Line voltage—120-volt household current, standard in North American homes.

Louver—A metal or plastic accessory used on a luminaire to help prevent glare.

Low-pressure sodium—A discharge lamp that uses sodium vapor as the light-producing element. It produces an orange-gray light.

Low-voltage lighting— A system that uses a current less than 50 volts (commonly 12 volts), instead of 120 volts, the standard household current in the United States. A transformer is used to convert the electrical power to the appropriate voltage.

Lumen—A unit of light power from a light source: the rate at which light falls on one square foot of surface area one foot away from a light source at one candlepower or on candela.

Luminaire—The complete light luminaire with all lamps (bulbs) and parts necessary for positioning and obtaining power supply.

Mercury vapor lamp—An HID lamp where the light emission is radiated mainly from mercury. It can be clear, phosphor-coated, or self-ballasted. It produces a bluish green light.

Metal halide lamp—An HID lamp where the light comes from radiation from metal halide. It produces the whitest light of the HID sources.

Mirror reflector (MR16 and MR11)—Miniature tungsten-halogen lamps with a variety of beam spreads and wattages, controlled by mirrored facets positioned in the reflector.

Motion sensor— A control that activates luminaires when movement occurs.

Museum effect—An environment with only accent lighting that makes the art seem more important than the people in the space.

Mushroom light—An exterior pathway and garden luminaire whose shape resembles that of a mushroom.

NEC (National Electric Code)—The rules for electrical installations that must be followed to ensure a safe installation, used throughout the United States.

Neon—A glass vacuum tube filled with neon gas and phosphors formed into signs, letters or shapes.

Opaque—Solid, permitting no light to pass through.

Open hearth effect—Lighting that creates the feeling of a glowing fire.

Pagoda light—An exterior pathway luminaire that resembles a pagoda.

Panic switch—An on-off switch to activate security lighting, usually located by the bed for emergencies.

PAR lamps—Lightbulbs with parabolic aluminized reflectors that give exacting beam control. There are a number of beam patterns to choose from, ranging from wide flood to very narrow spot. PAR lamps can be used outdoors due to their thick glass, which holds up in severe weather conditions.

Pendant—A luminaire that is suspended from the ceiling by wires, chains, or metal rods.

Pharmacy-type luminaire—A portable floor or tabletop luminaire that is used for reading. It normally has an opaque shade.

Photo-pigment bleaching—The mirror like reflection of the sun on a shiny surface, causing glare.

Photosensor—A control device that activates luminaires depending on surrounding light levels.

Planetarium effect—The look of too many holes in the ceiling resulting from an overabundance of recessed fixtures.

Puck light/puk light—A very shallow luminaire in the shape of a small hockey puck.

R lamp—An incandescent source with a built-in reflecting surface.

Receptacle—A point of access for electrical power.

Reflectance—The ratio of light reflected from a surface.

Reflected ceiling plan—A lighting or architectural plan drawn as if you are lying on the floor looking up at the ceiling.

RLM—A luminaire designed to reflect light down and prevent upward light transmission.

Security lighting—Exterior illumination intended to flood the property with bright light.

Silhouetting— The backlighting of an object.

Scone—Something that you eat with tea. This is not a wall mounted decorative luminaire but often used by people in the place of "sconce" (see below).

Sconce—Wall-mounted decorative or architecturally-integrated luminaire.

Socket—The receptacle that a lamp base screws into.

Socket dimmer—A dimmer that screws into a socket and into which a lamp is then screwed.

Spotlighting—Using a focused beam of illumination to draw attention to an object.

Spread lens—A glass lens accessory used to diffuse and widen beam patterns.

Stake light—A luminaire mounted on a stake to go into the ground or a planter.

Step light— A luminaire used to illuminate steps or pathways.

Stud finder—A device that detects the location of joists behind walls and ceilings by measuring differences in density or the presence of metal nails.

Swiss cheese effect—The look resulting from too many holes in the ceiling resulting from an overabundance of recessed fixtures.

Switch—Control for electrical device.

Task lighting—Illumination designed for a work surface so that good light, free of shadows and glare, is created.

Timers—Control devices to activate luminaires at timed intervals.

Torchère—A standing floor lamp that is portable.

Track lighting—A electrified metal channel onto which individual luminaires are attached.

Transformer—An device that can raise or lower electrical voltage, generally used for low-voltage lights and neon.

Translucent—Semitransparent, allowing some light pass through.

Transparent—Clear, allowing light to pass through.

Tungsten-halogen—A tungsten incandescent lamp (bulb) that contains gases and burns hotter and brighter than standard incandescent lamps.

UL—An independent testing company, Underwriters Laboratories.

Uplight—A portable luminaire used to project light toward the ceiling.

Uplighting—Illumination projected toward the ceiling.

UV—Ultraviolet light.

UV filter—A coating or lens that reduces ultraviolet emissions in order to reduce sun damage or damage caused by artificial light sources.

Veiling reflection—A mirror like reflection of a bright source on a shiny surface. This causes a difficulty in reading, as if looking through a veil.

Voltage—A measurement of the pressure of electricity going through a wire.

Voltage drop—The decrease of light output in fixtures farther from the transformer in low-voltage lighting systems.

White light—Usually refers to light with a color temperature between 5,000 and 6,250 degrees kelvin and composed of the whole visible light spectrum. This light allows all colors in the spectrum on an object's surface to be reflected, providing good color-rendering qualities. Daylight is the most commonly referred to source of white light. This is not a good color for skin tones.

Xenon—An inert gas used as a component in certain lamps to produce a cooler color temperature than standard incandescent. It is often used in applications where halogen may normally be specified, because of a longer lamp life.

Appendix One

RESOURCES: HOW TO USE THEM

Lighting design is a relatively new and emerging field. A basic lighting course cannot begin to cover all aspects of lighting design. It is important that you feel comfortable utilizing all the resources available to you.

Organizations

Please take advantage of the opportunities to expand your education. There are associations (listed below) that host classes or seminars around the country on all aspects of lighting design. The American Lighting Association (ALA), Illuminating Engineering Society (IES), Designer Lighting Forum, and American Society of Interior Designers (ASID) are all open to design professionals and students.

Hands-On

Take time to visit your local lighting showrooms; investigate and learn how to use their lighting labs. Most showrooms now have recessed, track, and outdoor labs of some sort, along with full displays of dimming options.

Interior design market centers put on seminars in conjunction with their annual, or semiannual, market events.

Getting Work Experience

Intern with or try to work with a particular individual or lighting design company that is knowledgeable and willing to teach in a real-life situation. The International Association of Lighting Designers (IALD; www.iald.org) has a listing of positions available.

Accreditation

The American Lighting Association has a Certified Lighting Consultant program, and IES has a program in place for Certificates of Technical Knowledge.

Code Requirements

Check with your local building department to verify local and state code requirements. Most have handbooks available at your library. It is far better to ask questions than to have to replace a ceiling because you specified the wrong placement of recessed fixtures.

Professional Organizations

International Association of Lighting Designers
Suite 9-104
The Merchandise Mart
Chicago, IL 60654
312-527-3677
312-527-3680 (fax)
www.iald.org

lluminating Engineering Society of North America (IES)
345 E. 47th Street
New York, NY 10017
www.iesna.org

American Lighting Association (ALA)
PO Box 420288
Dallas, TX 75342
800-274-4484
www.americianlightingassoc.com

American Society of Interior Designer (ASID)
608 Massachusetts Ave., NE
Washington, DC 20002-6006
202-546-3480
202-546-3240 (fax)
www.asid.org

LightFair International (Annual Lighting Conference)
Produced by AMC, Inc.
240 Peachtree Street, NW
Atlanta, GA 30303
404-220-2221
404-220-2442 (fax)
www.lightfair.com

The Bottom Line

You can never know too much, so take advantage of this emerging field. New and exciting lamps are rapidly being developed, and keeping up is as important as knowing new fashion styles or colors.

Appendix Two

SAMPLE ANSWERS AND LAYOUTS

The following are samples answers to the review examination given in Chapter 16:

1. What is meant by layering light? Explain and give examples._____
   The use of a combination of luminaires to create a cohesive overall design. A blend of task, ambient, accent, and decorative sources.

2. What 3 things are lit in a space? Which is the most important? Why?_____
   People, art, architecture. People are the most important. They need to feel comfortable, look their best, and have access to controllable, functional illumination.

3. What are color temperature and CRI? How would you use them to choose a lamp?
   Color temperature measures in degrees of Kelvin the color quality of a lamp. The CRI (color rendering index) compares the lamp source to daylight and its ability to mimic daylight.

4. How do finishes and light sources interact in a space? Explain by giving examples?
   Lamps and luminaires must be selected based on the finishes in a particular space. Dark surfaces absorb light, while light colored surfaces reflect light, so deeply hued rooms need more light.

5. What are some of the things to consider in specifying a fluorescent luminaire? How do they affect your decision? _____
   Consider using an electronic ballast, so that the luminaire is as quiet as possible. A dimming ballast would allow for varying light levels.

6. If you were setting the scenes for a 4-scene preset dimmer system, what scenes might you use? Why? Describe _____
   Scene One - normal - everyday setting
   Scene Two - pass through (a low light level - enough to see)
   Scene three - party - a little more accent and less ambient
   Scene four - clean-up - all lights up to full

7. How does Title 24 affect kitchen and bath lighting in California?_____
   The general illumination in new construction or remodel that exceeds
   50% must use fluorescent as the general illumination and be on the
   first switch as you enter the room.

8. What are some of the considerations (other than Title 24) used when designing lighting for kitchens? Explain. _____
   Provide good general illumination to help reduce shadowing.
   Locate task lighting between your head and your work surface, such
   as under-cabinet lighting.
   If entertaining includes the kitchen area, make the lighting as
   comfortable and controllable as the rest of the public spaces.

9. When lighting landscapes, safety, security and beauty are to be considered. Choose one of these and describe some of the techniques used to accomplish this?
   Where beauty is concerned, work on lighting the plantings, without
   drawing attention to the luminaires themselves. Let the decorative
   lanterns just be a glow and give the illusion that they are providing
   the light.

10. Why is it important to know the plant material being used when doing landscape lighting?
    Trees that lose their leaves may be lighted differently than ever-
    greens. Fast-growing plants may overtake a luminaire; extra lengths
    of cable would allow the luminaire to be moved as the plants mature.

11. What are some of the architectural constraints one must deal with in doing lighting design? Give an example?_____
    Existing structures can take advantage of luminaires made especially
    for remodel, but make sure that there is enough ceiling depth to
    accommodate a recessed can.

12. Describe the steps you would take in doing a lighting design from start to finish.
    1. Sit with the client to talk about their needs and their budget.
    2. Draw up a furniture plan.
    3. Draw up a preliminary lighting plan and specifications to review
    with the clients.
    4. Draw up the finished plan and specifications.
    5. Review with the installing contractor.

13. Color temperature is measured in degrees of __*Kelvin*_____

14. Do green plants look better under a cooler or a warmer color temperature? _cooler_

15. Name 2 benefits of ambient light?
    1. _Softens shadows on people's faces so that they look their best._

    2. _Fills the volume of a space to make it seem larger and more inviting._

16. Give 2 examples of task lighting in:

    An office: 1. _A desk lamp directed towards the keyboard of a computer_
                 2. _A ceiling-mounted luminaire in the supply room._

    A kitchen: 1. _Lighting under the overhead cabinets_
                 2. _A ceiling-mounted luminaire in the pantry_

17. How would you improve on the lighting in a dining room that is lighted only by a chandelier?
    Add a recessed adjustable fixture on either side of the chandelier to cross-illuminate the table. Install wall sconces or torchères to provide the much needed ambient illumination.

18. What does the "MR" stand for in an MR16 lamp? _____
    Mirror Reflector
    (The answer is not "mister")

19. What is the diameter of an MR16 lamp? _2" (16 eighths of an inch)_

20. To dim a quartz (tungsten halogen) lamp without significantly shortening its life, what percentage of time must it be burning at full capacity? _20%_

21. Why are clients afraid of fluorescent and what can you do to enlighten them? _____
    Fluorescents come in many wonderful colors.
    Fluorescents give 3 to 5 times more light than comparable wattage incandescents.
    Fluorescents last 10 to 30 times longer than standard incandescents.

22. For task lighting at a vanity, where is the best place to locate the luminaires? _____
    Flanking the mirror, mounted at eye level.

23. H.I.D. stands for _High intensity discharge_

24. Mercury vapor lamps produce what color light? _bluish-green_

25. High-pressure sodium lamps produce what color light? _yellow-orange_

26. People tend to look rather unattractive under High Pressure Sodium light. What might look good under this light? _____
    Brick, sandstone, the Golden Gate Bridge
    _____
    _____
    _____

27. Is "daylight" a warm color or a cool color temperature? _Cool_

28. What does the "R" stand for in a 75R30 lamp? _reflector_

29. Name two disadvantages of the compact fluorescent.
    1. _Some hum._
    2. _Some don't have rapid-start ballasts._

30. The three lamp categories are incandescent, fluorescent and H.I.D. Which category does a quartz lamp fit into? _____
    Incandescent
    _____
    _____

31. What are two advantages of fluorescent over incandescent?
    1. _Longer life_
    _____
    2. _Greater variety of colors_
    _____

32. Describe the "black mirror" effect: _____
    When a lighting design has neglected to light the exterior spaces,
    windows can become "black mirrors" at night. Exterior lighting helps
    eliminate this problem.

33. Describe the "moonlighting" effect: _____
    Positioning exterior fixtures so that they filter through
    the branches of the trees creates an effect similar to light cast
    by the moon.

34. Why is it necessary to light the clients as well as the art and architecture in a home?
    The space needs to be humanized, so that the homeowners can feel comfortable in the space. Lighting the people in a space helps them look and feel their best.

35. If you were glowing from within, what color light would you emit to attract bugs?
    Blue-white

36. Give three advantages of low-voltage lighting?
    1. *Compact lamps*
    2. *Tight beam spreads*
    3. *Energy-efficient*

37. Give three disadvantages of low-voltage lighting?
    1. *Hum*
    2. *Voltage drop*
    3. *Limited wattage*

38. True or False? All "pagoda lights" should be sent to Wichita, Kansas to be used as landing lights. *True*

39. Describe the term "veiling reflection." *The mirror-like reflection of a light source on a shiny surface when light comes from the ceiling directly in front of you, hitting the paper at such an angle that the glare is reflected directly into your eyes, as if trying to read through a veil.*

40. What does not change significantly when you dim fluorescent? _____
    The color temperature

41. What is the best way to light a piece of art with a reflective face (such as glass or Plexiglas™)? *Cross-illumination is best, using two luminaires. The one on the right is directed towards the left side of the art and vice-versa.*

42. When a client says, "How much light do I need for this room?," list at least three questions you need to ask them about the space:
    1. *What color will the walls and ceilings be painted?*
    2. *Will they be doing tasks, such as reading, in the space?*
    3. *Will they be entertaining in the space?*
    4. *Are there skylights?*
    5. *What is the finish or trim?*

43. What is a panic switch and where is it best located? _____
   A switch located next to the bed to turn on exterior lights.
   _____
   _____

44. What is the most important element to any design project? _Lighting is great, but_
   money ends up being the true most important element.
   _____
   _____

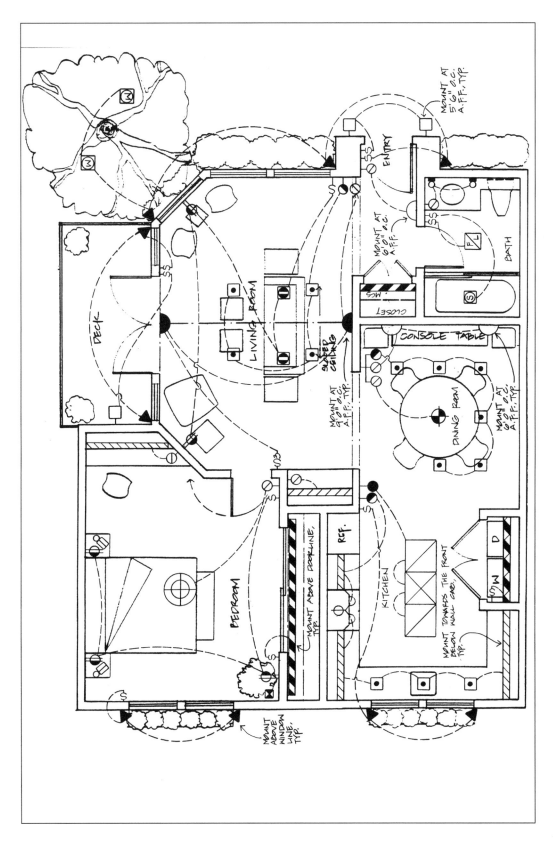

Sample lighting layout for the condo project in Chapter 16. Check these symbols against the ones listed in Figure 16.5 to get a better understanding of what has been designed.

Appendix Three

A Sampling of Luminaire Manufacturers

AAMSCO Manufacturing, Inc.
 (vertical vanity lights)
 15-17 Brook St.
 P.O. Box 15119
 Jersey City, NJ 07305
 201/434-0722
 FAX: 201/434-8535
 www.aamsco.com

Arroyo Craftsman Lighting, Inc.
 (period exterior luminaires)
 4509 Little John Street
 Baldwin Park, CA 91706
 818/960-9411
 FAX: 818/960-9521

ALKCO
 (under-cabinet task lights)
 11500 West Melrose Street
 Franklin Park, IL 60131
 312/451-0700
 FAX: 847/ 451-7512
 www.alkco.com

Artemide Inc.
 (Italian pendants & wall sconces)
 1980 New Highway
 Farmingdale, NY 11735
 516/ 694-9292
 FAX: 516/ 694-9275
 www.artemide.com

Banci
 (traditional decorative luminaires with
 hidden indirect halogen lamps)
 Rep: Casella Lighting
 111 Rhode Island St.
 San Francisco, CA 94103
 415/ 626-9600
 FAX: 415/ 626-4539
 www.banci.it

Bega/US
 1005 Mark Avenue
 Carpinteria, CA 93013
 805/ 684-0533
 FAX: 805/684-6682
 www.bega.com

Norbert Belfer Lighting Mfg. Co.
 (compact fluorescent strip lights, halogen-
 strip lights)
 PO Box 2079
 Ocean, NJ 07712
 732/ 493-2666
 FAX: 732/ 493-2941
 www.belfer.com

B-K Lighting, Inc.
 (recessed step lights)
 40429 Brickyard Dr.
 Madera, CA 63638
 559/ 438-5800
 FAX: 559/ 438-5900
 www.bklighting.com

Boyd Lighting Company
 (decorative wall sconces, torchères,
 pendant luminaires)
 944 Folsom St.
 San Francisco, CA 94107-1007
 415/ 778-4300
 FAX: 415/ 778-4319
 www.boydlighting.com

Capri
 (recessed light luminaires)
 776 South Green St.
 Tupelo, MS 38804
 662/ 842-7212
 FAX: 662/ 680-6619
 www.caprilighting.com

Casella
(mini-torchères)
111 Rhode Island St.
San Francisco, CA 94103
415/ 626-9600
FAX: 415/626-4539

Exciting Lighting
(light sculpture)
14 E. Sir Francis Drake Blvd.
Larkspur, CA 94939
415/ 925-0840
FAX: 415/ 925-1305

Fiberstars
(fiber optics)
44259 Nobel Dr.
800/ 327-7877
FAX: 510/ 490-3247
www.fiberstars.com

Flos USA
(European-modern interior wall &
ceiling-mounted fixtures)
200 McKay Road
Huntington Station, NY 11746
800/ 939-3567
FAX: 516/ 549-4220
www.flos.net

Halo
(recessed light luminaires, daylight blue
filters)
1121 Highway 74 South
Peach Tree City, GA 30269
770/ 486-4800
FAX: 770/ 486-4533
www.cooperlighting.com

Hans Duus Blacksmith, Inc
(traditional exterior and interior wall and
ceiling mount lanterns)
73 Industrial Way
Buellton, CA 93427

805/ 688-9731
FAX: 805/ 688-1793

Johnson Art Studio
(traditional ceiling and wall-mounted
fixtures)
3120 Capitola Road
Santa Cruz, CA 95062
831/ 464-0567
FAX: 831/ 464-1325
www.johnsonartstudio.com

Juno
(track and recessed luminaires)
1300 S. Wolf Rd.
PO Box 5065
Des Plaines, IL 60017-5065
847/ 827-9880
FAX: 847/ 827-2925
www.junolighting.com

Justice Design Group
(bisque wall sconces)
11244 Playa Court
Culver City, CA 90230
310/ 397-7170
www.jdg.com

Kim Lighting
(landscape light luminaires)
16555 East Gale Ave.
Industry, CA 91749
818/ 968-5666
FAX: 818/ 369-2695
www.kimlighting.com

Koch and Lowy
(vodka pendant luminaires, wall sconces,
torchères)
487 West Main St.
Avon, MA 02322
508/ 588-4700
FAX: 508/ 587-7592
www.kochlowy.com

Lightolier

(recessed low-voltage adjustable luminaires, decorative luminaires)
631 Airport Rd.
Fall River, MA 02720
508/ 679-8131
FAX: 508/ 674-4710
www.lightolier.com

Lucifer

(miniature low-voltage cove light and
recessed luminaires)
414 Live Oak Street
San Antonio, TX 78202
210/ 227-7329
FAX: 210/ 227-4967
www.luciferlighting.com

Lutron

(low-voltage, line-voltage and solid-state
fluorescent dimming systems)
7200 Suter Road
Coopersburg, PA 18036
800/ 523-9466
FAX: 215/ 282-3090
www.lutron.com

Phoenix Day

(decorative plaster wall sconces,
torchères, vanity luminaires, opaque
pendant luminaires)
1355 Donner Avenue
San Francisco, CA 94124
415/ 822-4414
FAX: 415/ 822-3987

Poulsen

(modern interior and exterior luminaires)
5407 NW 163rd Street
Miami, FL 33014-6130
305/ 625-1009
FAX: 305/ 625-1213
www.louispoulsen.com

Prescolite

(low-voltage recessed adjustable
luminaires)
1251 Doolittle Dr.
San Leandro, CA 94577
510/ 562-3500
FAX: 510/ 577-5022
www.prescolite.com

Zaneen

(European-modern interior ceiling and
wall mount fixtures)
65 Densley Avenue
Toronto, Ontario M6M 2P5
800/ 388-3382
FAX: 416/ 247-9319
www.zaneen.com

Zelco

(European style decorative luminaires,
recessed wall sconces)
630 S. Columbus Ave. C.S. #4445
Mt. Vernon, NY 10551-4445
800/ 431-2486
914/ 699-6230
FAX: 914/ 699-7082
www.zelco.com

Appendix Four

Top Ten Lighting Tips

Sometimes clients like to be provided with "bullets" of information that give them an idea of your level of expertise and also help them to feel that they will be able to easily understand the information you will be offering them. Here is an example of a good list:

1. There is no single light fixture that can satisfy all lighting needs. Light layering is a design method in which a number of light sources are blended together to create a successful design.

2. Put together a furniture layout before attempting to create a lighting system. The lighting should relate to the way each room is going to be used.

3. Try to get all the players (homeowners, architect, interior designer, lighting designer, landscape designer, and contractor) together. This is called a "team approach" to design. The result is a cohesive design where all the elements work with each other.

4. Check all the door swings in the house. Make sure that switches do not end up behind any of the doors.

5. Choose one adjustable recessed ceiling fixture that can serve as a downlight, accent light, or wall washer and use it throughout the house. Don't mix trims. It draws too much attention to the recessed fixtures themselves.

6. Put interior lights on dimmers whenever possible. This will allow an unlimited number of light levels for all the people living in the house.

7. Always try to include some exterior lighting in the overall design. It not only keeps windows from becoming "black mirrors" at night, but also visually expands the interior spaces.

8. Do not put exterior lights on dimmers. Standard incandescent light, when dimmed, becomes even more amber in color. Green plants look sickly under yellow light.

9. Locate a panic switch for security lights in the master bedroom. It's no fun running to the front door in the middle of the night to turn on the outside lights.

10. Don't put light switches for the main rooms and landscaping just at the front door. Most people enter single-family homes from the garage. This is where a second set of switches should be located.

Appendix Five
TOP TEN TIPS FOR OUTDOOR LIGHTING

Even if you end up choosing interior design or architecture as a profession, don't think that the exterior spaces can't fall under the umbrella for your design expertise. Homeowners are really sinking big bucks into the exterior spaces surrounding their homes. Keeping this in mind use this punch list to open the door to additional work.

1. There is no single exterior light fixture that can satisfy all lighting needs in the garden. The moonlighting effect is a design method in which a number of light sources are blended together to create a natural-looking design.

2. Put together a planting plan, outdoor furniture layout, and sculpture or water feature locations before attempting to create a lighting design. The lighting should relate to the way the outdoor spaces are going to be used.

3. Try to get all the players (homeowners, lighting designer, landscape designer, and contractor) together. This is called a team approach to design. The result is a cohesive design in which all the elements work with each other.

4. Create two levels of light: one for when the client is inside looking out, and one for when the client is actually in the garden.

5. Choose one style of adjustable shielded exterior fixture that can serve as a downlight, accent light, or wall wash. Don't mix fixture types; it draws too much attention to the fixtures themselves. Only the decorative fixtures, such as the lanterns flanking the doors, should be seen.

6. Always try to include some exterior lighting in the overall design, even if you are working on lighting the inside of the house first. It not only keeps windows from becoming "black mirrors" at night, but also visually expands the interior spaces.

7. Do not put exterior lights on dimmers. Standard incandescent light, when dimmed, becomes even more amber in color. Green plants look sickly under yellow light.

8. Locate a panic switch for security lights in the master bedroom. It's no fun running to the front door in the middle of the night to turn on the outside lights.

9. Don't locate light switches for the main rooms and landscaping just at the front door. Most people enter single-family homes from the garage. This is where a second set of switches should be installed.

10. Use a daylight-blue or color-correcting filter on the outdoor lights, which will eliminate the amber quality of incandescent light. This will keep the plants looking healthy.

Appendix Six
FREQUENTLY ASKED LIGHTING QUESTIONS

As a designer, you will find that you will get asked the same lighting questions over and over. This list of frequently asked questions would be a good handout to prospective clients to get them thinking about lighting as an integral part of any interior or exterior project.

What are the functional applications of lighting?
The four types of lighting are *decorative, task, accent, and ambient.*

Decorative describes fixtures, such as chandeliers and exterior lanterns, that add visual sparkle to a space. Task is lighting by which we do work, such as lighting under the cabinets in the kitchen or a light for reading next to a chair. Accent is light used to highlight objects in a room, to help create depth and dimension. Ambient is the gentle fill light for a space that softens shadows on people's faces and creates the feel of a glowing fire.

An effective lighting design layers these four functions together to create a cohesive overall design. Sadly, it is the ambient light that most often gets overlooked.

What does lighting do for design?
A lighting designer's job is to make the work that interior designers, architects, and landscape designers do come to life at night. You can call it "painting with light."

How do you define drama in an interior design?
Dramatic lighting makes a statement, sets a mood, and creates visual excitement. This is not the type of lighting that people can function with on a day-to-day basis. It is for entertaining. Effective lighting designs offer levels and layers of light so that clients have a great variety of lighting scenes for working, playing, cleaning, and socializing.

How does the lighting create drama in a room?
The accent lighting punches up art objects to give a visual show that draws a visitor's eyes around the room. Wall sconces can create a secondary ceiling line that helps humanize the scale of a very large room. The sconces can also lead guests down the various passageways like glowing torches. Decorative fixtures definitely play a role in adding drama to a space. For example, a perforated metal star-shaped fixture in an entry can throw a wonderful pattern of light across the ceiling and walls. The warm color of the incandescent light provides a dynamic contrast against the twilight blue sky seen through the windows as dusk approaches.

What lighting trends are popular now?
The biggest trend is the increased interest in landscape lighting. People want to create outdoor rooms for entertaining at night. Also, lighting outside visually expands in interior spaces beyond the "black mirror." This is the term for the effect of seeing your own reflection in the window instead of the view beyond.

How can technology be incorporated into lighting design?
Use of a four-scene preset dimming system allows the clients to have four different scenes at the touch of a button. This provides the option of many different light levels, depending on how the room is being utilized.

What are good design goals for a project?
What many clients want is a flexible lighting system that gives them the most bang for their buck. For accent lighting I normally specify recessed adjustable low-voltage fixtures that use a very energy-efficient 50-watt halogen source, called an MR16 (the MR stands for mirror reflector). The decorative fixtures are the "jewelry" in a project. If budget comes into play, we can recommend reasonably priced fixtures that have the look of much more expensive versions.

What is a major factor that makes a lighting design successful?
The creation of a collaborative atmosphere among all the design professionals and clients on a project. An active exchange of ideas really makes all the elements work together. This is why it is important to bring a lighting designer in early on a project instead of waiting until the end. The best lighting design is architecturally integrated into a building.

How is lighting design different from other interior design elements?
It is not so much different as it is another element in a well-designed space. Lighting makes a room's elements come alive at night. We are drawn to light in a very primitive, ancestral way. Light, when used correctly, creates an instant level of comfort.

When thinking about lighting a given space, there are three things to be illuminated: the art, the architecture, and the people. Good designer always start by lighting the people first.

Appendix Seven

RECORDING YOUR WORK: TIPS ON PHOTOGRAPHY

Once you have a few projects under your belt, even if it is your own house or apartment, you should consider using the services of a professional photographer. These people are artists in their own right and can make your work utterly publishable. Feel free to take the "before" pictures — they are supposed to look awful — but let a pro make a lasting and beautiful record of your design prowess.

Working with a Professional Photographer

Don't wait for a magazine to come to you and pay for the photographer's fee. It happens only with a select few and usually only if you have a big-name client. Plus, if someone else pays the photographer, that person controls the images, which prevents you from using them in different venues.

Building a rapport with a good architectural photographer or two is very worthwhile. You will get to know each other after a few projects, establishing a long-term partnership that will produce the type of top-quality images that you want.

Be open to their ideas. They have a great deal of experience in composing a successful shot. They know what sells.

Finding One

Look at design magazines to see who is doing photography that you like. If light plays a big role in your design, give particular attention to who is good at capturing light for dramatic night shots. Call other design professionals to see whom they use and would recommend.

Choosing One

Have the photographers show you a portfolio of their latest work. Select one who can give the feel and quality you want to the finished product.See what magazines they are connected with and where else they have been published, such as books on design. Hooking up with a photographer who regularly gets into the magazines that you would like to be seen in is a smart move. They can be a good foot in the door.

Cost Factors

Ask what formats they use. There are three film sizes in common use: 35 mm (small format), 2 1/4 inch or 70 mm, and 4 inch by 5 inch (large format). Now many professional photographers are using high-resolution digital cameras that have many advantages over traditional photography. Photo shoots using larger-format cameras are more expensive because the setup time is longer. The reason for using a medium or large format is a higher image quality. Digital photography requires less equipment, so the shoots tend to go more quickly. This means that you can get more shots within the time frame of a photo shoot.

Smaller-format transparencies can produce grainy images when blown up for publication. Using 35 mm is okay for "before" shots and detail shots that won't be enlarged greatly. Do ask for medium-format because it has good image quality, but is not as costly as 4 inch by 5 inch. One large-format shot, using traditional film, can take up to 1 1/2 hours to set up and shoot. You should request 4 inch by 5 inch though, when you want the results to be absolutely breathtaking.

Get a clear statement of all the charges. Even though you pay photographers for their services, they typically own the rights to the photos. You are normally required to pay a usage fee each time they are published. These fees can vary depending on the photographer and where the images are placed. Usage fees for photos reproduced on the inside pages of a magazine vary from those used on the cover. A different fee may apply images published in books.

Magazines and book publishers sometimes pay these fees, but not always. Consider it as part of your advertising budget. Discuss the possibility of a buyout, where you will pay a larger up-front fee but then have the freedom to use the photos in any way you deem suitable for promotion.

Piggy backing
Consider sharing the cost of the photo shoot with the other design professionals involved, such as the architect, lighting designer, and contractor. Establish an agreement stating that all the players, especially the photographer, get credit each time the project is published. This way everyone wins and reconfirms the value of the team approach to design. Normally the photographer's fee in this arrangement will be higher because they are giving publishing rights to more than one individual.

Make That Dollar Holler
If your project gets into publication, don't stop there. If you got the project into a consumer publication then get it into a trade publication. Get the work into the HOME section of the local paper. Put one of the images on a postcard and send it out to old clients and potential clients. Add the images to your Web site. Work those images every way you can.

The Bottom Line
Great photography is one of the best ways to document and promote your work.

Appendix Eight

TIPS ON PUBLIC SPEAKING

Public speaking is a terrific way of drumming up new business. It helps to establish you as an authority in your field and gives you good name recognition. One or two of the people in the audience will become your clients. Others will tell their friends. Don't miss this opportunity to make yourself known. It costs you nothing but a little time.

For most people the thought of getting up in front of a crowd of people is terrifying. A recent survey showed that when given a choice of public speaking or death, an amazing majority chose option number two. Now is a good time to deal with those fears. Here are some techniques that will help you become more comfortable when giving a talk:

1. As the crowd is gathering, talk with four different people. Ask why they are there. Get a little insight on what they hope to get from the presentation. Then when you are up in front of your audience you will have four friendly faces to make eye contact with instead of being overwhelmed by a sea of strangers.

2. Keep making eye contact. Don't look over people's heads and don't look down.

3. If you tend to shake, then make sure that you have a podium to hold on to. The nervousness will subside as you get into your subject matter.

4. Don't read from notes. Just have a list of points that you want to cover.

5. Take off your watch and put it on the podium. Constantly looking at your watch is distracting and makes people feel that you have something more important to do that you seem to be running late for.

6. Let the audience know that it is okay for them to ask questions during the presentation. It helps them to become active participants in the process and takes some of the focus off you. Always repeat the question for the rest of the audience so that everyone gets to hear it clearly. This also gives you a few moments to formulate a clear answer.

7. It's okay not to know the answer to everything. If a question stumps you, put it out to the crowd. See if someone else has the answer.

8. Tell little stories about projects you have done to illustrate a point. Admit to some mistakes; it makes you more human and accessible to the audience.

9. Ask if anyone has had a similar experience. It lets the people become engaged in the presentation and gives you a little break from the spotlight.

10. Provide handouts. This should be a summary of what the talk was about. List all your contact information at the bottom, including your e-mail address and Web site.

11. Always have a pocket full of business cards to hand out.

12. At the end of the talk, remember to thank the audience members for coming.

The Bottom Line

Face it—you are entering a field that requires selling yourself. This entails convincing potential clients that you have the knowledge and creativity to produce designs that look great and meet their needs. Think of public speaking as an infomercial for a really good product. That product is you.

Appendix Nine

The Business of Being in Business

What Designers would Have Liked to Have Known Before Starting Their Businesses

Here's a checklist of pointers from people who work for themselves. Fifty self-employed designers were asked what they would like to have known when they first set up their businesses. Here are the things that came up most frequently.

Self-assessment. You must be highly motivated and willing to work long hours to get yourself established. If you think you can do that, then you are a candidate for self-employment. Business has it own rules. It's all-important to understand what it means to run your own business. Keep on top of things. You need to make sure that accounting, billing, filing, returning phone calls, and answering correspondence are handled expeditiously and efficiently. Design is 20% of your workload; 80% is the paper chase.

It's also imperative to develop systematic ways of handling your tasks and prioritizing them. Most people depend on the supervisor or owner to tell them how to do their jobs and keep them on the ball. If you are the owner, you'll need to discipline yourself to make sure everything runs smoothly.

Don't be shy. Publicity and networking are essential. A small business just starting up won't have clients walking in the door. The major part of your work will be making contacts and getting your name out to the public. Otherwise the business won't survive.

Tips on Starting Your Business

1. Find an area in design that's interesting, such as kitchens and baths, store planning, or senior residence centers. Learn everything you can in that certain area. Be the best in that one area—don't generalize. Think of yourself as a fine French restaurant with a limited menu, don't be a Denny's.

2. When you open a new checking account, start your check numbering with a high number like 2000, not 100. It makes you look like you've been in business longer.

3. Consider not using your name in the business name, such Jane Doe Design. It offers a buffer between you and the salespeople who want to be your long distance carrier, office supplies distributor, and so on—a hundred other phone calls that keep you from getting work done. Plus, if you decide to expand the business to more locations, you can't physically be at all of them. It also helps prevent the situation where clients always want to speak only to you, not your associates. If you want to sell a business built on your name, it's worth much less without you. If you end up selling your name, you can't use it again in a related business. Consider what happened to Colonel Sanders and Famous Amos.

4. Think of a name that reflects an image you want associated with your company, like Green Space Design, Design on a Dime, or Home and Hearth Interiors. If you do choose to use your

name, always use "and Associates", even if you don't have any. It will make your company seem larger.

5. Hire people to do what you can't do. If you charge $100 per hour, you can't bill out to your clients that amount when you are doing the books, filing or writing checks. It's better to hire someone at $40 or so per hour. Then at the same time you can be doing something at $100 per hour.

6. Voice mail is your friend. Leave a daily message to let clients know when you will be back in the office. Offer an optional selection that gives your address, fax number, and e-mail address.

7. Have two in-office days a week when clients definitely know they can reach you. Keep your out-of-the-office appointments on the other days. For example, on Mondays and Thursdays you will be in the office. Tuesdays, Wednesdays, and Fridays you will be out of the office. If Fridays are an out-of-office day, this also gives you the opportunity to take an occasional three-day weekend.

8. Be computer-literate. It saves hundreds of hours, as time is expensive. Most of your correspondence will be by fax or e-mail.

9. Print up stationery on your laser printer from a template you have set up on your computer. Don't go to a printer and get multicolored embossed letterhead. It's costly and you will need all the business capital you have. Also, you will have moved, changed phone numbers, or added a Web site long before you use up that expensive stationery.

10. Be prepared to work six- and seven-day weeks for the first two to three years, at least.

11. In the course of a job, you will sometimes throw in some time or materials for free. Send an invoice marked "no charge" for all the freebies. Clients love it. It's like getting a gift in the mail. Clients will tend to forget everything you gave them for free when it comes time to collect on a bill. These gift invoices are solid documentation of your generosity.

12. When doing a remodel project, let your clients know ahead of time what's in store. Remodel virgins tend to go into cardiac arrest. You are messing with their nest. The more they know up front, the less crazed they will become.

13. Put together contracts that cover your butt without scaring the clients away. There are lawyers that specialize in contracts for designers.

14. Network by going to design association meetings that are in related fields. Be sure to exchange business cards.

15. Be prepared to jump at the chance anytime you're offered a way of getting free publici-

ty through speaking, articles, or other such methods. Not only do you get the publicity, but also people will think about you first the next time they need a designer.

16. Document all your client or contractor communications with faxes, transmittals, or e-mails. This will come in helpful when the inevitable problems or questions arise, as well as keeping all the team members in the loop.

17. The team approach gathers up related professionals who refer each other. If you get a referral, be sure to thank the person who referred you. If you are an interior designer, get to know two architects and two lighting designers who will be good team members. This helps when another design professional gets on the job first.

The Bottom Line
Take a good look at yourself before taking the plunge. Design is serious business.

Appendix Ten

Getting Published: The Game Plan

One of the best ways for design professionals to establish themselves is through publication. Being seen in print validates our work and impresses the heck out of potential clients.

Bite the bullet

Invest in a real architectural photographer to shoot your work. They are artists and experienced technicians. They will make your projects look their best. This will be money well spent. Sometimes you can piggyback with the other design professionals who worked on the project to share the cost of the photo shoot. Sometimes even the clients are willing to chip in, since they may really want to be in a magazine. Don't try to get a magazine to photograph your project. They then hold all the cards.

Reality check

If you are just starting out, your first job may be your own apartment or a room in your parents' house. In addition to whole-room shots, get a series of vignette shots as well. These could include tablescapes, room corners, and close-ups. Take "before" shots with a good 35 mm camera.

Plan ahead

Make sure that the photographer shoots large-format transparency (either 70 mm or 4 inch by 5 inch). These provide the best clarity and detail when the images are enlarged. Prints can be made from these transparencies, but magazines, book publishers, and newspapers want transparencies. Pretty soon most will want digital images that can be sent by e-mail and downloaded.

Protect your investment

Don't ever send original transparencies to magazines. Always send first-rate duplicates — 4 inch by 5 inch dupes are the best but very expensive, around $37 each. 35 mm slides are okay and run about $3.50 apiece. But a more recent option is the 70 mm –mini dupe. It is twice the size of a 35MM and produces a better-quality enlargement. They run in the $6 range.

Getting in the Door (It's OK to Use the Back Door)

Play detective

Most magazines have an editorial calendar that shows the subjects for each monthly issue through the end of the year. This is done mainly to attract advertisers to a specific issue that relates to the product or service they are selling. Call the advertising department of the magazines you want to be in and tell them that you are interested in possibly running an ad. Ask them to send or fax you a copy of their editorial calendar so that you can determine which issue relates best to your product. You can also contact the editor to get this information, but I have found that the advertising people are much quicker in responding to your request.

You gotta have a gimmick

Decide which issue will work best for your project. It may be the kitchen and bath issue, the remodel issue, or the garden issue. Next, create a "hook". What makes your kitchen project different from all the other kitchens that will be submitted? Maybe it's using fiber optics or recycled materials ,or maybe it was completed on a very limited budget.

Find the contact

Check the masthead of the magazine to which you want to submit. Find the name of the features editor. Put together a cover letter and address it to that person. The cover letter should state that you have the perfect project for their upcoming kitchens and baths issue in July. Write a short description of the project, provide captions for the images, and list the other players (the architect and other design professionals involved in the job). Put "please return to [your name and address]" on the sheet that holds the transparencies. And always give the photographer credit.

Be pushy

Don't limit yourself to one publication. Submit you project to both trade and consumer magazines. Also submit it to the home and garden section of your local paper. It is a great way to target your local client base.

Persist

One week after sending out the package, give the editor a follow-up call to make sure that he or she received the package and to see if the editor needs any additional information. The editor wants to publish the project, he or she will normally have a staff or freelance writer call to interview you. Build a rapport with that writer and let them know that you have other project coming up. Freelance writers are especially valuable because they get paid per article, so you are seen as a source of future income.

The Bottom Line

Remember that these publications are hungry for new projects. They have to put out a new magazine every month. They need you as much as you need them.

Index

Randall Whitehead, today's leading authorty on residential lighting design, has gained international renown for his humanizing approach to lighting living spaces. He is one of a small group of lighting design professionals who helped introduce a style that emphasizes illuminating people as well as art and architecture. Randall has received many professional design awards for his lighting design work and has lectured and written extensively on the subject. His articles and projects have appeared in numerous national design magazines. His firm, Randall Whitehead Lighting Inc., has designed commercial and residential lighting for projects all over the world. His first book on lighting was *Residential Lighting: Creating Dynamic Living Spaces*. Randall is known for his fresh, innovative, practical approach to lighting, and for his inimitable sense of humor.

Randall's company, Randall Whitehead Lighting Inc., can be located on the internet at: www.randallwhitehead.com.

Book and cover design: Clifton Lemon
Photography: Dennis Anderson